Contents

Preface

We are pleased to present here 16 of the 27 papers presented at the eighth annual Theoretical Roman Archaeology Conference held at the School of Archaeological Studies, Leicester University in April 1998. Following the trend of last year's volume, we have tried to allow for more substantial contributions rather than 'soundbites', whilst publishing as many of the papers as possible within the space available. The chronological scope of the papers ranges from the late Republic to the end of the Empire and beyond, utilising a wealth of evidence to explore a wide assortment of issues, from shoes to cities, and historical 'experience' to archaeological practice. However, we would like to highlight a remarkably persuasive theme concerning the construction of identities in the Roman world.

Starting with the politics of the centre, Ralph Häussler's paper demonstrates how the ideology of the Roman state and Imperial Cult was, quite literally, constructed through the built environment of the local municipalities of the Empire. Imperial cohesion was also maintained by the community of soldiers, whose distinctive identity as a corporate body within Empire is considered by Simon James. However, the hegemony of Rome was also dependent upon a negotiation of power between Roman and Other; the next four papers foreground this dialogue, in the context of Gaul (Kenny Aitchison), the northern frontier (Simon Clarke), the Fenland Iceni (Garrick Fincham) and the Silures and Cornovii of western Britannia (Louise Revell). Unlike traditional accounts of 'romanization', these papers demonstrate the active participation of the Other in the definition of identities.

Next, the papers by Richard Bayliss and Mark Jackson explore the construction of new Christian identities within the later Empire and emphasise how pagan religions were appropriated rather than destroyed in order to achieve this. The end of the Empire was marked by further transformations of identity, following divergent courses in different provinces. In sub-Roman Britain, David Petts shows how the Bible was used by the Britons to negotiate new definitions of self, whilst Howard Williams and Geoff Harrison consider the ambiguities of becoming Saxon through the contested interpretations of material culture and burial rite. Meanwhile, in North Africa, Anna Leone considers the redefinition of built space at Carthage consequent to the arrival of the Vandals and the removal of Roman power.

Next the symbolic significance of shoes as emblems of individual identity is considered by Carol van-Driel Murray, whilst Patricia Baker offers an intimate examination of Roman women as reflected in contemporary medical literature. John Pearce then assesses the rural burial evidence of Roman Hampshire and argues for a range of different mortuary identities to those found in the context of the better known urban cemeteries. Finally, we return to the centre of the empire, with Giovanni Ricci and Nicola Terrenato, to look at the self-identity of the archaeologist and the hopeful prospects for archaeology in the city of Rome itself.

Thanks are due to the all of contributors to the original conference and for the participation of delegates; we also thank the authors published here for adhering to our tight schedules. We are immensely grateful to staff, postgraduates and others, especially from Leicester and Southampton, for helping to organise and chair sessions and generally ensuring the conference ran smoothly – special mention must go to Mel Barge, Sam Burke, Neil Christie, Ken Dark, Simon Esmonde-Cleary, Lin Foxhall, Mark Gillings, John Hawthorne, Kris Lockyear, David Mattingly, Deirdre O'Sullivan, David Petts, Sarah Poppy, Jane Webster, Howard Williams and Rob Young. Thanks are also due to the referees and to Mike Durkin, Philip van der Eijk, Alice Hiley, Jeremy Patterson and Pam Thornett for their assistance and support.

TRAC98 was generously sponsored by the School of Archaeological Studies, Leicester University, the Society for the Promotion of Roman Studies and English Heritage, for whose support we express our gratitude. Finally, thanks are due to David Brown of Oxbow Books for his continuing commitment to the rapid publication of these proceedings.

Patricia Baker, Colin Forcey, Sophia Jundi & Rob Witcher   February 1999

Published by
Oxbow Books, Park End Place, Oxford OX1 1HN

ISBN 1 900188 86 4

This book is available direct from
Oxbow Books, Park End Place, Oxford OX1 1HN
(Phone: 01865–241249; Fax: 01865–794449)

and

The David Brown Book Company
PO Box 511, Oakville, CT 06779
(Phone 860–945–9329; Fax: 860–945–9468)

or from the Oxbow Books website

www.oxbowbooks.com

Printed in Great Britain by
The Short Run Press, Exeter

Architecture, Performance and Ritual:
the role of state architecture in the Roman Empire

by Ralph Häussler

Introduction

This paper examines how Rome's *superior* role was manifested in local communities in order to tie them to the centre of the empire. Road building, architecture and art are considered more than just a practical necessity or a physical expression of 'imperialism'. They play an often pivotal role in 'materialising' imperial ideologies, and coercion, as the most visible means through which to present the Roman state, a social construction, physically throughout the empire (cf. Mitchell 1991; Yiftachel 1998). Moreover, imperial architecture, or political architecture, as we shall see, provides the setting for rituals, and especially rituals related to Rome. The scale and elaboration of monumental architecture, which exceeds any functional requirements, is intended to impress subjects by displaying the power of the centre (Trigger 1990). The 'centre'–that is the *princeps*, the senate, and Roman magistrates – actively promote this type of architecture, most apparently at places such as Athens or Lugdunum which were of major concern to the Roman emperors. Here, they clearly 'imposed' architecture as a medium through which to communicate with and influence their subjects (cf. Alcock 1993:172–214).

All empires need to consolidate their dominions, colonies or provinces and all therefore face similar problems of coercion, control and communication. It is also a feature of empires to incorporate what are considered to be distinct ethnic units. The army, or even the long-term threat of military intervention, cannot have been an efficient means of control, as it is too costly. Instead, 'colonialism…is an operation of discourse,' which 'interpellates colonial subjects by incorporating them in a system of representation' (Tiffin & Lawson 1994:3). The Roman empire is no exception. There is a large range of influential media to promote imperial ideologies aimed at keeping the empire together. The function of ideology can be defined as 'to disguise the arbitrariness of the social order, including the uneven distribution of resources…' (Leone 1984:26) by promoting advantages, such as the protective role of individuals or the state, peace and order, or 'civilizing' missions. Yet if bureaucracy and direct force seem almost negligible in most pre-industrial empires, how did empires achieve the necessary degree of unity and coercion? The Roman empire seems to create a 'common Roman identity', at least among the élites, a development that had already started in the time of Cicero (who, in his *de legibus* 2.5, points out that everybody has two *patriae*, one of nature and one of citizenship) until the time of Aelius Aristides, during the second century AD, the empire had increasingly become like a single country whose people – or the wealthy strata of society at least – were unified by Roman citizenship (cf. Ael. Arist., *εἰς Ρώμην*, 49–50, 53–6, 93–104).

The emphasis of this paper, however, will be on a single medium of integration, namely public architecture as an expression of imperial ideologies, and as setting for events of an integrative nature. Tilley has pointed out that architecture and other objects:

> are affected by their place in the space of others. Presence, position and absence or 'negative presence' are of crucial importance. Places stand out and are vested with meaning and significance. They are far more than merely locational nodes in a spatial lattice. Places exist through time and space, and sacred places … command awe and respect and this is an obvious reason for their monumentality

(Tilley 1994:122)

And Leone shows how architecture and landscape reflect the ideology of the time:

> ideology takes social relations and makes them appear to be resident in nature or history, which makes them apparently inevitable. So that the way space is divided and described, including the way architecture, alignments and street plans are made to abide by astronomical rules, or the way gardens, paths, rows of trees ... appear to be trained and under the management of individuals or classes with certain ability or learning, is ideology

(Leone 1984:26)

Nowhere else is this more obvious than in the art and architecture of the Augustan period. With its symmetry and regularity it mirrors the political will for order after the chaotic years of the Civil War (cf. Zanker 1988), while at the same time aspiring to order both time and cosmos, as reflected in Augustus' sundial. The emergence of another autocratic regime, where state and ruler become identical, shows clear parallels. The architecture of Louis XIV (1638–1715), especially his palace at Versailles, mirrors his political aims. The scale and technical accomplishments demonstrate the achievement of what could be called 'civilisation', the geometric layout of the palace represents the socio-political conditions, the iconography inserts the king into a mythical system of representation, with Apollo as allegoric representation of Louis XIV (Farrenberg 1996:54–8). Similarly, the Augustan regime created accomplished building works of unprecedented scale which astonished contemporaries like Horace; private, public and religious sphere can no longer be separated, for example, the merger of the temple of Apollo and Augustus' house on the Palatine. It is in this period that Rome became a true capital city, whose architecture reflects Rome's superior role, as well as the omnipresence of the emperor (Zanker 1988).

Rather than merely *reflecting* or *reproducing* ideologies, imperial architecture is intended to *communicate* – more, it wants to *persuade*. Rhetoric is always one element of architecture, i.e. the wish to communicate and to convince (cf. Farrenberg 1996:28; Hauser 1973:122). By physically *materialising* ideologies, imperial dogmas cannot only be communicated and more easily understood, but can be experienced by their intrusion into everyday life through the creation of new spaces and perspectives, and points of focus. During the early Principate, landmarks in the urban landscape of Rome are increasingly related to events and personalities related to the *princeps*. Augustus' dynasty physically occupies space, but not only in Rome, but throughout Italy and the provinces.

The scale and diversity which Rome's empire had acquired during the late Republic demanded a very different approach to create long-term peace and harmony. For instance, the Civil Wars of the first century BC introduced a new chapter in Roman imperialism. An Italy of Roman citizens – united in legal terms, as well as by their experience in the wars – showed the way for an intensifying direct interference from the centre. Also the process of understanding Greek architecture only started in the Late Republic – characterised by instances of an aggressive alienation, i.e. the deliberate re-use of Greek art and architecture in a very different Roman context. For instance, Corinthian columns from the Olympieion in Athens were used for the reconstruction of the Jupiter temple on the capitol (Pliny *HN* 36.45). Moreover, the meaning of architectural forms changes, as Bammer has demonstrated in the case of the monument of C. Memmius at Ephesos. There, by combining different architectural motifs, a new political symbolism was devised which alienates existing motifs; the Romans use this new iconography to represent their relationship with conquered people (cf. Bammer 1985:116–9).

The public architecture of the Principate has to be considered a vital aspect for integration during the first and second centuries AD. While taking up existing symbols and iconography, the monumentality of buildings across the empire created powerful symbols that emphasised Rome's superiority, creating a visible presence of the central government and enhanced ties with the centre. It is essential for a vast state, such as Rome, to be present in the consciousness of its people through its actions, symbols, festivals, parades, and public holidays, in order to create moments of widespread integration and identification with the state.

Roman landscapes

Rather than looking at individual provincial cities in isolation, it is necessary to remember the wider relationships, namely the provincial landscape created by Rome. It should not escape the enormous symbolic meaning to emphasise Rome's place at the centre of this road-system. Not unlike the Inca empire (cf. Hyslop 1985), road building and the introduction of Roman rule always seem synonymous and during the Principate, the network of *viae publicae* was extended throughout the empire (Purcell 1990; Witcher 1998). Itineraries and the *tabulae Peutingeriana* show the road network from Britain to Syria as an efficient communication system. Having improved communication throughout the empire, cultural boundaries were likely to diminish.

Along the roads, there emerges a network of Roman sites, including a countless number of *mansiones* (Pliny *HN* 6.102, 12, 52) and *mutationes* (e.g. Amm. Marc. 21.9.4) which were constructed to facilitate transport and communication. The political importance of roads is reflected by emperors assuming responsibility for their maintenance. Following the lines of Roman roads, the empire became monumentalised, not dissimilar to the monumentalisation of Rome herself. Throughout the empire, the ideology of Augustus' regime has been *materialised* in architecture and iconography. The passage led through triumphal arches and along monuments. Ascending to the Alpine passes one passed through Cottius' triumphal arch at Segusio (Susa) – a passage experienced by Ammianus Marcellinus (15.10.7) (cf. Bartolomesi *et al.* 1994) – or through Augustus' arch at Augusta Praetoria (Aosta) and the sanctuary to Iupiter Poeninus where votive inscriptions reflect the cosmopolitan nature of this route (Cavallaro & Walser 1988). Along the via Aurelia between Ventimiglia and Nice, the *tropaeum Augustae* celebrates Augustus' conquest of the Alps (Lamboglia 1983). Outside Aurasio (Orange), another triumphal arch – celebrating the conquest of Gaul – marks the passage north into Gaul. The popularity of arches can be explained by their symbolic meaning: subjugation – prisoners-of-war were driven through the *iugum* and the triumphal arch was a symbol for the purification of the army (*sub iugum*, cf. Bammer 1985:120; cf. Cic. *Off.* 3.30; Caes. *BG.* 1.12). The 'propaganda' function of imperial architecture was acknowledged by contemporaries, for example in Maecenas' speech, recorded by Cassius Dio, who advised Augustus to use monumental architecture in order to make Rome's allies respectful and to frighten Rome's enemies (Cass. Dio 52.30.1; cf. Hammond 1932). Winter has already noticed that the emperor's buildings 'thus became an important factor in the Romanisation processes in the provinces' (1996:235). By the first century AD Rome and the imperial family had become omnipresent and the empire had acquired a sense of homogeneity and unity, at least along roads.

These memorials to imperial glory are supplemented by urban monuments. When one approached a Roman town, necropoleis lined the suburban roads. Often there were impressive funerary monuments, like at Glanum (St. Remy-de-Provence), which followed fashion and types common at Rome at the time (cf. Häussler 1998b), and exemplified the presence of social groups with putative links to Rome and the *princeps*. Many Roman towns are re-foundations of existing settlements – part of Roman strategy to take accommodate existing social and religious structures and transform their meaning. Contrary to Millett (1990), I believe that the Romans deliberately transformed existing socio-economic patterns by reshaping existing 'indigenous' settlements and created Roman towns as part of a deliberate strategy to *assimilate* the local population, i.e. to integrate them in Roman forms of representation. This is not dissimilar to the Spanish policy to place, wherever possible, churches and main squares on the sites of an indigenous focus of either worship or power (Fraser 1990:64–5).

Entering a Roman town, provincial architecture is intended to communicate and persuade. On the one hand, it was a strategy of 'unification' to provide Roman citizens throughout the empire with urban amenities, such as aqueducts and bridges, *fora* and baths – at the same time, these were characteristics of 'order' and 'civilisation'. On the other hand, it was a display of power, a demonstration of Rome's superiority – which local élites could profit from (Winter 1996:54–61); though sometimes provincials resisted violently, as in the case of Claudius' temple at Camulodunum which Tacitus described as *arx aeternae dominationis* (Tac. *Ann.* 14, 31, 6, 3–4). Scale represents wealth and power; the standardised geometrical perfection intimidates and impresses (for Assyria, cf. Reade 1979), whereas the street-grid represents, in sharp contrast to La Tène settlements, aspects of order (one of the reasons it was adopted for sixteenth century Spanish colonies was that the grid plan was 'a visible manifestation of ordered Christian society' (Fraser 1990:46)). As a result travelling along Roman roads architecture, art, and the names and languages of inscriptions, all have acquired Roman characteristics – supplied by means of an efficient communication network which diminished cultural boundaries (Häussler 1998a).

Only with Caesar and Augustus, does Rome's concept of urbanisation spread on an unprecedented scale throughout the Western Empire. Previously, Roman urbanism was more restricted: *coloniae* were, in Cicero's view, not *oppida*, but *propugnacula imperii* 'bastions of the empire' (Cic. *leg. agr.* 2.73) and provided land for veterans and proletarians. By contrast during the Principate, provincial cities included Rome's colonial foundations and re-foundations, as well as numerous indigenous sites, the *civitas* capitals. Why had urbanism become so important, considering that Rome had previously been able to control many peoples, such as the Samnites, Insubres and Taurini, without the need for municipalisation? This answer must lie in people's experience of the Late Republic, which stimulated changes in the relationship between the city of Rome, the 'centre', and the provincial or allied municipality.

There were practical reasons for Rome's direct involvement. Especially in the case of Italy it is obvious that an efficient taxation presupposed a cadastre in order to achieve a reliable census assessment (cf. Nicolet 1988); hence the need for large-scale land surveys or centuriation by Roman *gromatici* (Gabba 1985; Inaudi 1976). Similarly, the grant of Roman citizenship stimulated a process of municipalisation in Italy. Indeed, a municipalized Italy was so important that non-urban communities (e.g., many Alpine peoples) had to be attributed to an urban centre (on *adtributio*, cf. Laffi 1966; on the *reducciones* of 'natives' in sixteenth century Peru, cf. Fraser 1990:42); Augustus' *tota Italia* was symbolised by the re-organisation of Rome and Italy into *regiones*. Decision-making processes were transferred to Rome, i.e. the *praetor* had become the highest juridical institution and the *lex de Gallia Cisalpina* mirrors a process where the role of local authorities had to be defined vis-à-vis the Roman *praetor* (Laffi & Crawford 1996). At the same time, it is interesting to see that Roman magistrates took a strong interest in the running of local government, for example by imposing forms of *euergetism* into municipal charters, such as the *lex de coloniae Genetivae* of Urso obliging magistrates to spend a certain amount of money for *pane et circensem* public buildings (Gabba & Crawford 1996). Through this Roman cognitions of *euergetism* are actively imposed on communities throughout the empire. Fundamentally, this notion might not seem dissimilar to what Gluckman called the 'spirit of generosity' in 'tribal' communities (Gluckman 1965:50–2), though the Roman system encouraged the accumulation of wealth for the few (as compensation for loss of statesmanship). Wealth had to be redistributed through forms of *euergetism;* this became a fundamental essence of the Roman Empire during the Principate since it aimed at limiting social strife and political unrest under the auspices of Rome.

Many of these mechanisms had been developed during the Republic, but it was during the Principate that one can recogise their more efficient application. Moreover, links between the local community and Rome becomes increasingly institutionalised. Besides the official chain of command – from the senate, via the provincial governor to the local municipality – patronage links always were highly important in order to represent the individual community's interests at Rome. Among the new mediators between the *princeps* and the local municipality, were the *flamines* and the *seviri*; the relationship was therefore based on a religious foundation, which enhanced its official role (cf. Price 1984). Similarly, in cities throughout the empire, urban plebs set up inscriptions to the emperor. This reflects that the urban and rural plebs acquired a group identity, as well as a direct link to the emperor bypassing existing hierarchies and thus undermining the authority of local élites and councils.

It appears that urbanism provided a setting for a certain kind of lifestyle and society that was unique to the Principate, where social structures were based on an urban lifestyle (cf. Owens 1991:146). In the context of a Roman town, the cultural and economic assimilation of people of various social and ethnic origins was promoted, while the link with the 'centre' could be fostered in institutions situated at the core of any regional centre. Indeed, places were constructed to create a setting for shared rites involving large groups of people. Forum, theatre, and amphitheatre are particular spaces in the urban landscape. Their design is highly standardised, increasingly copying examples at Rome, rather than Greece, which is not accidental, but reflects the strong focus on Rome, most apparent in the rebuilding of Greek theatres during the Principate (cf. Alcock 1993). Under the Roman premise of *utilitas publica* (cf. Winter 1996:42–53) it was the practical achievements of Roman engineering – aqueducts, bridges, roads, baths, etc., which became cultural symbols of *romanitas* (Bammer 1985:129–30; Waldherr 1989:38–9).

The Forum – a particular piece of social space

Not all places have the same design or cultural intent. Different kinds of square stimulate different forms of experience. A square is a place for human interaction, whose mode is produced or reproduced by size, location and access patterns. There are various forms of public interaction, such as processions, commercial exchange, executions or games. In this respect, the Roman *forum* can be defined as 'a particular piece of social space, a place socially and ideologically demarcated and separated from other places,' – a place which 'conveys and evokes a range of responses. The importance of these sites is not only their manifest and distinctive appearance, but their qualifying and latent meaning...' (Kupfer 1972:420). The forum, as such, was a key place in the urban landscape. In Zucker's typology, it is both a dominated square, with the temple as focal construction and a closed square in which the space is surrounded by repetitive built forms (Zucker 1959). Access becomes prestigious as the restricted number of entrances, usually two, allow social control. During the Republic, the focus of *fora* in Rome's colonies was on the capitolium and the voting assembly as shown by the example of Cosa. Through time, a distinct architectural feature emerges in which the *fora* of Caesar and Augustus at Rome are archetypes by having just one or two entrance gates, repetitive colonnades incorporating the basilica, and the temple (cf. in general, Anderson 1984). This structure is not accidental, nor does it originate as such from known Greek predecessors. Zanker has demonstrated in the case of Forum Augustum how Greek architectural models were taken up and modified to become expressions of Roman *Machtdenken;* the architectural frontage had become a ritualised demonstration of Roman authority (Zanker 1970:11–2; Winter 1996). The visitor was engaged in a dialogue – art and architecture of imperial *fora* intended to communicate the *imperator*'s grandeur and his achievements (for the Forum Iulium, cf. Westall 1996). This usage of architecture seems characteristic of autocratic regimes and is exemplified in baroque and renaissance architecture whose rectangular squares show order and harmony (just like in Augustan art); through the scale of buildings one intends to intimidate, to overwhelm; buildings induce respect and fear. It is society that shapes buildings, but buildings also impose constraints on future social actions (cf. Hillier & Hanson 1985), that make them a useful tool for a new regime.

Both emperors and local élites were involved in building. For instance, local élites were motivated by the need for self-representation, for example, the capitolium, underlines the *romanitas* of a town (cf. Dohna 1997), Roman examples are imitated, most obvious the copy of

Augustus' forum at Mérida (de la Barrera & Trillmich 1996). On the other hand, the emperor's direct involvement is frequently attested (Winter 1996; even using the army for civil building, e.g., *SHA Prob.* 9.3; 18.8). The emperor's activities are often concentrated at 'cosmopolitan' sites where his image and message can be seen by many people, as in cities like Nikomedeia and Nikaia in Bithynia, Trapezous in Pontos, Ankyra in Galatia (Winter 1996:234).

To the visitor of any Roman forum, there unfolds the picture of power relationships (with the exception of Propertius, for whom the splendour and charm of the Forum of Augustus was merely an excuse for him being late for a date (Prop. 2.31: *Quaeris, cur ueniam tibi tardior? aurea Phoebi porticus a magno Caesare aperta fuit*; cf. Klodt 1998)). Already the controlled flow of movement along the rectangular axes of the Roman town, the controlled access to the forum, the overwhelming size of architecture must have provided a claustrophobic and intimidating emotion. Entering the forum – usually through triumphal arches, a common metaphor for relationships of power and subjugation – the visitor's view was focused on the dominating temple, on the basilica, as well as the colonnades and statues. As an icon of Roman urbanism the forum provided the stage and the facilities for an urban way of life. It allowed people to stroll along the colonnades and pavements, creating the 'civilised' atmosphere which contemporaries considered an essential aspect of *humanitas* (Tac. *Agr.* 21).

The statues visualised imperial power relationships – from the *princeps* to the local *patronus* and other local magistrates. The relatively uniform patterns of statue arrangement is no accident, as shown by the similarities from geographically distinct regions, such as Africa (Zimmer 1989) and Spain (Alföldy 1979). Similar to the forum of Augustus, statues communicate a particular view of history – centred around the *princeps*. There also seems to have been the need to represent the ruler's family (e.g., cult of Livia (cf. Gross 1962)). While coins had a more 'secular' message, statues were identified with the person, so that honours paid to the emperor in person and to his statue were interchangeable (Price 1984:204–5). For instance, Apuleius referred to the emperor's statue as a haven of refuge (*Metamorphoses* 3.29; cf. Price 1984:119). How better to include Rome and the emperor in everyday life?

Entering the forum, people's view had to be focused on the temple or *capitolium* as the centrepiece of the layout. Vitruvius demanded that the temple had to be visible from anywhere in the city; hence its prominent location on a podium overlooking the surrounding structures (Vitr. 1.7.1; e.g., at Aosta (Viale 1967)). This temple reflected the continuous presence of Rome, whether worshipped in form of the Capitoline Triad or on behalf on the deified emperor. The importance of this dominating focus on the temple can be seen, for example, at Roman Athens, where the layout of the *agora* was radically altered providing a more penetrating focus on a Roman-style temple (Alcock 1993:192–8). The creation of these imperial points of reference in the heart of public places was clearly considered important, and emperors continuously added dominant buildings, for example, in Athens where the imperial *familia* was visible throughout the *agora* (Alcock 1993; Whittaker 1997).

The forum is also the venue for one of the most Roman activities: jurisprudence. During the Republican period, fora were constructed in Italy, Spain and the South of France as 'scenes of *iudicia publica*' (Ruoff-Väänänen 1978:9); many of these fora later acquired the status of *colonia* or *municipia* (e.g., CIL 5.7375; 11.1059)), and every juridical person belonged to a certain forum (e.g., *suum forum* in Cic. *Verr.* 3.38). Indeed, jurisdiction had to be one of the forum's prime functions. In Rome, all trials took place in the Forum Romanum during the Republic and because of their increase Caesar and Augustus started the construction of two new fora (App. *BC.* 2.102; Suet. *Aug.* 29.2). The basilica is only occasionally attested as a venue for jurisdiction (as argued by Welin 1959:447), but it was there (basilica or forum) that people in cities throughout the empire were actually able to see the Roman magistrate in action; the closest most people would get to representatives of the central government. The superior role of Roman jurisdiction, allowing the appeal to governor and emperor (cf. Apuleius, *Metamorphoses*

3.29) are essential in ideologically justifying the benefit of Roman rule. One should not underestimate the absolutely essential role of Roman law and jurisdiction for the integration process since it allowed control of 'indigenous' people by involving them in legal practice. Stern (1982) has demonstrated the possibilities of jurisdiction in the case of Spanish colonialism in South America, where in the long run, "indigenous' litigation weakened capacities for independent resistance by fostering rivalry and conflict, and by integrating 'native' society more tightly into the power structure of the conquerors' (Stern 1982:291). At various levels Roman juridical institutions created ties with local communities and élites. Already in the second century BC permanent courts for extortion were created aimed at suppressing any military resistance of an exploited province by transferring occasions of strife to the law courts. Similarly, inner-élite power struggles are decided by Roman magistrates, as in the case of Genoa and the Veturians (CIL 1².584) or between Magnesia and Priene (Sylloge 3.679). Juridical institutions integrated local communities and brought them close to Roman authority which sought coercion, i.e. law could be used by local communities to defend their interests at Rome, but also by the centre to enable compliance.

Besides the forum being a representation of the Roman emperor and State through its statues, its intimidating architecture and the presence of Roman magistrates, we have to focus on the cult activity as a major event involving people in ceremonies related to the emperor. It is necessary to emphasise the ritual function of cult; be it the Capitoline Triad or the so-called Imperial cult, i.e. the cult to Roma and the deified emperors which existed throughout the empire – not as a standardised, 'alien' imperial imposition, but as a more or less integral part of existing religious practices (cf. Beard *et al.* 1998:313–63; Price 1984). Philo already suggests that the name and the temple for the emperor had acquired an all-dominating place in the transformation of any *polis* (Phil. *Leg. Ad Gaium* 149–50), so that Rome became omnipresent (also cf. Price 1984:133; Owens 1991:140–5). Part of the success of the Imperial cult is its integration with existing cults. For instance, at Thugga the Imperial cult was almost completely fused with the Capitoline Triad (Dohna 1997:476; *AE* 1949:109), while in many Greek cities other deities were worshipped on behalf of the emperor (cf. Price 1984). What is important is that throughout the empire people participated in cults and worship which were directly or indirectly connected to the welfare of the *princeps* and the empire. The constant focus on the emperor is mirrored in imperial religious calendars (e.g. third century AD Dura Papyrus 54).

The *princeps* used, consciously or not, religious power as a means of coercion; its importance becomes more apparent in periods of crisis, as reflected in the sources of the third century AD. Though often seen as 'homage', rather than 'worship' (cf. discussion in Price 1984; Beard *et al.* 1998:313–63), as a cult the communal activity includes sacrifice and consumption of the sacrificial food by the community. Our evidence for sacrifices to the emperor is restricted. There were libations, ritual cakes, burning of incense and the killing of an animal, usually a bull (cf. Price 1984:208–9 for further bibliography). The communal focus is underlined by processions (e.g., SEG 9 923; Price 1984:210–1), but more importantly through feasting: for example, a feast alone is mentioned for an imperial birthday celebration. We can expect feasts for the whole local population after sacrifices, so that sacrifice 'was integrated into the life of the city' (Price 1984:230). This is a form of conspicuous consumption, a display of power of the emperor and his supporters who could invest in monumental architecture, in luxury goods, as well as sacrificial goods (cf. Trigger 1990).

In this way, not just symbolically *sharing* but, for many, *profiting* in a form of reciprocity of the spoils of empire made it into a festival of integrative and legitimising nature. Is it possible that the linkage between the state and the local populace heavily relied on ceremonial aspects – ceremonies in which large numbers of people were brought together in rites of legitimisation? Especially in a society where bureaucratic activities hardly exist, the relationship between 'centre' and regional centre can expect to be shaped by ritual activities. In the Inca empire, for example, it was suggested that the distribution and consumption of food and other goods by the state are an essential aspect of these legitimisation rituals and that *generosity* forges a relationship between Inca leaders and locals (cf. Moore 1996). It is common for rulers to sponsor elaborate ceremonies that often require special equipment and large quantities of foodstuff (cf. Murra 1962). At this stage, one should bear in mind the importance of élite generosity and *euergetism* in societies other than the Roman empire such as the Vijayanagara Empire in Southern India (Sinopoli & Morrison 1995). *Euergetism* was heavily supported by Roman emperors who increasingly had to coerce local élites, i.e. for the cohesion / coercion of the empire, it was seen necessary to avoid any de-stablilising factors, such as internal strife between rich and poor, by promoting forms of reciprocity and redistribution.

Is it therefore possible to lodge the administrative function of larger provincial centres mainly in traditional forms of reciprocity? Empires face similar problems of coercion. Within this system of political and economic control, artificially created regional centres, such as the Inca city of Huánuco Pampa, provided the ceremonial context and physical layout which was designed to articulate various local units in their relationship to each other and their relationship to the centre (Moore 1996). From their layout and facilities, the cities of the Roman empire are not that dissimilar. One could attribute a central role to the forum. While temple and basilica physically materialise the link with Rome, the forum also provides the setting for Roman rituals and Roman activities, such as large scale ceremonies in honour of the emperor and the Capitoline Triad. The existence of storage space under the forum (*cryptoporticus*), for example at Aosta and Arles, might reflect the forum's role in redistributive rites. Within this setting, local magistrates were visibly integrated and subordinated into the civic and religious role of maintaining the ties with the (deified) emperor. Power structures are thus represented on the basis of a cult that interpreted the local communities' place in the Roman world, although we should not ignore the increasing bureaucratic control, for example by the *curatores*.

Theatre and Amphitheatre

In this respect, theatre and amphitheatre reflect a more specialised venue, though of increasing importance over time. For the sake of the plebs, Augustus would not miss any theatre performance, which became a rite of legitimisation. Indeed, the theatre audience increasingly reflected the social order. This was also the venue for pro-Augustan poetry, Horace, Virgil, etc., to be read out loud (cf. Yavetz 1969, 1983). *Ludi* and *munera* 'functioned as institutions in Roman life' (Edmondson 1996: 71), so that theatres seem increasingly to take over some of the functions of the forum. It is not surprising that monumental theatres and amphitheatres often dominate the urban landscape, for example at Orange where the theatre is clearly the central focus of the urban landscape. But there was no clear division between entertainment, politics, jurisdiction and ritual: plays and games had a religious context, since festivals took place in honour of deities, while the gathering allowed for political participation. For the Roman State it was necessary to involve the public – a public who took a lively interest in capital trials and executions (Potter 1996: 151-2).

The functions of theatres and amphitheatres are largely analogous with those of the forum: to include large parts of the population in common rituals, i.e. performances which were staged by the local élite and often had a focus on the emperor or the empire as a whole (e.g., the emperor's birthday) (in general, cf. Geertz 1980; Edmondson 1996; Potter 1996). There was an increasing level of specialisation. During the second century AD, *fora* acquired more commercial functions; often, permanent stalls were built within the forum square, or specialist *merkatos* were constructed. Theatres and amphitheatres allowed the public display of society as inserted in an imperial hierarchy, with imperial magistrates taking the best seats, with public executions under imperial auspices. The theatre also allowed the inclusion of an even larger part of the urban and rural population than the forum.

The importance of the forum as a symbol of an independent city state within the empire declined and there was a shift away from politics during the first and second centuries AD. Inscriptions reflect this change with *duoviri* and *quattuorviri* becoming less prominent in the epigraphic record than *flamines* and *seviri*, i.e. the relationship with the princeps became more important than political *libertas*. The general socio-political climate had changed and local decision-making increasingly became unpoliticized. Instead, the emphasis shifted to other communal institutions, hence the increasing importance of *collegia*, of theatres and amphitheatres during the first and second century AD, largely stimulated by fashion at Rome. Eventually, with difficulties in maintaining supply and communication with the centre, urban life style increasingly turned to forms of personal bondage ('colonate'), as mirrored in the decline of many theatres, amphitheatres and even fora.

Conclusions

Self-representation, for example by means of architecture, and consolidation of group identities and group interests through common activities (rituals, festivals) are essential to consolidate and maintain social order (cf. Quaritsch 1993:1070). This is especially the case for an economically, historically and ethnically diverse society, such as the Roman empire. Through art and architecture, state and society are represented by concrete representations, both *intentional* and *unintentional* (Krüger 1977). This also implies that as architecture reflects the *Selbstverständnis* of architecture and/or patron (cf. Goffman 1959), the architecture and layout of a city reflects changing societal and political order.

The city of Rome herself appears like a macrocosm of the whole empire. Deities from all the provinces were worshipped; artefacts and products were imported from around the Mediterranean; Roman culture increasingly incorporated elements from all over her empire. Rome's superior role is convincingly communicated by its symbolic architecture of the Principate. On a basic level, the numerous provincial centres employed a similar visual language; every provincial city looked onto Rome (Dion. Hal. *Orat. Vet.* 3). They encompass important aspects of Roman ideology. Location and street-grid are generally composed of a 'disassociated' architecture that neglects natural bearings, while the forum, temple, basilica, theatre are the key settings for Roman rituals, as well as being representative of the Roman state. Meier-Dallach had shown how, on the background of what he describes as political culture, architecture imprints images of state and society and hence an element to legitimise the existing order (cf. Meier-Dallach, quoted in Gottschall 1987:42–3) and not just at the centre.

But Roman architects have not just created exclusive monuments, but places that were incorporated into everyday life, whether they were arches to pass through or bustling market squares. These places were meant to be *experienced* and different peoples in the empire experienced them in a different ways, thus, explaining the variations in typologies and the chronologies of their use. Most importantly, for the Roman State, these places were designed as venues for certain social activities. While colonnades and pavements made it possible to wear the Roman *toga*, the theatre/amphitheatre made social divisions public. Above all, festivals and rituals created both regional gatherings and focus points and helped to form a 'Roman' identity, which was essential to keep the empire together. In previously non-urbanised territories, Roman architecture had the twofold aim of stabilising newly created regional centres, whose population could then be integrated into an imperial network.

It can be assumed that aspects of reciprocity and redistribution are essential, not only to maintain social order, but to create empire-wide structures. *Euergetism* and *annonae* helped to redistribute wealth, mostly from people of imperial rank, i.e. senators and knights, who spent most money in a local community (Frézouls 1990). The importance of the Imperial cult should not be underestimated. Ceremonies and festivals in the honour of the deified emperor created moments of 'national' integration and sharing in the spoils of the sacrifices. The concept of the emperor as semi-god is one way to create superiority and to communicate it in a way that could be understood throughout Rome's provinces.

There are of course, certain concerns which Roman ideology convincingly communicated as being beneficial. Imperial coinage frequently refers to peace, concord, prosperity, and victory; whose major agent was the *princeps*. It is hardly surprising that the deities of Fortuna or Victoria, so typical for Roman society of the first and second century AD, dominate provincial inscriptions. Aspects of unity and the focus on the *princeps* become important issues with the coming of the monarchy that facilitated and stimulated cultural and political 'homogeneity'.

All this underlines that urbanism, as promoted in the first century BC/AD was considered essential for the integration process. Imperial ideologies and hierarchy aimed at undermining local authority. This is characteristic for any 'new' state, because the ties with the centre need to be increased, automatically disturbing existing social geographies.

With the emergence of the Principate, urbanisation, imperial ideologies and state/political architecture are promoted on an unprecedented scale. Throughout history, in periods of significant socio-cultural change the new social order has to be publicised, maintained and consolidated. This phase of intensive promotion is most visible in architectural terms. In regard to Augustus, this is not to deny that many developments and architectural forms had Republican predecessors, but the political will reflects an autocratic regime that wanted to indoctrinate its power all over the empire. Architecture is a tool that enabled the new regime to create a physical presence of the Roman State, while creating the stage for legitimating rituals. One can only speculate on the overwhelming effect of Roman architecture, especially in the Roman West where monumental architecture of this scale was previously unknown – there, Roman architecture must have been considered intimidating and mirroring Rome's claim to eternal rule. But because Roman architecture had practical purposes, which intruded everyday life, as well as representing Rome, it was essential as a means to legitimise Roman rule.

Wolfson College, University of Oxford

Bibliography
Aelius Aristides *Smyrnaei quae supersunt omnia, vol.2.* (ed. B. Keil, 1898). Second edition, 1958. Berlin: Weidemann.
Alcock, S. E. 1993. *Graecia Capta. The landscapes of Roman Greece.* Cambridge: Cambridge University Press.
Alföldy, G. 1979. Bildprogramme in den römischen städten des Conventus Terraconensis. Das Zeugnis der statuenportamente. *Rev. Univ. Complutense (Homenaje García y Bellido)*, 28 (118) 4: 177–275.
Ammianus Marcellinus *Histoire, Tome 3, Livres 20–22.* (ed. J. Fontaine, 1996). Paris: Les Belles Lettres.
Anderson, J. C. 1984. *The historical topography of the imperial fora.* Bruxelles: Coll. Latomus 182.
Bammer, A. 1985. Architektur *und gesellschaft in der antike.* Second edition. Wien, Köln & Graz: Böhlau.
Bartolomasi, N., Forno, T., Lambert, C., Nesta, P., Patria, L. & Ponzio, G. (eds.) 1994. *Susa. Bimillenario dell'arco. Atti del convegno (2–3 ottobre 1992).* Susa: Segusium, Società di ricerche e studi valsusini.
Beard, M., North, J. & Price, J. 1998. *Religions of Rome 1: a history.* Cambridge: Cambridge University Press.
Caesar *Commentarii rerum gestarum. Vol. 1. Bellum Gallicum.* (ed. O. Seel, 1961). Leipzig: Teubner.
Blänsdorf, J. (ed.) 1990. *Theater und Gesellschaft im Imperium Romanum.* Tübingen: Mainzer Forschungen zu Drama und Theater 4.
Caesar *Bellum Gallicum,* ed. W. Hering 1987.
Camps, W. A. (ed.) 1967. *Propertius, Elegies, Book II.* Cambridge: Cambridge University Press.
Cavallero, A. M. & Walser, G. 1988. *Iscrizioni di Aosta–Inscriptions de Augusta Praetoria.* Aosta: Musumeci.
Cicero *De legibus.* (ed. K. Ziegler, 1978). Third edition. Freiburg/Würzburg: Ploetz.
Cicero *De lege agraria.* (ed. V. Marek, 1983). Leipzig: Teubner.

De la Barrera, J. L & Trillmich, W. 1996. Eine Wiederholung der Aeneas-Gruppe vom Forum Augustum samt ihrer Inschrift in Mérida (Spanien). *Mitteilungen des Deutschen Archäologischen Instituts (Rom)*, 103: 119–38.

Dio Cassius *Historiae Romanae* (ed. U. P. Boissevain, 1895–1931). Berlin

Dionysius of Hallicarnassus (ed. G. Aujac, 1978). Paris: Les Belles Lettres.

Dohna, F. 1997. Gestaltung des öffentlichen Raumes und imperiale Ideologie am Beispiel des Kapitols von Thugga. *Mitteilungen des Deutschen Archäologischen Instituts (Rom)*, 104: 467–76.

Edmondson, J.C. 1996. Dynamic arenas: gladiatorial presentations in the City of Rome and the construction of Roman society during the early Empire. In W. J. Slater, (ed.) *Roman theatre and society: E. Togo Salmon papers 1*. Ann Arbor: University of Michigan Press, pp.69–112.

Farrenberg, B. 1996. *Staatsarchitektur. Die Selbstdarstellung des Staates. Beispiele staatlicher Architektur in Europa*. Ludwigshafen: BDK-Brief-Verlag.

Fraser, V. 1990. *The architecture of conquest. Building in the Viceroyalty of Peru, 1535–1635*. Cambridge: Cambridge University Press.

Frere, S. 1987. *Britannia. a history of Roman Britain*. Third edition. London & New York: Routledge & Kegan Paul.

Frézouls, E. 1990. Évergetism et construction publique en Italie du Nord (Xe et Xie régions augustéenes). In AAVV. (eds.) *La città nell'Italia settentrionale in età romana: morfolofie, strutture e funzionamento dei centri urbani delle regione X e XI. Atti del convegno Trieste, 13–15 marzo 1987*. Trieste: Università di Trieste & Roma, École française de Rome, pp. 179–209.

Gabba, E. 1985. Per un'interpretazione storica della centuriazione Romana. *Athenaeum* 63: 265–84.

Gabba, E. & Crawford, M. H. 1996. Lex Coloniae Genetivae. In M. H. Crawford (ed.) *Roman Statutes*. London: Bulletin of the Institute of Classical Studies Supplement 64, pp.393–454.

Geertz, C. 1980. *Negara: the theatre state in nineteenth century Bali*. Princeton & New York: University Press.

Gluckman, M. 1965. *Politics, law and ritual in tribal society*. Oxford & New York: Blackwell.

Goffman, E. 1959. *The presentation of self in everyday life*. Edinburgh: University of Edinburgh Social Sciences Research Centre, Monograph 2.

Gross, W. H. 1962. *Untersuchungen zur Grundlegung einer Iulia-Ikonographie*. Göttingen: Vandenhoeck & Ruprecht (Abhandlungen der Akademie der Wissenschaften zu Göttingen 3, 52).

Hammond, M. 1932. The significance of the speech of Maecenas in Dio Cassius, Book 52. *Transactions and Proceedings of the American Philological Association*, 63: 88–102.

Hauser, A. 1973. *Kunst und Gesellschaft*. München: Beck.

Häussler, R. 1998a. Motivation and ideologies of Romanization. In C. Forcey, J. Hawthorne & R. Witcher, *TRAC97. Proceedings of the seventh annual theoretical Roman archaeology conference*. Oxford: Oxbow, pp.11–19.

Häussler, R. 1998b. Resta, viator, et lege. *Papers of the Institute of Archaeology*, 9: 29–45.

Hillier, B. & Hanson, J. 1985. *The social logic of space*. Cambridge: Cambridge University Press.

Hyslop, J. 1985. *The Inca road system*. New York: Academic Press.

Inaudi, G. 1976. Il problema della centuriazione e della duplice deduzione di 'Augusta Taurinorum'. *Bollettino Storico-Bibliografico Subalpino*, 74: 381–98.

Klodt, C. 1998. Platzanlagen der Kaiser in der Beschreibung der Dichter. *Gymnasium*, 105: 1–38.

Kolb, F. 1984. *Die Stadt im Altertum*. München: Beck.

Krüger, H. 1977. Die Selbstdarstellung des Staates. In H. Quaritsch (ed.) *Die Selbstdarstellung des Staates. Vorträge und Diskussionsbeiträge der 44. Staatswissenschaftlichen Fortbildungstagung 1976 an der Hochschule für Verwaltungswissenschaft Speyer*. Berlin: Duncker & Humbolt, pp. 21–49.

Kupfer, H. 1972. The language of sites in the politics of space. *American Anthropologist*, 74: 411–25.

Laffi, U. 1966. *Adtributio e contributio. Problemi del sistema politica-amministrativo dello stato romano*. Pisa: Nistri-Lischi.

Laffi, U. & Crawford, M. H. 1996. *Lex de Gallia Cisalpina*. In M.H. Crawford (ed.) *Roman statutes*. London: Bulletin of the Institute of Classical Studies Supplement 64, pp. 461–482.

Lamboglia, N. 1983. *Le Trophée d'Auguste à la Turbie*. Fifth edition. Bordighera: Institut international d'études ligures.

Leone, M. 1984. Interpreting ideology in historical archaeology: using the rules of perspective in the William Paca Garden in Annapolis, Maryland. In D. Miller & C. Tilley (eds.) *Ideology, power and prehistory*. Cambridge: Cambridge University Press, pp.25–35.

Millett, M.J. 1990 *The Romanization of Britain: an essay in archaeological interpretation*. Cambridge: Cambridge University Press.

Mitchell, T. 1991. The limits of the state: beyond statist approaches and their critics. *American Political Science Review*, 85 (1): 77–96.

Moore, J.D. 1996. The archaeology of plazas and the proxemics of ritual. Three Andean traditions. *American Anthropologist*, 98 (4): 789–802.

Morris, C. 1982. The infrastructure of Inca control in the Peruvian Highlands. In G. A. Collier, R. I. Rosaldo & J. D. Wirth (eds.) *The Inca and Aztec states, 1400–1800, anthropology and history*. New York & London: Academic Press, pp.153–71.

Murra, J.V. 1962. Cloth and its functions in the Inca state. *American Anthropologist*, 64: 710–28.

Nicolet, C. 1988. *L'inventaire du Monde: Géographie et Politique aux Origines de l'Empire Romain*. Paris: Arthème Fayard.

Owens, E.J. 1991. *The city in the Greek and Roman world*. London: Routledge.

Pliny *Naturalis historia*, (eds. L. Jan & C. Mayhoff, 1889–1905). Leipzig: Teubner,.

Potter, D. 1996. Performance, power, and justice in the High Empire. In W. J. Slater, (ed.) *Roman theatre and society: E. Togo Salmon papers 1*. Ann Arbor: University of Michigan Press, pp.129-59.

Price, S.R.F. 1984. *Ritual and power: the Roman imperial cult in Asia Minor*. Cambridge: Cambridge University Press.

Propertius *Elegies* (ed. W.A. Camps, 1967). Cambridge: Cambridge University Press.

Purcell, N. 1990. The creation of provincial landscape: the Roman impact on Cisalpine Gaul. In T. Blagg & M. Millett (eds.) *The early Roman Empire in the West*. Oxford: Oxbow, pp.7–29.

Reade, J. 1979. Ideology and propaganda in Assyrian art. In M. T. Larsen (ed.) *Power and propaganda*. Copenhagen: Akademisk Forlag, pp.329–43.

Quaritsch, H. 1993. Weiteres zur 'Selbstdarstellung des Staates'. *Die Öffentliche Verwaltung*, 24: 1070–1075.

Radke, G. 1979. Viae Publicae. In K. Ziegler, W. Sontheimer, H. Gärtner (eds.) *Der Kleine Pauly. Lexikon der Antike,* 5: 1244–46. München: Deutscher Taschenbuch Verlag.

Ruoff-Väänänen, E. 1978. *Studies on the Italian fora*. Wiesbaden: Franz Steiner Verlag (Historia Einzelschriften 32).

Sinopoli, C.M. & Morrison, K.D. 1995. Dimensions of imperial control. The Vijayanagara capital. *American Anthropologist*, 97 (1): 83–96.

Stern, S.J. 1982. The social significance of judicial institutions in an exploitative society: Huamanga, Peru 1570–1640. In G. A. Collier & J. D. Wirth (eds.) *The Inca and Aztec states, 1400–1800*. New York & London: Academic Press, pp.289–320.

Tacitus *Annales. Livres 13–15* (ed. P. Wuilleumier, 1978). Paris: Les Belles Lettres.

Tiffin, C. & Lawson, A. (eds.) 1994. *De-scribing empire: post-colonialism and textuality*. London: Routledge.

Tilley, C. 1994. *A phenomenology of landscape. Places, paths and monuments*. Oxford: Berg.

Trigger, B.G. 1990. Monumental architecture: a thermodynamic explanation of symbolic behaviour. *World Archaeology*, 22, 2: 119–32.

Viale, V. & Viale M. 1967. *Aosta romana e medievale*. Torino: Istituto bancario San Paolo di Torino.

Vitruvius *Vitruve de l'architecture, livre 1*. (ed. P. Fleury, 1990). Paris: Les Belles Lettres.

Waldherr, G. 1989. *Kaiserliche Baupolitik in Nordafrika. Studien zu den Bauinschriften der diokletianischen Zeit und ihrer räumlichen Verteilung in den römischen Provinzen Nordafrikas*. Frankfurt: Lang.

Welin, E. 1959. *Studien zur Topographie des Forum Romanum*. Frankfurt: Gleerup.

Westall, R. 1996. The Forum Iulium as representation of Imperator Caesar. *Mitteilungen des Deutschen Archäologischen Instituts (Rom)*, 103: 83–118.

Whittaker, C.R. 1997. Imperialism and culture: the Roman initiative. In D. J. Mattingly (ed.) *Dialogues of Roman imperialism. Power, discourse, and discrepant experience in the Roman Empire*. Portsmouth, Rhode Island: JRA Supplementary series 23, pp.143–63.

Winter, E. 1996. *Staatliche Baupolitik und Baufürsorge in den römischen Provinzen des kaiserzeitlichen Kleinasien*. Asia Minor Studien 20. Bonn: Rudolf Habelt Verlag.

Witcher. R. 1998. Roman roads: phenomenological perspectives on roads in the landscape. In C. Forcey, J. Hawthorne & R. Witcher (eds.) *TRAC97. Proceedings of the seventh annual Theoretical Roman Archaeology Conference*. Oxford: Oxbow, pp.60–70.

Yavetz, Z. 1969. *Plebs and princeps*. Oxford: Clarendon Press.

Yavetz, Z. 1983. *Julius Caesar and his public image*. London: Thames & Hudson.

Yiftachel, O. 1998. Planning and social control: exploring the dark side. *Journal of Planning Literature*, 12 (4): 395–406.

Zanker, P. 1970. *Forum Augustum. Das Bildprogramm*. Tübingen: Wasmuth.

Zanker, P. 1988. *The power of images in the age of Augustus* (trans. by A. Shapiro). Ann Arbor: University of Michigan Press.

Zimmer, G. 1989. *Locus datus decreto decurionum: Zur Statusaufstellung zweier Forumsanlagen im römischen Afrika*. München: Abhandlungen der Bayerischen Akademie der Wissenschaften, Phil.-hist. Klasse, 102.

Zucker, P. 1959. *Town and square. From the agora to the village green*. London & New York: Oxford University Press & Columbia University Press.

The Community of the Soldiers: a major identity and centre of power in the Roman empire

by Simon James

Introduction

We tend today to conceptualise the Imperial Roman military as a monolithic state institution. In this paper, which concentrates especially on the second and third centuries AD, I will argue that such a view has rendered largely invisible, a fascinating and very complex social entity of profound importance in the history of the Roman world. The military consisted of people, not cogs in a machine, and it is quite clear that, distinct from the military institutional structures of the state, 'the soldiers' (*milites*) formed a major, well-defined identity-group which constituted a recognised and self-aware empire-wide 'imagined community'.

This community, segmented into hundreds of discrete military formations scattered across the empire, each with its own substantial train of dependants and unique pattern of external social interactions, played a profound role in the history of the Roman world and its neighbours, distinct from that of 'the army' as an organisation. However, as yet this complexity is only partly understood.

What follows is a consideration of the community of *milites*, and the nature of soldierly identity which underpinned it – especially the bodily expression of that identity, where archaeological, representational and documentary evidence allows us to approach aspects of the ideology and symbolic lives of the *milites*.

The anachronism of current terminology

The Imperial Roman military is widely envisaged as a monolithic instrument of state power, its nature closely analogised, more or less overtly, with the armed forces of modern nation states. We commonly speak of 'The Roman Army', implicitly capitalised, and a mechanical analogy is frequently employed, that of 'the Roman war machine' (e.g. Peddie 1994); its units conceptualised as chess-pieces, Roman soldiers as brutally disciplined, and brutal, automata.

I suggest that such a conception of 'The Roman Army' is a modern reification which significantly distorts the evidence. The concept of '*The* Army' seems to me to imply elaborate centralised institutions, a unified hierarchy of command, perhaps a permanent general staff, etc., which did not exist under the Republic or the Principate (the only standing central command institution was the emperorship itself). Certainly, it implies a single unified organisation; but, tellingly, during the later Republic and down to the middle imperial period at least, the Romans appear to have had no such term, and no such concept: 'army' (*exercitus*), singular, was used for a particular grouping of forces, such as the standing army of a province or a corps specially assembled for a particular campaign. When generalising about the military, they employed plurals, writing of 'the armies' (*exercitús*), 'the legions' (*legiones*), 'the regiments' (*numeri*), etc., and not least of 'the soldiers' (*milites*), denoting a socio-political category.

In place of the monolithic/machine model, it is suggested that we should start to think and speak of 'the soldiers', and of Roman armies in the plural, as better ways of conceptualising the Roman military, ways which are much closer to ancient understandings of the military: as a social entity and not just a state institution.

Not 'the army' but 'the soldiers'

It has been widely assumed that discipline made imperial soldiers unthinking military thugs; they may often have been brutal, but they certainly were not robots. Here the current theoretical emphasis on individuals in the past as self-aware social agents is highly valuable, and provides a perspective which makes good sense of a lot of ignored or downplayed data. In fact there always has been plentiful evidence that Roman soldiers were active agents. The way soldiers appear in the surviving literary sources is very far from an image of unquestioning obedience. Under the empire, soldiers in society were represented as feared, dangerous, arrogant outsiders (Carrié 1993:105), a class of men with their own peculiar codes who exploited their position for personal ends with virtual impunity (e.g. MacMullen 1963:84–9). The evidence for the wilfulness and unruliness of soldiers has been played down under the long-prevailing, top-down, officer-centred view of the Roman military; incidents of indiscipline and mutiny have tended to be seen as aberrant or signs of bad leadership. But there is good reason to believe that such behaviour by the troops was normal, even expected by those in authority, a fact of life to be managed and controlled as far as possible. The roots of this situation seem fairly clear. The arrogance, unruliness and sometimes rebelliousness of the troops were surely rooted not only in the violence implicit in their identity, and the privileged place they enjoyed in imperial society, but in the traditional rights to free speech of Roman citizen soldiers of the republican era and in the traditions of warrior classes of other peoples from whom many soldiers continued to be recruited.

Soldiers under the empire had a highly visible special status and resultant professional pride. Their right to bear arms in public symbolised their unique position as guarantors of the Roman order through the threat, probably more often than the delivery, of lethal force on behalf of the state. They held privileges regarding control of property and inheritance denied to others, and occupied a unique legal position, with their own military courts (Campbell 1984:207–42). This special status and official power also gave the brotherhood (or Mafia) of the soldiers unofficial local power, without redress, over civilians (Campbell 1984:246–54). They stood outside the local civil hierarchies; alternately despised and feared, soldiers (and particularly wealthy veterans) were nevertheless courted by civilians of many levels (MacMullen 1963:99–118). The *milites* grouped in regiments scattered across the Roman world were very much aware of their special, shared status, forming a self-conscious 'imagined community' (a concept I will explore further below).

Clearly then, the military was not simply a hierarchical machine controlled with ease from the top; framed by an inordinately complex organisational structure manifested in its hundreds of permanent units, and the amazing proliferation of ranks, grades and offices (Domaszewski 1967), it constituted an equally complex social system (e.g. MacMullen 1984). 'Class-divided' like Roman society as a whole (Giddens 1985:1), the army was a field of continual contention and renegotiation between a variety of cross-cutting interest-groups: the rank-and-file soldiers; centurions and other prominent groups such as standard-bearers; regimental and provincial army commanders; and the emperor, or those who would be emperor. All this resulted in a web of mutual obligation, mutual dependence and mutual implicit threat in which the ordinary soldiery was a key player; maintaining the goodwill and consent of the *milites* at large was obviously vital to military (and so to imperial) authority; the political power of the soldiers was potentially very real, if usually unfocused and not clearly articulated by the men themselves (Campbell 1984:383). Stability and control was achieved, at least most of the time, by constant indoctrination, training, surveillance and discipline, but surely also by the prospect of rewards and personal patronage extended by the emperor, provincial governors/generals and regimental officers.

Soldiers' awareness of their own implicit power was greatly enhanced by the Civil War of the 190s, and the reign of Severus, which showed with glaring clarity the dependence of the emperor on the support of the armies. Thereafter, it became ever more difficult for emperors to maintain strong discipline, because they were constantly obliged to curry the goodwill of the soldiers. Hence the ever-growing importance, which Campbell has examined (1984:32–59), of the soldiers perceiving the emperor as *commilito* ('fellow-soldier'), revealing the concern of the emperors to court the loyalty of the troops as much as to demand it (Campbell 1984:191–8).

What was the nature of this huge and powerful entity, the *milites*? Perhaps the question is best answered through a consideration of how the soldier's identity was actually created and reproduced.

Creating and reproducing Roman soldierly identity

Beyond obedience, encouraged by both simple material rewards and the threat of savage punishment, a sense of personal attachment to regiment, emperor and Rome was achieved by inducing in the recruit (*tiro*), whether volunteer or conscript, a profound ontological shift; his entire sense of being was systematically changed as he acquired a new identity, or more accurately, changed some of his multiple existing identities, and perhaps acquired additional ones. The process of joining a regiment affected his cultural/national/ethnic identities, social status, 'professional' and perhaps religious identities, and indeed the definition of his masculinity. Of course, the degree of change and the profundity of the shock involved will have varied according to the recruit's personal background, and the unit he was joining (legions, and 'ethnic' auxiliary units, for example, seem to have maintained quite varied and distinctive traditions). Unless he had grown up at a camp and was already half-integrated, everything about military life was initially alien.

Attachment of the soldier to the imperial regime was achieved through exposure to propaganda and ideological indoctrination, from saluting the standards to the perhaps subliminal impact of imagery on the coins in his pay. His new existence was framed within carefully created theatres of control; he found himself in the special physical environment of a military base – in my view commonly designed more with surveillance and control of the soldiers in mind than with external functions or defence against perceived external threats. He was also immersed in new practices and routines in space and time, according to unfamiliar diurnal and annual cycles of life and ceremonial, including official Roman and specifically military festivals, rooted in the distant past of an Italy the recruit had probably never seen. As part of their own particular regimental traditions and identity, auxiliary units may also have continued to venerate cults of their place of origin (Figure 1).

It was of course an overtly masculine environment, governed by a distinctive warrior value system, into which he was integrated through indoctrination and, varying according to degree of personal enthusiasm, through conscious voluntary effort, in the re-creation of his sense of self. The potential depth of psychological impact of the transformation may be gauged from the fact that many soldiers acquired a new Romanized name on enlistment, itself a profound expression of the imposition/adoption of a new persona, and assimilation to Roman hegemony.

He had also joined a community with its own special language, the *sermo militaris*, which he would have to learn and use correctly to be a member of the group. This was much more than just bad Latin; it was of course full of jargon and technical expressions, many of which were taken from Greek and languages of other peoples recruited into the army (Carrié 1993:127–8).

The *tiro* also experienced a radical physical transformation of his own body, in terms both of visual appearance and personal habits and practices. He was introduced to a perhaps new hygiene and grooming regime, including the routines of Roman baths and particular military fashions regarding hairstyle and patterns of facial hair; dietary and drinking habits may also have been alien, depending on his origin. And, of course, he was also put into military uniform which, as will be seen, is no anachronistic term.

Through physical exercise, weapons training, and especially drilling in squads and rhythmic marching, the recruit was made to feel a part of a corporate group with a high purpose, and sense of its own potency and worth. Arising from immersion in the synchronised, rhythmic

Figure 1 Painting from the Temple of Bel, Dura-Europos, Syria, showing Roman soldiers of cohors XX
Palmyrenorum attending a sacrifice. Note the swagged belts, white tunics with (now faded, but visible)
purple trimming, dark breeches and cloaks (brown except for officers). Probably AD230s.
(Reproduced by kind permission of Yale University Art Gallery).

actions of a group, the emotional power of this process of 'entrainment' can be enormous, and is key to understanding how the sense of solidarity in a group, especially one facing physical dangers, is established and maintained (Ehrenreich 1997:184).

Transition of a man to the new status of *miles* was sacramentalised via the oath of personal loyalty to the emperor. Periodically renewed on accession days, and taken afresh to each new emperor, it imposed both religious and legal obligation (Campbell 1984:19–32). Yet, emotionally, perhaps the most important step of all was one we can infer, but have no direct evidence of, to my knowledge; this was the acceptance (rapid, slow or grudging) of the individual into long-term membership of a particular small, fairly stable, all-male warrior group, his *contubernales*. Units were generally divided into *contubernia*, sections nominally of eight men who shared a barrack room, and who seem to have formed basically fixed groupings on duty as well, sharing a tent in the field, and perhaps standing together in line of battle (Goldsworthy 1996:257). Such small stable sub-groups have been shown to be of central importance to the dynamics of modern soldierly behaviour–especially to the unit cohesiveness vital to success on the battlefield (Goldsworthy 1996:257), and I suspect that the formation of such groups is probably a universal trait of warrior behaviour, although this remains to be investigated. While, as in most human groups, each regiment will presumably have had its permanent misfits, in general the personal social bonds between men who shared experiences, who knew and often trusted each other intimately, will have formed the basic glue which held the regiment together in peace and war.

From the point of view of the system, the object of all this was to disconnect, as far as possible, the soldier from his own provincial roots and to connect him body and soul to the emperor through complete immersion in, and identification with, Roman military in the form of his unit. The regiment formed a self-contained society complete in almost all respects except the literal, physical ability to reproduce itself, amounting to a good approximation of a 'total institution' (for a detailed case study applying this notion to the Roman garrison of Dura-Europos, see Pollard 1996). From the point of view of the soldiers themselves, it may be argued that things were rather different.

Soldiers apparently did generally accept this hegemonic framework of indoctrination, and saw themselves as part of an 'imagined community' of *milites*. The concept of the imagined community was developed to explain features of modern nationalism (Anderson 1991), but seems equally applicable here: such a community is imagined because it cannot be experienced directly–most soldiers rarely saw more than their own, and a few neighbouring regiments, and even in major wars, they rarely set eyes on more than a few percent of their *commilitones* ('fellow soldiers'; significantly, a widely used term: Campbell 1984:32–59: e.g. at Vindolanda, Bowman & Thomas 1996:324, No. 3). This widespread common identity was expressed through a system of shared symbols, from the image of the emperor, the eagle of Jupiter, to the clothes they wore and the language they spoke. Soldiers could instantly recognise each other.

Milites were active participants in creating this military culture, within which they interpreted, developed and probably subverted many elements in their own ways, and made their own contributions at its various levels, to mainstream official regimental identities, and to their own identities as individual soldiers. Out of sight of military officialdom, they probably instigated local 'military subcultures' of their own, at the level of their immediate peer-groups, the visible social community of their *commilitones* in their own unit, and the imagined community of *milites* at large (for a sociological study of such a 'military subculture' in a modern British battalion, see Hockey 1986). Indeed soldierly identity looks to be internally complex, with 'nested' levels: the soldier conceptualised himself in relation to his immediate *contubernales*; to his century, *turma*, or cohort; especially to his regiment as the immediately perceptible, bounded community of daily experience; probably to his provincial army group; as well as to 'the soldiers' at large. As with other dimensions of identity, the particular aspect or level emphasised at a given moment will have depended on context; for example, provincial army loyalties flared in times of civil war, but at other times, it was probably the small group and the regiment which were most important, with the 'imagined community' as the ideological substrate. I believe that soldiers' contributions to the resultant military culture can be seen in the documentary, archaeological and representational evidence.

The nature and expression of soldierly identity

It is possible to examine the identity of the soldier in more detail than almost any other identity in the Roman world, especially those outside the political elite. It was peculiar and complex: a particular masculinity, under the empire usually monopolising the traditional free, propertied male role of bearing weapons for the state; a social status; a professional identity, which was also political (warrior as Roman citizen) and at once involved with national identity (legally speaking, imperial soldiers were, or were becoming, Roman citizens), while also being to an important degree multi-cultural–the army was drawn from many peoples, both within and beyond the frontiers, and many units preserved elements of these cultural origins as part of their regimental identities, from regimental cult (Figure 1) to equipment and language.

The particular dimension of this identity that I want to explore in this provisional treatment is the bodily expression of soldierliness, specifically in the first half of the third century AD. The richness of the data-set permits mutual elucidation of a range of documentary data, archaeology and representations, such as military tombstones, commissioned by soldiers to project images of themselves or close comrades, and so effectively self-representations of soldiers.

Military dress of the third century AD is quite well understood, through a combination of highly detailed representations created for, if not by, individual soldiers (including funerary portraits and other depictions on stone and in paintings) and archaeological finds (weapons, dress fittings, footwear and textiles). These categories of evidence are mutually illuminating, the archaeological finds corresponding exactly to many details of the representations, the latter permitting reconstruction of the often-fragmentary archaeological remains. The result is a finely detailed and nuanced understanding of military dress across most of the empire.

A fair repertoire of variation in more decorative components is seen, overlying a remarkable basic homogeneity which literally is a uniform. It is currently believed that this uniformity did not derive from modern-style dress regulations, and there is no evidence for centralised manufacture of clothing or equipment at the time. It seems to me that homogeneity arose due to movement between units of commanders and other officers, especially centurions, and not least of large numbers of troops across the empire on campaigns, and the exchange and copying of soldierly fashions and symbols between units. We are seeing the development of widespread military customs, which are a material expression of the 'imagined community' of *milites* discussed above: other non-material traits of this identity, such as special language, modes of behaviour, attitudes and values, were surely transmitted from unit to unit, adopted and adapted via the same contacts.

In the third century soldiers are usually depicted in so-called camp dress – seen on tombstones and other representations, some in colour; this was apparently regular dress when on duty, but not full fighting kit (Figures 1 & 2). It consisted of a long-sleeved tunic (white with characteristic purple bands and patches), dark trousers/hose, hobnailed footwear, an elaborate waist-belt, a longsword on an equally elaborated baldric, and a rectangular cloak with prominent, often highly decorative brooch. In various ways this ensemble was, it seems, immediately distinguishable from the dress of any other group of males in or around the Roman world, as will be seen. Such military dress contained important characteristics which expressed aspects of soldierly ideology, and the relation of the wearer to other social groups. Individual garments, and especially the ensemble, clearly and specifically denoted a soldier, not only by visual appearance, but also by sound.

For example, it may be argued that the apparently universal wearing of white tunics, with small patches of purple (including notched bands over the shoulders and other components) corresponded to the same features seen on the dress of Graeco-Roman and other male civilians (Jews also wore such garments: Roussin 1994:186). Further, such garments, like suits in the West today, were probably a marker of relatively privileged males (who could afford to buy, and who had the means to keep clean, white/purple garments?). In these respects, then, military tunics conveyed visual messages regarding gender and status.

The other major items of military clothing were generally plain and drab; cloaks, usually brown in colour, and dark breeches. There were probably good practical reasons for this, relating to the visibility of inevitable dirt on such garments, their vulnerability to damage and perhaps the need frequently to replace them, and hence maybe the employment of coarse, drab textiles: but further symbolic associations are discernible. For example, plain, drab outer garments correspond appropriately to common motifs of soldiers' service, characterised by toil and sweat (Carrié 1993:115–6) and, therefore, by implication dust and dirt. It is interesting that physical effort is emphasised rather than combat and bloodshed; baths notwithstanding, it is likely that Roman soldiers also smelt strongly, again perhaps in characteristic ways, especially on campaign. Apart from bodily odours, they will have smelt of leather, sheep–from the lanolin-rich raw wool of their water-resistant cloaks, and often of horses. Perhaps by extension of such symbolic associations, soldiers are recorded scorning the extravagance of 'foreign' dress, which 'is not admired by the Roman troops, appearing to be more appropriate to barbarians and women' (Herodian 5.2.4; B. Goldman 1994:167). This was a traditional prejudice going back to the republic, which saw elaboration in dress as 'unroman', and suggests that these dimensions continued to help denote both gender and national identities.

Yet for all this ideological rhetoric apparently embodied in his garments, the soldier did wear small areas of intense colour, precious materials and/or elaborate ornamentation, over and above the purple thread embroidered into his tunic: buckles, strap-ends, attachment-rings, *fibulae*, and a range of non-functional studs and plates were made of bright metal, sometimes

Figure 2 The tombstone of L. Septimius Valerinus, a Praetorian Guardsman. He is shown in 'camp dress'. Note the 'Caracalla'-like hairstyle and beard, the ring buckle and carefully depicted double strap-end on his belt, and his fringed cloak (Rome). (Drawn by Simon James).

Figure 3 Reconstructions of mid-third century AD military belts, based on archaeological finds from Dura-Europos, Syria, tomb groups from Europe and representational data such as Figure 2. The waist-belt was very often (but not always) extended into a long swag to the right hip, and hung down the right thigh, terminating in a pair of terminals, sometimes heavy and perhaps hinged, which would clash as the soldier moved. The uppermost example shows the ring-buckle, a common form but in this case the ring, and attendant studs and strap-terminals, are of ivory. The fittings on the other examples are copper alloy. (Drawn by Simon James).

silver; buckles and strap-pendants could be of these metals or ivory (or bone, as a substitute, as tinned copper alloy imitated silver?). Metal fittings were often elaborate decorative castings, quite often with brightly-coloured glass inlay, including *millefiore*. However, significantly, such display was confined to the very items which symbolised his military status *par excellence* – the waist-belt (*cingulum*), the sword on a baldric (ultimate symbol of warrior status), and the cloak-brooch.

The military symbolism of such dress made its way into general language. Long established as a metaphor for going to war was the expression 'to put on the *sagum*', i.e. the soldier's cloak (and originally his campaign blanket: N. Goldman 1994:232). Also generally understood, at least by the end of third century, was the symbolic act of rejecting military service by discarding the *cingulum*, the military belt (Woods 1993:55–60).

Dress also influences, indeed frames, bodily posture and movement: the military ensemble actually helped generate the feeling of being a soldier. In trying by experiment to understand how such military dress was made and worn, I have been struck how wearing a long-sword on a baldric, and a carefully-draped cloak, compel an upright bearing, and encourage a swagger and rhythmic pace (compare the difference one feels today when wearing formal dress such as a suit, compared with jeans and a sweatshirt). One can see–feel–how the characteristic military ensemble was active in constituting the embodiment of soldierliness, in the mind of the wearer, and to the eye, and indeed to the ear, of the observer: the crunch of hobnailed boots announced the arrival of a soldier (which, it has been suggested, was the reason for the ban on hobnails instituted in Jewish law of the period: Roussin 1994:188), while it seems to me evident that a common form of military waist-belt, with a pair of (usually metal) strap-ends, was knowingly intended to make a characteristic jangle as the soldier walked, a sound like that made by a small bunch of keys (Figure 3).

There was a fairly broad, but nonetheless bounded, range of permissible variations in the detail of military dress, mostly in the decoration of the fittings mentioned above. It apparently constituted a kind of private semiotics, loosely similar to that seen in the badges on modern military dress, providing the insider with some of the visual cues required to distinguish between units, ranks, and statuses, even if not as systematically as with modern uniform symbols. But the *general* uniformity and distinctiveness of military dress and appearance also encouraged and expressed collective difference from outsiders, and internal cohesion and the sense of solidarity of the *milites*.

Roman, but 'de-Italianized' soldiers

By the third century AD many regiments had long become part of local civilian life in the frontier provinces. The private ties of their men were much more along and across the frontiers than with the core provinces. Hence the need for a high intensity of continuous propaganda and indoctrination from the centre, to foster a sense of corporate cohesion and separation from the provincial matrix, and to maintain ideological identification with the person of the emperor and the state. This process may be seen in the celebration of the birthdays of long-dead emperors and obscure Italian festivals in the military base at Dura-Europos on the Euphrates during the third century (the *Feriale Duranum*, *c*. AD 225–235: Welles *et al.* 1959:191–214; *P. Dura* 54).

At the level of the individual soldier, and the daily interaction of small groups of *milites*, the material culture they inhabited, the language they used, were all increasingly incomprehensible to Roman civilians, especially those of the 'core' provinces. Incomprehensible not just because these represented the *habitus* of another, separate community, but because so much of it was no longer really Italian-derived. Paradoxically, although the persona of the *Roman* soldier remained unmistakable, during the 200 years the armies had been based away from Italy, it had undergone a profound transformation; a 'provincialisation' or 'de-Italianization', just as, politically, legally and culturally, the term 'Roman' itself no longer equated to 'Italian'.

A good example is provided by the nature of the military uniform discussed above. Archaeology and representations reveal that military dress no longer represented the male

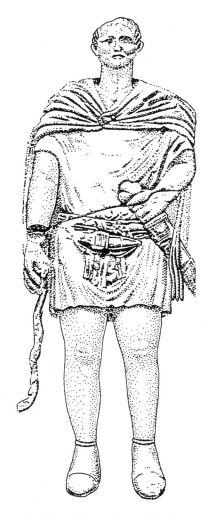

Figure 4 Italian military dress of the late republic: figure of a centurion from a tombstone, Padua. Note the simple, short-sleeved tunic, and bare legs. (Drawn by Simon James, after Franzoni, 1987 46, No. 26, Tav. XIII).

Figure 5 A 'barbarian' from the Column of Marcus Aurelius, later second century AD. He wears a version of the (specifically free?) male dress common across much of Europe north of the Mediterranean world: long breeches, long-sleeved tunic and cloak fastened at the right shoulder. Compare with Figures 4 & 2. (Drawn by Simon James, after Caprino et al. 1955, Scene LXVIII, Tav. O).

clothing traditions of the Mediterranean core, but those of the provincial periphery and beyond: the standard 'barbarian' dress of the North and East had displaced Italian garments. Instead of a simple tunic which left the limbs bare, and various types of cloak (Figure 4), the soldiers now wore essentially the same garments as males (at least, free warrior males?) of the peoples along and beyond the frontiers; long-sleeved tunics, long trousers, and the northern blanket-cloak (Figure 5).

These 'foreign' garments, and other traits, are assumed to have came into the Roman military repertoire by recruitment of units from peoples newly conquered, or not directly annexed at all, joining up with their own equipment, and warrior traditions. Elements of these became encapsulated within specific regimental traditions, or were generally adopted as part of the living culture of the Roman armies. This process can be seen in the special language of the soldiers, the *sermo militaris*, which was infused with terminology and expressions from subject peoples; for example, terms describing cavalry manoeuvres, and especially bodily postures and movements of individuals, were largely adopted from Celtic (Arr. *Tact.* 33.1; 37.5; 42,4; 43,2; 44,1: Hyland 1993:69–78).

Although such developments were undoubtedly seen at the time, at least in the metropolitan core, as barbarisation of the armies, paradoxically such adoptions and adaptations were, of their nature, time-honoured Roman custom, indeed arguably a characteristic of military *romanitas*. Roman armies had always been composite, including a large percentage of foreign soldiers from allied or subject peoples; and since republican times they had adopted useful or attractive ideas from friends and foes, from Spanish swords to Gallic mail and helmets (Bishop & Coulston 1993:204), Greek siege technology and so on. The common culture of the *milites* was a particular, peculiar, empire-wide case of *romanitas*, which, as will be seen, was intimately related to the many local trajectories of Romanization throughout the provinces where soldiers were stationed.

The wider military communities of the Roman world

The person of the emperor and the notion of Rome provided the overt *raison d'être* for soldiers and regiments, while the empire-wide imagined community of the *milites* expressed their identity. But the reality of their routine existence, in peacetime and to a large extent in war as well, turned on the corporate life of the particular unit to which the soldier was attached (whether in a major legionary base, an auxiliary or *numerus* fort, or away with a vexillation or on some lesser detachment). Each unit formed the kernel of a more-or-less sharply bounded, living, directly experienced *local* military community. The structure and life of each such community intimately involved many other agents who did not appear on the regimental rosters: these included a host of regimental dependants and many external connections, particularly among the local population, but also to varying degrees with more distant places (e.g. the home communities of individual soldiers, even of entire ethnic units, in other provinces or lands).

Documentary evidence makes it quite clear that, even before it was legalised by Severus, official soldiers' marriages were more-or-less commonplace. While it is likely that the majority of the soldiers at any one time were still single–especially younger ones–even single soldiers often had other dependants, whether blood-relatives or servants: slaves or freedmen/freedwomen (Carrié 1993:114; Speidel 1992; Maxfield 1995; Varon 1994). In the Roman world, women, children and servants seem generally to have taken much of their social standing from that of the male head of the family. Given that these people were also supported, largely if not wholly, by the soldiers' pay, we should think of them, too, as fully members of the military communities, in a social rather than institutional sense. Beyond these, there were also groups not personally attached in these ways to individual soldiers, but to varying degrees tied to the unit more than the host civil population, even when the regiment concerned was in the middle of a city: such was the case, it seems, with the group of 'dancers and entertainers' from Zeugma who took up residence for some months in a house at Dura-Europos, where graffiti make it clear they were dealing intimately with military personnel: it seems likely that they were providing services for a legionary vexillation on detachment from Zeugma whence, perhaps, they had followed it (Rostovtzeff *et al.* 1952:46). These regimental communities, then, were probably fairly distinct entities within the local civil context, even in cities.

Conclusions

If we consider the formal and personal connections of any established group of ordinary soldiers, they evidently stood at the centre of a complex network of often conflicting influences and pressures. It is notable that the 'official' military culture to which they were exposed on duty, emanating from the centre, and 'top down', was still largely of the Italian tradition – state ideology, ceremonial, command structures, regimental organisation and the names of units, etc. were all drawn primarily from roots deep in the Roman republican past. It was centralising and normative, although imperial norms were themselves evolving, with the increasingly provincial backgrounds of the emperors. Yet, as we have seen, more and more of the *habitus* of the ordinary soldier came 'from the bottom up', incorporating not only the existing Italian warrior values and traditions of the legions, but increasingly those of other peoples as well, from the frontier regions and even beyond them, primarily via recruitment of provincials and 'barbarians'.

The long stationing of particular units, and entire army groups, in the same place and the interaction of each with its own particular social matrix of provincials and 'barbarians', ecologies and climates, resulted in a tendency to regionalization, with differences between armies accentuated by their long separation. Individual soldiers, and then whole units, developed personal ties with people of the frontier regions, not only through marriage but other legal, financial and commercial interchanges. They seem often to have recruited local men into their ranks as well, further strengthening such ties. The connections of men and unit were increasingly within, across, and even beyond the frontier provinces rather than with the geographical or state core of the empire. Some units preserved connections even with distant provinces where they had been raised, as in the case of the Syrians of Intercisa (Fitz 1972).

It was these divergent, localising tendencies which the imperial centre sought to counteract through its unceasing bombardment of indoctrination. Yet it was a by-product of the imperial systems of command and control of the soldiers which, in my view, provided the real glue which maintained the military as a distinct entity, and prevented it becoming a series of regionally-minded armies, at least until the disasters of the 260s: this was the soldiers' highly developed sense of common identity and solidarity across the empire, constantly renewed by frequent, inter-provincial movements of *milites*, which helped to cross-cut, or better to cross-link, these 'radial' (imperial-convergent and local-divergent) tendencies.

The men of each regiment, of each stretch of frontier, of each provincial or regional army stood at the centre of unique trajectories of social development, at once both components of aggregate imperial history, and also of innumerable distinct local histories, each of which demands consideration in its own particular terms. In the frontier provinces, the military communities – distinct from, and in addition to the state institution of the armies – constituted a major component in those wider processes known as Romanization. The soldiers scattered across the empire numbered over 400,000 in the early third century AD, at least in theoretical establishment (Campbell 1984:4). With their dependants, including slaves, freedmen and freedwomen as well as wives, children and other kin, they will surely have exceeded a million, a grouping as large in numbers as the City of Rome and, it seems to me, a community just as influential in the social, political and economic history of the middle imperial period as the capital itself.

Acknowledgements

I would like to thank the Leverhulme Trust and Durham University for funding the Special Research Fellowship on the military archaeology of Dura-Europos, Syria, which permitted me to conduct the research behind this paper. Thanks also to Pat Baker who organised the TRAC session at which the original version was presented and the editors for inviting me to publish it. I should also like to thank Yale University Art Gallery for kind permission to reproduce Figure 1.

Bibliography

Anderson, B. 1991. *Imagined communities: reflections on the origins and spread of nationalism.* (revised edition). London & New York: Verso.

Arrian *Ars Tactica* (trans. F. Brudenall). In A. Hyland 1993. *Training the Roman cavalry.* London: Grange Books, pp.69–77.

Bishop, M.C. & Coulston, J.C.N. 1993. *Roman military equipment.* London: Batsford.

Bowman A.K. & Thomas, J.D. 1996. New writing-tablets from Vindolanda. *Britannia*, 27:299–328.

Campbell, D.B. 1984. *The emperor and the Roman army, 31 BC–AD 235.* Oxford: Oxford University Press.

Caprino, C., Colini, A. & Gatti, G., 1955. *La colonna di Marco Aurelio.* Rome: Bretschneider.

Carrié, J.-M. 1993. The soldier. In A. Giardina (ed.) *The Romans.* Chicago & London: University of Chicago Press, pp.100–137.

Domaszewski, A. von 1967. [1908] *Die Rangordnung des römischen Heeres, 2.* Durchgesehene Auflage. Köln & Graz: Einführung, Berichtungen und Nachträge von B. Dobson, Böhlau.

Ehrenreich, B. 1997. *Blood rites: origins and history of the passions of war.* New York: Henry Holt.

Fitz, J. 1972. *Les Syriens à Intercisa.* Brussels: Latomus.

Franzoni, C. 1987. *Habitus atque habitudo militis. Monumenti funerari di militari nella Cisalpina Romana.* Rome: Bretschneider.

Giddens, A. 1985. *The nation-state and violence: volume two of a contemporary critique of historical materialism.* London: Polity Press.

Goldman, B. 1994. Graeco-Roman dress in Syro-Mesopotamia. In J.L. Sebesta & L. Bonfante (eds.) *The world of Roman costume.* Madison: University of Wisconsin, pp.163–181.

Goldman, N. 1994. Reconstructing Roman clothing. In J.L. Sebesta & L. Bonfante (eds.) *The world of Roman costume.* Madison: University of Wisconsin, pp.213–237.

Goldsworthy, A.K. 1996. *The Roman army at war 100 BC – AD 200.* Oxford: Oxford University Press.

Herodian *History* In B. Goldman 1994. Graeco-Roman dress in Syro-Mesopotamia. In J.L. Sebesta & L. Bonfante, (eds.) *The world of Roman costume.* Madison: University of Wisconsin, pp.163–181.

Hockey, J. 1986. *Squaddies: portrait of a subculture.* Exeter: Exeter University Press.

Hyland, A. 1993. *Training the Roman cavalry: from Arrian's Ars Tactica.* London: Grange.

MacMullen, R. 1963. *Soldier and civilian in the later Roman empire.* Cambridge, USA: Harvard University Press.

MacMullen, R. 1984. The legion as a society. *Historia*, 33: 440–56.

Maxfield, V.A. 1995. *Soldier and civilian: life beyond the ramparts.* Eighth Annual Caerleon Lecture, Cardiff: National Museum of Wales.

P.Dura. Welles, C.B, Fink, R.O & Gilliam, J.F., 1959. *Excavations at Dura-Europos, final report 5, part 1, the parchments and papyri.* New Haven: Yale University Press.

Peddie, J. 1994. *The Roman war machine.* Stroud: Sutton.

Pollard, N. 1996. The Roman army as total institution in the Near East? Dura-Europos as a case study. In D.L. Kennedy (ed.) *The Roman army in the East.* JRA Supplementary Series 18, pp.211–227

Rostovtzeff, M., Bellinger, A., Brown, F., & Welles, C. 1952. *The excavations at Dura-Europos, preliminary report on the ninth season, 1935–6, Part 3: the Palace of the Dux Ripae and the Dolicheneum.* New Haven: Yale University Press.

Roussin, L., 1994. Costume in Roman Palestine: archaeological remains and the evidence from the Mishnah. In Sebesta, J.L. & Bonfante, L. (eds.) *The world of Roman costume.* Madison: University of Wisconsin Press, pp.182–190.

Speidel, M.P. 1992. The soldiers' servants. In M.P. Speidel (ed.) *Roman army studies* 2, Mavors 8, Stuttgart, 342–352 [originally published in *Ancient Society*, 20:239–248].

Varon, P. 1994. Emptio ancillae/mulieris by Roman army soldiers. In E. Dabrowa (ed.) *The Roman and Byzantine army in the East.* Krakow: Universytet Jagiellonski, pp.189–195.

Welles, C.B, Fink, R.O & Gilliam, J.F. 1959. *Excavations at Dura-Europos, final report 5, part 1, the parchments and papyri.* New Haven: Yale University Press.

Woods, D. 1993. The ownership and disposal of military equipment in the late Roman army. *Journal of Roman Military Equipment Studies*, 4:55–65.

Monumental Architecture & Becoming Roman in the First Centuries BC and AD

by Kenneth Aitchison

Introduction

Major social changes took place around the beginning of the first century BC in western and central Europe, and part of the way they were enacted was through large-scale alterations to the settlement pattern. New settlements were established, for the most part in previously unoccupied locations such as hilltops. It can be argued that '...in order to give material expression to the development of their way of life, the inhabitants of second century BC villages returned to the traditional model of the hillfort' (Audouze & Büchsenschütz 1992:235), but transformed it with the use of new techniques, – such as the general use of metal – and through reference to the urban models of the Mediterranean.

These new centres were the *oppida* – enclosed proto-urban sites, but which were not simply developed hill forts; the two systems were '...mutually exclusive phenomena, with no evidence of one developing into the other' (Collis 1984:69). The development of the *oppida* can be seen as a reference to the past, to what had become a mythical time when fortified occupation of high places was the way in which heroic ancestors lived.

One such site is on Mont Beuvray, in the Burgundian highlands of central France. Two massive ramparts encircle this site; the outer forms a perimeter of about 7km, enclosing a total area of 200ha. A number of buildings have been excavated, mostly in the last century, and particular 'quarters' of specialised activity have been identified (Goudineau & Peyre 1993:35). *Bibracte*, described as the chief town of the Aedui in Caesar's (*B.Gall.*) account of the Roman military adventure in Gaul in the 50s BC, has been confidently equated with the site.

Early work on Beuvray was historically driven, relating in particular to events described by Caesar such as the Pan-Gallic Council at *Bibracte*, when Vercingetorix took command of the Gallic armies in 52 BC (Caes. *B.Gall.* 7.63), and Caesar's subsequent over wintering at the site, 52–51 BC (Caes. *B.Gall.* 7.90). The other important historical event is the founding of *Augustodunum Aeduorum*, modern Autun, 22 km east of Beuvray, which has a traditional founding date of around 15 BC (Goudineau & Peyre 1993:195).

It has been considered that the founding of *Augustodunum* was the motive force that led to the abandonment of *Bibracte*. But the founding of *Augustodunum* should not be looked on simply as an externally imposed event; it should be seen as part of the ongoing historical process that had created *Bibracte*. Mid-first century society was in the process of becoming increasingly stratified; Roman intervention did not end this process, nor did it impose a new, foreign, militarily backed elite upon central France. New ideas were unquestionably introduced, but this was not novel; ideas had been taken from the Mediterranean urban centres for several generations by this time. The same people, from the same families, exercised authority and control in *Augustodunum* as they had in *Bibracte* and for a time the two towns co-existed as thriving centres.

This paper aims to present a comparison of the ways in which monumental architecture was used in these two towns, and how ideas that drew upon elements of each town were used in the development of the other. In particular, it aims to show the manner in which *Augustodunum* was not an artificial, new, town but that its structure was a reflection and re-construction of the urban form of *Bibracte*.

Chronology

Recent work on Mont Beuvray has divided the occupation of the site into six phases. The first of these phases is from the beginning of the third century to the mid-first century BC, and predates the urbanisation of the hilltop. The final recognised phase is from about AD 15 to 30, when the site was progressively abandoned (Flouest 1995:14).

The earliest excavated evidence from the ramparts suggests that they were initially constructed late in the second century or near the beginning of the first century BC (Aitchison *et al.* 1996:81). Important dates of the development of the *oppidum* in the context of this paper are the construction of a monumental basin between 40 and 30 BC, the infilling of that basin in the final decade BC, the remodelling of a major gate, the Porte du Rebout, around the middle of the first century and the digging of small ditches parallel to the rampart inturns at the same gate late in the first century (Aitchison *et al.* 1996:82).

Augustodunum was founded late in the first century BC. Goudineau and Peyre (1993:195) offer a date of around 15 BC, while MacKendrick (1971:118) suggests 12 or 7 BC; however, it is not disputed that the town was founded in the final two decades of the century.

Monumental architecture at Bibracte and Augustodunum

The theoretical argument behind this comparison is based on ideas relating to the way in which people understand the world they live in, how they express this understanding through ritualised behaviour and how such behaviour pervades the everyday experiences of people. Bourdieu (1977) uses the concept of *habitus* as a practice or way of doing things which follows social structures and which either alters or reinforces these structures, and I choose to use this approach to consider the experiences and understandings individuals had of monuments and landscape.

In addition to knowledge of how to deal with everyday situations, people develop belief systems to rationalise the complexities of the world as they experience it (Barrett 1991). The mechanism by which these systems are reproduced is ritual; the transformation of experience and behaviour into formal patterns of action, which is achieved through the use of fixed, habitual forms of conduct (Brown 1961:9). Ritual need not be the preserve of special occasions, – through repetitive experience and actions the activities of the everyday become ritualised and can preserve symbolic values. It is thus that ritual remains foremost in the minds of individuals, and the symbolic content of places and actions is maintained.

As ritual and repetitive action structure daily life, it is the routine encounters of the everyday that create these repetitive actions. Within any settlement, daily encounters with architecture structure activity in the most obvious and physical of ways. The repetitive process of encountering architecture leads to a formalised understanding of it – following Bourdieu (1977), the strategies that are adopted for these encounters influence individuals' overall objective comprehension; *habitus* is linking people with their immediate landscape – and as ritual refined a significant formal pattern from experience, it can equally be seen to refine a significant formal pattern from space, engendering architectural form.

There are two themes in the architecture of *Bibracte* and *Augustodunum* that are of particular interest. The first is in the way that solar observations have been used to orientate and structure the layout of the towns, and the second is the use of monumental ramparts and the gateways through these ramparts

Bibracte

Not all of the enclosed area of *Bibracte* was given over to the construction of buildings; there remained extensive open areas within the ramparts. There was, however, an urbanised core to the site, based on a semi-regularised pattern of streets, which became more regular over time. Unfortunately, many of the later buildings were built with cellars, so much of the information pertaining to the earlier phases of the settlement is lost.

Streets

The street layout was deliberately planned, allowing for regularly shaped and sized plots which have been recognised in the Parc aux Chevaux area of the site (Meylan 1997:30). The excavation of a monumental stone basin in the centre of the 'main street' at Pature du Couvent, at the intersection with the 'rue des caves' has cast some light on the rationales behind the street layout.

The basin is oval (10.48m by 3.65m), is surrounded by the paved surface of the road, was built from red granite blocks (Goudineau & Peyre 1993:43) and was waterproofed with clay (Almagro-Gorbea & Gran-Aymerich 1991:240). While a supplying conduit at the south end has not been identified, the basin's outlet is easily identifiable at the north end and its drain can be traced for 30m. This would appear to suggest that the basin was a pool of constantly flowing water, rather than a still reservoir.

The long axis of the basin is that of the main road that surrounds it, but this is secondary to the short axis that has been aligned on solar observations. This axis of the basin coincides with a line drawn between the point of sunrise on the winter solstice to the south-east and the point of the summer solstice sunset to the north-west (Almagro-Gorbea & Gran-Aymerich 1991:240).

The basin was also a central spot around which the town plan was ordered. The main street of *Bibracte*, aligned on the long axis of the basin, must have been orientated after this place had been identified as being of significance. The basin appears to have been installed at the same time as road was enlarged to a width of over 12m (Szabó 1997:34).

The basin fell into disuse and silted up in the final decade of the first century BC. The stratigraphic evidence for its construction date is unreliable, but the excavators suggest a date, based on the pottery recovered from the fill, of between 30 and 40 BC (Goudineau & Peyre 1993:44). The excavators consider that the infilling of the basin was wholly natural; there seems to be no evidence for deliberate or structured deposition within it.

As a place of running water, the basin echoed the spring sanctuaries identified by Brunaux (1988) as being of religious importance, and so could be considered to have had some ritual significance. Through the solar observations, it was located by reference to the sky, and by its very excavation into the soil, to the earth. 'Sacred sites are connected with natural elements – water, the earth, forest, the sky...' (Audouze & Büchsenschütz 1992:149) and the elements of earth, water and sky combined at this point to create a locale of great symbolic significance.

By its solsticial references, the basin marked the longest and shortest days of the annual cycle from which the seasons and years were counted. Thus it measured the calendar, the means to order annual life, and so occupied a central place in time, as it was also a central place in space, around which the layout of streets and buildings was organised. The basin played a significant part in the definition of the settlement's urban character – it '...forms the *omphalos*, the navel of *Bibracte*, the sacred point from which the town has been founded and organised' (Goudineau & Peyre 1993:44).

But this was not an excluded place, separated from daily life. It lay in the middle of the main street of the town; only a few metres away were houses and workshops (Goudineau & Peyre 1993:45). People would encounter and pass the basin in the course of their everyday activities, yet they would always be reminded by it of the cosmological plan by which their town and their lives were ordered.

Enclosure

The massive and extensive ramparts of *Bibracte* have been surveyed topographically; they still survive to a height of over 4m in places, and one area of the inner rampart has been excavated, at the Porte du Rebout. This rampart is a timber laced and stone-faced construction, with the presence of large iron spikes, typically 200–250mm in length, which characterise it as a *murus gallicus*. Metal detector surveys (Hesse & Aitchison 1992, Niaux 1995) have confirmed the presence of such iron spikes at other places on the ramparts, although they do not appear to be universally present.

If this is the case, then the architecture becomes part of a dialectic process – firstly, the scale of Porte du Rebout determined the width of Porte d'Arroux, and then the details of Porte d'Arroux influenced a secondary remodelling of the Porte du Rebout.

Augustodunum is east of and slightly north of *Bibracte*; the most logical gate to leave *Bibracte* by in order to travel to *Augustodunum*, was the Porte du Rebout. Travelling from *Bibracte* to *Augustodunum* necessitates crossing the Arroux River; the logical place to do this would be at the bridge or ford at Porte d'Arroux. So after crossing the river arrival at *Augustodunum* would be at this gate: the point on which the town layout of *Augustodunum* was organised and the most significant visual way in which *Bibracte* was recalled in the architecture of *Augustodunum*.

It was familiar and understood that to enter or leave *Bibracte*, passage had to be made through an impressively monumental gateway in a massive rampart. As this enclosure was the understood way in which towns were built, so it was repeated at *Augustodunum*. Similarly, the accepted way in which the town's streets were orientated was on observations of sunrise and sunset on the longest and shortest days of the year.

Conclusions

'The more hierarchical a society was, the more readily it could be absorbed into the Roman empire' (Collis 1994:36). Iron Age society in central France was indeed very hierarchical, and was very readily absorbed into Roman society – but the creation of 'Gallo-Roman' society was not a mere imposition of Roman culture and values on a passive and conquered populace, nor was it a thin veneer of new ideas.

Society at *Bibracte* was centralised, hierarchical and above all *ordered*. The town was planned and laid out with a road network, drainage systems and parcels of land; but this was not all – the way that people lived their lives, the way they moved through the town and the wider landscape was ordered too. This order was based on the movement of the sun across the heavens and on the natural world, in a land where hills, forests and springs all had their own significance beyond simple topographic location.

Repetitive action and experience formed the basis of the ways in which people understood the world (Bourdieu 1977). As this repetitive action was formalised into ritual, so ritual was used to formalise space through architecture in both *Bibracte* and *Augustodunum*. The town plan grid and the main streets were the way to locate one's self in the Roman urban world, and so structured a particular way to think about that world as it was being experienced, or *habitus*. Thus whilst Roman town plans were very much part of *romanitas*, of being Roman – the plan was a construct based on ritual definition of the routine experiences of everyday life.

The plan of *Augustodunum*, so very Roman in style, was orientated on the rising sun at the summer solstice, when other Roman towns were organised by the passage of the sun across the sky, rather than on solsticial observations. The street plan of *Bibracte*, as far as it was based on the basin, was orientated on the sun as it rose on the winter solstice.

The rampart built in a Roman style, but unique in northern Gaul at *Augustodunum*, reflected the monumental and symbolic enclosure of territory at *Bibracte*. The principal gate of *Augustodunum*, Porte d'Arroux, was a physical recreation, again in a Roman style, of Porte du Rebout, the principal gate of *Bibracte*. Possibly subsequent to the creation of Porte d'Arroux, Porte du Rebout was again remodelled (with the insertion of the smaller ditches), to make it resemble more closely the new gate of *Augustodunum*.

At *Augustodunum*, a town was built that was unquestionably Roman but that also included many concepts that represented ideas held by the society that had built and inhabited *Bibracte*. While this can be seen as an attempt by the agents of Roman authority to legitimise their presence and control, it may well have been because the very people who were building *Augustodunum* and living there were the same people that had lived in and built *Bibracte*. As the lives of these people '...made themselves, [they] also remade the institutional arrangements within which they were lived' (Barrett 1997:60). If '...to become Roman was to adopt a discipline of life which confirmed with some overarching ideal and which was understood to do so by those who adopted it, as well as by others' (Barrett 1997:52) then the inhabitants of *Augustodunum* were becoming Roman, but very much on their own terms, with reference to the lives they had experienced and understood, with their traditions still in place. The development of *Augustodunum Aeduorum* reflected continuity in the lives of these people, not change.

Landward Archaeology, Sheffield

Bibliography

Aitchison, K., Ralston, I., Rieckhoff, S. & Urban, O. 1996. La Porte du Rebout. In V. Guichard (ed.) *Rapport annuel d'activité scientifique 1996*. Glux-en-Glenne: Centre archéologique européen du mont Beuvray, pp.46–126

Almagro-Gorbea, M. & Gran-Aymerich, J. 1991. *El estanque monumental de Bibracte (Mont-Beuvray, Borgoña)*. Madrid: Editorial Complutense.

Audouze, F. & Büchsenschütz, O.E. 1992 [1989]. *Towns, villages and countryside of Celtic Europe: from the beginning of the second millennium to the end of the first century*. (trans. H. Cleere). London: Batsford.

Barrett, J.C. 1991. The archaeology of social reproduction. In J.C. Barrett, R. Bradley & M. Green *Landscape, monuments and society: the prehistory of Cranbourne Chase*. Cambridge: Cambridge University Press, pp.6–8.

Barrett, J.C. 1997. Romanization: a critical comment. In D. J. Mattingly (ed.) *Dialogues in Roman imperialism: power, discourse and discrepant experience in the Roman Empire*. Portsmouth, Rhode Island: JRA Supplementary Series 23, pp.51–64.

Bourdieu, P. 1977 [1972]. *Outline of a theory of practice*. (trans. R. Nice). Cambridge: Cambridge University Press.

Brown, F.E. 1961. *Roman architecture*. New York: Braziller.

Brunaux, J, -L. 1988 [1987]. *The Celtic Gauls: gods, rites and sanctuaries*. (trans. D. Nash). London: Seaby.

Büchsenschütz, O.E. & Richard, H. 1997. L'environnement. In K. Gruel & D. Vitali L'Oppidum de Bibracte: un bilan de onze années de recherche (1984–95). *Gallia*, 57:13–14.

Caesar. *The conquest of Gaul*. (trans. S.A. Handford, 1951). Harmondsworth: Penguin.

Collis, J.R. 1984. *Oppida: earliest towns north of the Alps*. Sheffield: Department of Archaeology and Prehistory, University of Sheffield.

Collis, J.R. 1994. Reconstructing Iron Age society. In K. Kristiansen & J. Jensen (eds.) *Europe in the first millennium BC*. Sheffield: Collis Publications, pp.31–40.

Dehn, W. 1962. Aperçu sur les oppida d'Allemagne de la fin de l'époque celtique. *Celticum*, 3:329–86.

Flouest, J.-L. 1995. Cadres des recherches. In J,-L. Flouest (ed.) *Document final de synthèse: rapport triennal 1993–95: vol. 1*. Glux-en-Glenne: Centre archéologique européen du mont Beuvray, pp.1–15.

Goudineau, C. 1980. Les villes de la paix romaine. In G. Duby (ed.) *Histoire de la France urbaine: volume 1*. Paris: Seuil, pp.237–397.

Goudineau, C. & Peyre, C. 1993. *Bibracte et les Eduens: à la découverte d'un peuple Gaulois*. Paris: Editions Errance.

Grimal, P. 1983 [1954]. *Roman Cities*. (trans. G.M. Woloch). Madison: University of Wisconsin Press.

Hesse, A. & Aitchison, K. 1992. Recherche des clous de fer sur le rempart. In J.-P. Guillaumet (ed.) *Rapport scientifique: activités 1992 prévisions 1993*. Glux-en-Glenne: Centre archéologique européen du mont Beuvray, pp.181–2.

King, A. 1990. *Roman Gaul and Germany*. London: British Museum.

Mackendrick, P. 1971. *Roman France*. London: Bell.

Metzler, J. 1995. *Das Treverische oppidum auf dem Titelberg*. Luxembourg: Librairie Archéologique.

Meylan, F. 1997. Evaluation de la densité de l'occupation. In K. Gruel & D. Vitali L'Oppidum de Bibracte: un bilan de onze années de recherche (1984–95). *Gallia*, 57:26–30.

Niaux, R. 1995. Prospections sur le mont Beuvray et dans le pays Eduen. In J.-L. Flouest (ed.) *Document final de synthèse: rapport triennal 1993–95: volume 4*. Glux-en-Glenne: Centre archéologique européen du mont Beuvray, pp.1–19.

Rebourg, A. 1993. *Carte archéologique de la Gaule 71/1 Autun*. Paris: Académie des Inscriptions et Belles-Lettres.

Hunter, F. 1997. Iron Age hoarding in Scotland and northern England. In A. Gwilt & C. Haselgrove (eds.) *Reconstructing Iron Age societies*. Oxford: Oxbow, pp.108–133.

Jones, R.F.J., Cheetham, P., Clark, K., Clarke, S. & Rush, P. 1989. *The Newstead Research Project, 1989 interim Report*. Bradford: University of Bradford.

Jones, R.F.J., Cheetham, P., Clark, K., Dent, J. & Rush, P. 1990. *The Newstead Research Project, 1990 interim Report*. Bradford: University of Bradford.

Jones, R.F.J., Cheetham, P., Clark, K., Clarke, S. & Dent, J. 1991. *The Newstead Research Project, 1991 field season, preliminary report*. Bradford: University of Bradford.

Jones, R.F.J., Cheetham, P., Clark, K., Clarke, S. & Dent, J. 1992. *The Newstead Research Project, 1992 field season, preliminary report*. Bradford: University of Bradford.

Jones, R.F.J., Cheetham, P., Clark, K., Clarke, S. & Dent, J. 1993. *The Newstead Research Project, 1993 field season, preliminary report*. Bradford: University of Bradford.

Jones, R.F.J. & Clarke, S. 1994. *Melrose bypass part 3: archaeological report 1, field evaluation*. Bradford: University of Bradford.

Kurchin, B. 1995. Romans and Britons on the northern Frontier: a theoretical evaluation of the archaeology of resistance. In P. Rush (ed.) *Theoretical Roman Archaeology: second conference proceedings*. Aldershot: Avebury Press, pp.124–131.

MacDonald 1911 The coins. In J. Curle. *A Roman frontier post and its people*. Glasgow: Glasgow University Press, pp.385–415.

Manning W. H. 1981. Native and Roman metalwork in northern Britain: a question of origins and influences. In J. Kenworthy (ed.) Early technology in northern Britain. *Scottish Archaeological Forum*, 11:52–56.

Millett, M. 1990. *The Romanization of Britain*. Cambridge: Cambridge University Press.

Oswald, A. 1997. A Doorway on the past: practical and mystic concerns in the orientation of roundhouse doorways. In A. Gwilt & C. Haselgrove (eds.) *Reconstructing Iron Age societies*. Oxford: Oxbow, pp.87–95.

Piggott, S. 1953. Three metalwork hoards of the Roman period from southern Scotland. *PSAS*, 87:1–50.

Parker-Pearson, M. & Richards, C. 1994. Architecture and order: spatial representation and architecture. In M. Parker-Pearson & C. Richards (eds.) *Architecture and order*. London: Routledge, pp.32–78

Rapoport, A. 1990. Systems of activities and systems of settings. In S. Kent (ed.) *Domestic architecture and the use of space*. Cambridge: Cambridge University Press, pp.9–20.

Richmond, I.A.1952. Excavation at the Roman fort of Newstead, 1947. *PSAS*, 84:1–37

Robertson, A. 1970. Roman finds from non-Roman sites in Scotland. *Britannia*, 1:198–226.

Ross A. 1967. *Pagan Celtic Britain: studies in iconography and tradition*. London: Routledge.

Ross A. & Fencham, R. 1976. Ritual Rubbish? The Newstead pits. In J.V.S. Meadows (ed.) *To illustrate the monument*. London: Thames & Hudson, pp.230–237.

Scott, E. 1995. Women and gender relations in the Roman Empire. In P. Rush (ed.) *Theoretical Roman Archaeology: second conference proceedings*. Aldershot: Avebury Press, pp.174–189.

Sommer, C. S. 1984. *The military vici in Roman Britain: aspects of origins, their locations and layout, administration, function and end*. Oxford: BAR British Series 129.

Van Driel-Murray, C. 1995. Gender in question. In P. Rush (ed.) *Theoretical Roman Archaeology: second conference proceedings*. Aldershot: Avebury Press, pp.3–21.

Poverty or Power?
The native response to Roman rule in the Fenland

by Garrick Fincham

Introduction – Romanization and post-colonial theory

This paper is concerned primarily with the implications of discrepant experience, for our interpretation of the evidence for Romano-British settlement in the East Anglian Fens. Discrepant experience encourages us to consider the perspective of the conquered, as well as the conqueror. Therefore, it is necessary to begin with a discussion of the contentious issue of 'Romanization', as an understanding of what we mean by the term is central to any exploration of relations between different groups within the empire. The approach of Millett (1990) had been superseded, and Romanization can no longer be seen as a purely acculturative process (Webster 1996a:11). Yet, in an environment where the concept of discrepant discourse (Said 1993:35–50) has undermined fatally any concept of the Roman Empire as a unified experiential whole, and in which we are retreating from the comfortable absolutes that we have created in the past (Mattingly 1997a:11), attempting to define a widespread and generalised process of any kind sits uncomfortably with approaches which seek to emphasise difference and variability across the empire and within individual provinces and local communities (Terrenato 1998:24).

To try to redefine Romanization then, is to fall into the same trap of trying to find a prefabricated, simplified, and general set of rules to think about complex cultural interaction in many different situations: in effect to universalise the *process* of Romanization. To do so is to maintain a Rome centred, hegemonic view, in which Roman culture is given an overarching power to subsume and dominate native cultures. Such universalism fails to 'acknowledge or value [native] cultural difference' (Ashcroft *et al.* 1998:235). This, of course, leaves no room for the consideration of the uniqueness of the experience of individual communities subject to Roman imperial domination, but reduces those communities, no matter where they are in space or time, to identical units, their domination to be measured by identical criterion. A Roman pot, therefore, becomes an absolute indicator on a meta-scale of Roman imperial domination, and thus we have eradicated 'context' from any consideration of 'Romanization'. The presence (or absence) of Samian, for example, as an absolute indicator of Romanization (or non-Romanization), is to deny something which, on the smaller scale of an individual excavation, all archaeologists accept, that *context* is vital to understanding material culture. Once we begin to examine the individual contexts in which 'Romanizing forces' are playing themselves out, we must abandon any universal definition of Romanization, and move in a new direction in which we accept that 'Romanized' cultures deserve individual interpretations. Alcock (1997) and Mattingly (1997b) working in Greece and North Africa respectively have worked along these lines, characterising the regions that they have studied as landscapes of resistance, or opportunity. Whilst acknowledging that these landscapes are created within the system of empire, by terming them 'landscapes of imperialism' (Mattingly 1997a:11), the terms resistance or opportunity are empowering ones for the native, in that the landscape is primarily characterised by the contribution of native agency to their own condition. Thus, looking at my own data, the settlement pattern of the Fens is not simply the product of Roman colonisation. As agents acting upon their own condition, we must allow the native population of the Fens input into the process which created the landscape in which they lived. It may be characterised as a landscape of resistance or opportunity (both implying the exercise of native will), but the natives are not merely passive individuals in varying states of acculturation.

Deconstruction

The full title of the Royal Geographical Society publication *The Fenland in Roman Times, studies in a major area of peasant colonization* (Phillips 1970) encapsulates many of the elements of what has since become the orthodox view of the Roman period in the Fens, and is a clear starting point for any deconstruction. Phillips' use of the word 'peasant' has particularly intriguing connotations. This area is difficult, as no wholly value neutral term exists to refer to a subject population in the Roman Empire, and this difficulty has serious ramifications for our understanding of their experience (see Webster 1996b). *Peasant* in particular implies an inferior populace with a low standard of material culture (when compared to an idealised Roman norm), and in the manner of Webster's (1996b:111) discourse of the 'timeless primitive' abandons them to a steady state of being for which there is no history. The word *native*, although not without its difficulties (Ashcroft *et al.* 1998: 158–9) seems at present as good, or at least no worse, than any other, and is the term adopted here.

To move forwards, and begin to write a 'native' history, free from a Romanocentric conceptual framework and, thus, less entangled in modern value judgements, we must also consider the notion of poverty. The Fen farmers, to use classic terminology, failed to 'Romanize', and were poverty stricken (Hall & Coles 1994:121). However, this standpoint is clearly a modern value judgement based upon a reading of Roman material culture, something never clearly defined, as inherently superior to native culture, that is, something never fully justified. 'Poverty' as an archaeological concept reinforces the dis-empowerment of the native and enforces their marginality. A re-reading of the Roman failure fully to acculturate material culture in the Fens is key to our reconstruction of native history.

The foundations of re-construction

The area within the Fenland of which our current knowledge is most complete is the central fen area around the town of March, Cambridgeshire (Figure 1). This area has received extensive survey cover (Phillips 1970; Hall 1987, 1992) and has, by Fenland standards, a high proportion of published excavation data (Jackson & Potter 1997; Potter 1981). It is in this area that a closer look at the archaeological data is most profitable, and in particular it is helpful to examine the complex of sites on the fen island of Stonea (Figure 1).

Evidence has been recovered from this area of a ritual complex, which stretches back to the Neolithic. This was, at least periodically, in use up to the destruction of the Icenian client kingdom, in which, on the basis of the coin data, probably controlled the Central Fens (Jackson & Potter 1997:671–94). Whilst this region may have been marginal in a geographical sense, the scale of this complex argues against any vision of the area as being an uninhabited backwater. Indeed, as a source of a wide range of wetland resources, including salt, the area may well have been perceived as very valuable. The late pre-Roman Iron Age (LPRIA) earthwork at Stonea Camp, an impressive monument positioned in the central Fens, along with increasing evidence of Iron Age occupation in this area as a whole, can leave us in no doubt that activity of considerable intensity was occurring prior to the Roman conquest.

The Central Fens were not a vacant landscape when the Romans arrived. This is not a new suggestion (Hall & Coles 1994:103–4) but with existing structures that needed to be controlled, we are entitled to ask what the effect this Iron Age presence had upon Roman activity. Amongst the first actions of the Roman authorities were the building of a fort at Grandford (Figure 1), long theorised, and now proven by recent aerial photographs (T.W. Potter, pers. comm.), along with the development of a complex communications system consisting of canals and roads (Fincham, forthcoming).

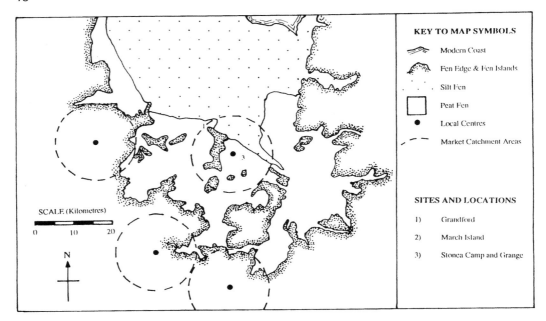

KEY TO MAP SYMBOLS

~~~~   Modern Coast

🐾   Fen Edge & Fen Islands

. . . Silt Fen

☐   Peat Fen

●   Local Centres

- - - Market Catchment Areas

SCALE (Kilometres)

0   10   20

N

SITES AND LOCATIONS

1)   Grandford

2)   March Island

3)   Stonea Camp and Grange

Figure 1 Area map showing the East Anglian Fens, sites mentioned in the text, and the catchment areas of possible local centre market places (After Hall & Coles 1994; Hingley 1989; Phillips 1970).

In the early second century AD a further feature was inserted into this core area. A planned settlement not far removed from Stonea Camp (Figure 1). This site at Stonea Grange also boasted a market place, a temple, possibly dedicated to Minerva, and a large stone tower (Jackson & Potter 1997:684). This last structure, built of imported stone, and containing a great amount of window glass, has been claimed as the administrative headquarters of the Fens, the possible base of a centurion with administrative authority (Jackson & Potter 1997:686). Other scholars have cast doubt upon the centrality of the Stonea site to the administrative infrastructure of the region (Mackreth 1996:234), but the unusual nature of the structure in the context of the Fens, must make it a strong candidate for an 'official' site of some nature. It is certainly true that the material culture of the site is not what we might expect of such a centre. Although there are artefacts such as amphora and glass bottles, quantities are low compared with other sites for which a similar status is claimed (Jackson & Potter 1997:685), though this need not dent (in fact, it may enhance) the 'official' interpretation of the site, as I shall later argue. The building and the temple were demolished around AD 220 but the settlement continued, lasting even beyond the end of the Roman presence in the area.

Several reasons for the decommissioning of the official core of the foundation have been advanced: the structure's isolation from main communication routes (Hall 1992:67), poor drainage, and the failure of the natives to take up the running of the centre due to a 'thin sense of *Romanitas*' (Jackson & Potter 1997:690). The latter of these suggestions at least gives some room for native involvement in the failure of Stonea, but paraphrased in language orientated to the Roman centre. We are left with the impression of recalcitrant Fen farmers, refusing to buy into the 'imperial ideal'. But *why* should this overt act of *colonialism*, defined by Said (1993:8), the act of a dominating metropolitan centre 'implanting...settlements upon a distant territory', have failed? Furthermore, what implications did that failure have for Roman *imperialism*, defined again by Said (1993:8) as 'the practice, the theory, and the attitudes of a dominating metropolitan centre' in the Fens, and how did this effect the lives of the native population?

It may be of significance to this question that the LPRIA site of Stonea Camp appears to have been at its most active during the period of the Icenian client kingdom, at the conclusion of which the site fell out of use (Jackson & Potter 1997:677). The absorption of the Iceni was not easy, or smooth. A wider glance at the Icenian *civitas* reveals that there were fewer villa structures here than in other areas of the South East, few urban centres, and the civitas capital, Venta Icenorum developed at a comparatively late date (Wacher 1995:25). It is, therefore, possible that violent Roman re-occupation of this area after the Boudican revolt had a long lasting impact upon the native experience of empire. However, couching this impact in purely negative economic terms and labelling it 'poverty' allows no positive role to the conquered population in influencing their own condition, and once more ascribes them a passive status. This is an approach, which ignores other possible interpretations of material culture that we label 'poor', and helps to prevent the recovery of a native perspective.

There appears to be little or no status differentiation within rural Fenland settlement, a feature most obvious in the region's lack of villas, and it is this aspect of the settlement pattern that has in part been responsible for the characterisation of the area as poor. We might advance an explanation for this lack of villas based upon the Boudican revolt: that in the aftermath of the rebellion's defeat the native aristocracy suffered most heavily (Jackson & Potter 1997:689). If this were so, there would be no one to construct villas. However, it is unlikely that there was no gradation of status within post-rebellion native society *at all*, and even if we envisage the complete destruction of the native aristocracy (for which, in any case, we have no evidence), we would expect the re-emergence of a native hierarchy over time. Even if this were, as Grahame (1998:7) envisages, not a formal native elite, but in the form of social bonds established between 'agents of Roman power...and those they had conquered', this still constitutes a gradation of status between those natives directly involved in such relationships, and those who were not. Thus, irrespective of the fate of the native hierarchy at the point of conquest, we must conclude that in the post-rebellion Fens, status was being demonstrated in ways that do not show as readily in the archaeological record as an elaborate stone building.

It has been suggested by Hingley (1989:100) that the majority of settlements in the Fens exhibit the characteristics of the 'girdle' pattern, that is to say a pattern in which the settlements surround an area of land, which is held in common. He also suggested that this form of settlement is indicative of the common descent of different elements of the community within those settlements (Hingley 1989:100). Such kin based extended communities are best interpreted as the survival of some aspects of the LPRIA social structure of the Fens into the Roman period. It can be argued, therefore, that what we see is a landscape characterised positively as one which had retained some pre-conquest features, and not a landscape which is characterised negatively by its lack of a certain feature of the normative version of the Romano-British landscape (i.e. the villa). This point is perhaps underlined by the lack of Roman period 'local centres' in the region. Hingley (1989:114) has suggested that in pre-modern agricultural societies there is a practical limit to how far a small farmer can travel to attend a market. He sets this limit at seven to ten kilometres and, although, the exact figure may be debatable, the distribution of such centres in the Fens leaves little doubt that the network of markets as currently understood was not sufficient to service the region (Figure 1). Indeed, the only known market from the Fens proper is located at Stonea, directly in front of the main building and positioned in such a location it is likely to have been heavily regulated. Exchange between settlements cannot have taken place through such 'official channels' across much of the Fens, as these channels never even developed in many places, and local trade must have remained largely informal, and thus difficult, if not impossible, for the Roman authorities to regulate. The physical presence of this market place in the central Fens, precisely the area where a trading network (perhaps centred on Stonea Camp?) must already have existed between LPRIA settlements, may be read as an attempt to symbolically control a pre-existing system, rather than to create a functioning economic market in a conquered territory. This act of *colonialism* was a key tool of Roman *imperialism*.

Having offered a picture of LPRIA activity in the central Fens as relatively vibrant and resilient in the face of a turbulent incorporation into the Roman Empire, we see a region which fails, or refuses, to adopt many of the material trappings acquired by neighbouring regions in the process we loosely label Romanization. This, together with the nature of settlement at which we have briefly glimpsed, appears to suggest that the Fens as a region did not succumb readily to Roman cultural influence. If we seek to explain this situation through an expression of native identity, we can create a reading of the evidence which allows room for the native population to engage with their condition as active agents, and advance the thesis that the people of the Fens consciously characterised themselves as being in a state of non-violent resistance to the Roman empire. Aspects of the material culture hitherto identified as symptoms of simple poverty may then be seen as pointers towards a vibrant native identity during the Roman occupation, and to an extent, the native response to that occupation. We may term this situation 'a landscape of resistance', a term used by Alcock (1997:105), when considering the 'unsuccessful' province of Greece.

In such a scenario, the very presence of the Stonea tower in this landscape becomes an overt act of imperial symbolism. It was this structure, and its accompanying temple and market, that the Romans constructed in close and obvious proximity to the equivalent LPRIA focus at Stonea Camp. In so doing, the imperial authorities sought to signal their control of administration, economic exchange and religion to natives who were engaged in cultural resistance. The small amounts of imported material at Stonea Grange, rather than weakening the interpretation of the site as an official centre, is rather an indication that the impact of the Stonea complex was as much to do with its simple presence, as with its actual function. The lack of material investment in the running of the site is an indication that although such a proto-urban settlement was implanted upon the central Fens, it was a hollow institution, an attempt to project imperial authority to an uncooperative populace, who in making positive cultural choices, had engaged in resistance to a way of life which was not their own.

Conclusions

To characterise the Fens as a poor area, a backwater in which the natives suffered from a lack of access to Roman material culture, is to present a Romanocentric view, which rests upon a simplistic understanding of cultural interaction and poverty. However, post-colonial theory allows us to construct a rival interpretation, and in doing so we not only take account of the perspective of the native, but also reach a better understanding of how Roman domination was enforced. The benefits of such an approach are to allow us to explore more fully the power relations symbolised by the official 'place' of Stonea Grange.

The image of empire that was projected into the Fens was characterised by the alien structures and institutions, and tainted by the violence that crushed the Boudican revolt. In these circumstances the local understanding of the meaning of 'Empire' was negative, something to be feared and actively resisted, rather than something to be participated in and embraced. In shaping their response to Roman rule the native populace rejected the symbolism and also the substance of Stonea, but accepted, if not a commitment to the imperial ideal, at least the minimum physical demands of imperial exploitation. From the Roman perspective, LPRIA structures were colonised principally to signal imperial domination, rather than to actually control the minutiae of administration, or the market place. Once domination was secure, Stonea became redundant, and the centrepiece of imperial architectural symbolism at Stonea was withdrawn, thus representing the positive conclusion of a 'negotiation between ruler and ruled' (Mattingly 1997a: 10).

In this paper I have tried not simply to deconstruct the colonial archaeology of the Fens, but to begin a reconstruction along post-colonial lines. What is presented here is only a first step in one-off showpieces of imposed Roman values. For example, the front portico and range of shops in the forum at Wroxeter were rebuilt after substantial damage from fire in the 160s (Atkinson 1942). Within both complexes, there is evidence of minor work that cannot be accurately dated, but points to their continued use: for example the partitioning and repainting of rooms and reflooring with *opus signinum* or mosaics. These episodes all warn against the argument that these buildings have a single event, their construction, and that their small size, comparative dearth of decoration or even their possible construction by external agents all indicate an evident lack of Romanization. Instead, these buildings demonstrate a history of continued use within their urban environments. As the local inhabitants incorporated these buildings into their daily lives, they also actively incorporated an ideology of urbanism and reproduced through practice elements of Roman society. Work on patterns of villa distribution, showing a tendency to cluster around the civitas capitals, indicates the extent to which urban centres were becoming a dominant focus for certain members of society (Gregson 1987).

A consideration of some specific elements of these buildings allows us to explore in greater detail how some of these themes might operate. For this I shall concentrate upon the basilica itself; rather than an art-historical description, we should ask how specific features become resources implicated in social reproduction. The first area I shall discuss is the 'tribunal'. At Caerwent (Figure 1), there is one at each end of the central nave, but the one at the east end can be more accurately reconstructed. It is blocked off from the north and south aisles by walls and so is visually only accessible from a single direction. The area is highlighted by an engaged column at the east end of the north *stylobate* which was rendered with plaster and painted white (Frere 1991:225). It was separated from the rest of the nave by either a screen or balustrade as indicated by a 30 cm wide groove (Frere 1988:422). Whether this screen was of stone or wood, and how tall it stood, is unclear. The area was approximately 7 metres deep, with a raised tessellated floor contrasting with the *opus signinum* of the rest of the nave. Access was either from the nave or through a door from the north aisle. A hypocaust was later added, and there is evidence of two phases of wall painting. There is less evidence for the tribunals at Wroxeter (Figure 2), but these were apparently also differentiated from the rest of the nave (Atkinson 1942:98). The northern tribunal seems to have been set in a rectangular apse with a raised floor, and again separated by a balustrade with a second entrance from the east aisle.

Thus, these areas are delineated and accentuated through architecture: setting certain people apart within the gathering, but also controlling the encounters both physically and visually. Different groups of the community would be differentiated by their right to enter this area, their means of access, either through the nave itself or from the aisle, and the length of time they might be permitted to linger. The other parts of the basilica from which this area can be seen is restricted by the internal rows of pillars and the walls of the apses. Thus the appearance of those with access to this area is very controlled: the audience is only to the front of them which then limits the possible experiences of the encounter. This area would have been used by the imperial representatives for the dispensation of justice, the promulgation of official announcements and other public duties (Wacher 1995:42). In this way, the authority of the Roman empire becomes established and reinforced within a specifically Roman context. However, these ideas can be taken further; this area becomes a resource, or technology, through which a Roman imperial magistrate routinely creates his own identity. As a magistrate he is empowered in a way which sets him apart from other members of the community and his ability to become a magistrate constitutes a way of defining his gender and his membership of a certain age group. Within the Roman system, only men were eligible for such office and progress through the ranks was linked with age (Beard & Crawford 1985:52–4); the performance of magistral duties was therefore a constituent part of both masculinity and adulthood. Furthermore, this area would become imbued with a particular meaning which would then be recalled when others, the local civitas magistrates, also used it. For them, their social identity becomes maintained through a new Roman technology, this identity again reflecting hierarchies of status, gender and age. We also need to acknowledge that these two types of encounter should not be separated, as the enactment of one becomes recalled and implicated in the enactment of the other, bringing added meaning to it. Within this approach, we have to acknowledge the role of the audience: the knowledge and the acquiescence on the part of other members of the community is central to this display of status.

For an imperial official, brought up within the ideology of Rome, the nature of such social encounters is constrained by ideas of theatricality. The works of Cicero (*De or.* 56.214, 59.220) and Quintilian indicate that there was an anxiety over the similarities between the activities of acting and oratory within élite circles, as the two were believed to be at opposite ends of a political and moral spectrum. Nevertheless, there were strict rules concerning the movement of the body during public speaking, and these were openly acknowledged as an important part of oratory. As Quintilian states:

> ... the arms may be extended in the proper manner, the management of the hands free from all trace of rusticity and inelegance, the attitude becoming, the movements of the feet appropriate and the motions of the head and eye in keeping with the poise of the body. No one will deny that such details form a part of the art of delivery, nor divorce delivery from oratory; and there can be no justification for disdaining to learn what has got to be done...

> (Quint. *Inst.* 1.11.16–7)

Here Quintilian explicitly uses the terminology of *urbanus-rusticus* ideology: to deliver a speech in the appropriate manner allows a Roman magistrate to establish and maintain his identity within that set of values. The role of the audience and the idea of performance are also implicit: this identity is expressed through the performance using the correct posture and gestures in the presence of an audience also aware of these rules. The tribunals provide the stage for this enactment and the architecture of the building reinforces the theatricality of the event, thus perpetuating the ideology governing it.

The second element of the buildings I wish to discuss is the rear range of rooms. Neither Caerwent nor Wroxeter possess a complete range, but each adds something to our understanding of their possible role. At Caerwent, room 3 has been identified as a probable council chamber (Frere 1989:264). It could only be entered via an antechamber, rooms 1/2, initially a single room, later divided into two. Thus access is not only limited to certain people, but it is also physically and metaphorically distanced from the rest of the building and the community through this increasingly convoluted approach. The room itself possesses slots in the floor for benches and the base for a large dais at the furthest end. Once again, comparative status is articulated through the layout of the room, with the most senior magistrates presumably having access to this dais. The high status attached to the room as a whole is indicated through the two phases of painted plaster and the later mosaic floor (Ashby 1906:128, plate 19). The right to enter the curia as a member of the élite class or as a serving magistrate would be limited. In the absence of a charter for a civitas capital, we can only surmise the exact criteria for eligibility: whether it was based solely on Roman law or represented a compromise between pre-existing and native traditions. However, we might expect that the criteria might incorporate distinctions of wealth, gender and age. The right to enter the curia becomes a way of expressing these aspects of identity: as a person of high rank in an society where status is based upon wealth; as a man in an era when the genders are given specific roles, and finally as having reached a certain number of years, where access to power is graded by age. But this also constitutes a way of actively perpetuating and promoting the ideology behind this system, and the inequalities underpinning it, that of the superiority of the adult, wealthy male.

The finds from room 1 in the Wroxeter basilica include locks, padlocks, hinges and samian inkpots (Atkinson 1942:101–3, 220–1 no. 6). The metal finds suggest the presence of wooden chests or cupboards, and together these suggest a possible clerk's office or archive. Recreating the daily use of this room is more difficult, but presumably it was connected with the administrative requirements of the imperial system: for example, the keeping of records, the census and tax details. Thus both the physical presence of these buildings and activities such as

Figure 1. Gerasa, the colonnaded street (photograph by Charles Daniels, courtesy of Miriam Daniels)

The stage for these urban dramas was the streets and monuments of the city. It was here in the city's public arena where expressions of civic identity and munificence were most highly manifest, and it was these monuments and the great streets between that channelled procession between points of significance and on to an ultimate goal (Figure 1).

By its very nature the colonnaded street created strong bounding edges, and anything punctuating the monotony, enforced its identification as a landmark in the mental map (MacDonald 1986:99–107; Yegül 1994). The projecting *propylea* of buildings along the street served to mark destinations from a distance. At Gerasa in provincial Arabia the only intrusions on an 800m stretch of colonnaded street between the north gate and south piazza were the *tetrapyla* on the two principal intersections and the propylea which marked the positions of the two principal temples (Browning 1982:80–6, map 3; MacDonald 1986:38–42; Wharton 1995:64–7). A colonnaded street that terminated in a temple as at Palmyra and again at Gerasa, could also bestow added potency to the vista of approach at a sacred time. Nor should it be ignored that these experiential qualities of what MacDonald called an 'urban armature' (MacDonald 1986:5–31) may well have been emphasised through distinctions in the colour of buildings and, particularly during festivals, in the decoration of significant buildings.

One of the most vivid portrayals of urban procession is provided by a long inscription from the early second century found at Ephesos, in which a wealthy benefactor Salutaris intends to provide funds for a regular procession in honour of the city's patron goddess Artemis (Rogers 1991). According to the inscription, approximately every two weeks a group of 31 gold and silver statues and images of mythological, imperial and local figures were carried in a circuit around the city by a procession comprising some 260 persons, organised into a strict hierarchy and following a fixed route (Rogers 1991:figs. 1–3). The procession would begin and end out-

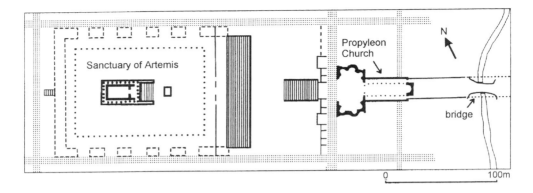

Figure 2. Gerasa, simplified plan of the Artemis temple complex and Propyleon Church (after Browning 1982: 83)

side the city at the temple of Artemis, symbolising the fundamental role of the goddess in the mythological foundation and the ultimate destiny of the city. Its route, the choice of statues and images carried, connected the three historic foundations of the city, from the Roman Imperial re-development of the upper agora, through the city's Hellenistic core, to the Ionian quarter by the Koressian gate, proceeding through them in a reverse chronological direction. Furthermore, by the status and ordering of participants, the images conveyed, its timing and its direct reference to the city's historic monuments and statuary which lined and punctuated the route, the Salutaris procession was clearly intended to perpetuate the foundation legends and social hierarchy, and by regular repetition to create an image, symbolic map and identity for the city (Rogers 1991:80–115).

The fundamental importance of procession in urban ritual can further be reflected in the ar-chaeological record. At Gerasa, there survives one of the most striking ensembles of proces-sional monuments in any Roman city; those associated with the second century Sanctuary of Artemis (Figure 2). The temple was situated at the conclusion of a 500m sequential architectural scheme, which combined a dominating approach vista with successive increases in elevation emphasising the temple as an urban landmark (Browning 1982:86–92; MacDonald 1986:70–1; Wharton 1995:65–75). The axial arrangement of these structures along the *Via Sacra* created a bounded ritual pathway that defined the heart of the city; from the bridge on the east side, along the street, through successive propylea and up a series of grand staircases to the sacred precinct. This route and the monuments associated with it were apparently composed to embellish and to emphasise the ritual approach to the temple.

Christian procession

By the end of the fourth century in the East, pagan public festivals had on the whole been superseded by Christian ceremonials led by the bishop and ecclesiastical hierarchy (Croke 1990:177–82; Markus 1991:97–121)[3]. Recent research in early Christian art and literature has clarified the central importance of procession in early urban Christianity, which developed to a large degree within the existing framework. Baldovin has defined the crucial role of stational liturgy in the formation of the Christian urban topography of Rome, Constantinople and Jerusa-lem, beginning in the late fourth century as personage-centred and participatory ritual proces-sion connected the increasing number of urban churches and monuments in many major cities (Croke 1981; Baldovin 1987:234–7, 253–68). In addition, Mathews has demonstrated how the convergent procession dominated the repertoire of Christian interior decoration in the fifth and sixth centuries, and how images of procession were sympathetic to the ritual activities of the

Figure 3. Diocaesarea (Uzuncaburç), temple and church.

viewers in a particular space (Mathews 1993; also Wharton 1995:60; Elsner 1995:221–39). By the fifth century the calendar of festivals in most eastern cities was predominantly Christian, although the logistics, timing and meaning of many processions had been adopted from antique predecessors. For example the procession of the Great Litany in Rome took place on the same date as the pagan Robigalia, with a similar route and composition (Baldovin 1987:236)

With the rise of the cult of martyrs, the gods as bearers of civic identity were succeeded in this role by 'protector' saints. Yet even as many old pagan centres withered in the mid to late fourth century, most still remained untouched by the church builders. With the growing attention given to the shrines of martyrs, Christian procession in the fourth century generally involved movement from within to without the city or vice versa and bore very little reference to pre-existing places. However, by the late fourth century a new intra-mural trend was emerging, as the martyrs relics were translated to new churches within the city walls and within the pagan centres (Hunt 1998:242–4, 250–7). Relics began to form the foci of elaborate processions, like the statues of Artemis in Salutaris' procession, which in turn gave buildings, churches and places new Christian meanings. It was only from this time that the Church really made its mark on the innermost fabric of the cities (Markus 1991:139–155; Milojević 1996).

We have seen how pagan procession bore a direct relationship to the monuments that defined the route, and how at Gerasa for example, the monuments themselves demonstrate the importance of procession. Accepting the centrality of procession and processional architecture in the urban religious experience, archaeology can reveal aspects of the usurpation rather than obliteration of the symbolic map. I will proceed to examine the spatial and what I see as the experiential qualities of these changes.

Temple conversions and re-invented topographies

The late fourth to sixth century was the most active period of temple conversions, many of which resulted in only visually superficial changes to the pre-existing monument (Deichmann 1939; Vaes 1986:fig. 48; Milojević 1997). In many instances the temple peristyle was preserved in the new church building, either on the interior, forming the church colonnades as at Aphro-

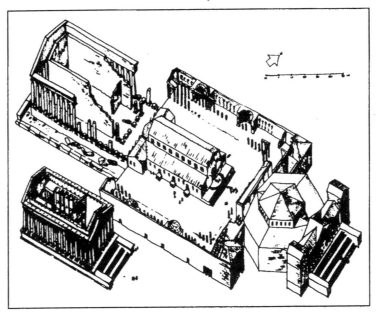

Figure 4. Sanctuary of Jupiter Heliopolitan and the Church of St. Peter at Baalbek (after Ragette 1980: 70)

disias in Caria (Cormack 1990b) or in the outer fabric as at Diocaesarea in Cilicia (Hill 1996:252–4). In the latter case the intercolumniations were walled up with blocks probably from the temple cella and the upper portions of the columns modified to accommodate a new roofing system (Figure 3). The scale, essential form, surrounding architectural context and strong verticality imposed by the peristyle were maintained in the church. Temples converted in this way therefore still retained many of their pre-existing visual qualities, and are in a sense similar to some of the later conversions in Rome which reflect efforts to resurrect the city's ancient identity (Krautheimer 1980).

In a great number of other temple conversions, when the church was built entirely within the peristyle or cella, the transformation may not have been possible to detect from a distance, as may perhaps have been the case with the temple conversions of Ancyra, Assos and Didyma (Deichmann 1939:128–9). The more famous examples at Agrigento and Syracuse are worth mentioning in this context, as are the later conversions of the Parthenon and the Hephaiston in Athens. It is important to remember that temples such as these were located in prominent, highly visible urban positions.

Other examples of temple conversions are equally as illuminating in terms of what is preserved. At Baalbek in Phoenicia the altar and viewing platform of the massive and dominating temple of Jupiter was destroyed at the end of the fourth century and the material used to build a church in front of the temple steps (Figure 4). To maintain the existing approach from the east, the apse of the church was oriented unusually westward. The temple *propyleon* and hexagonal court were restored and continued to provide a grand entrance. It was only some time later, when more rigorous building traditions were apparently enforced, that the apse was moved to the east side and the approach to the church became disarticulated (Ragette 1980:68–71).

The late antique re-development of Aezani in Phrygia has also been realised with some clarity by recent excavation (Rheidt 1995). This included the construction of a church within the peristyle of the Temple of Zeus and a major rebuilding programme on the street that led to it.

Material from a nearby temple dedicated to Artemis was used extensively in the porticoes of the street, which from at least the second century had formed part of a processional way connecting both temples with an important extra-mural rock-cut shrine.

As highly visual urban landmarks, temples were an important element of the city's imaging and orientation (Price 1984:136–46; Favro 1996:168–9). With a conversion that was often little more than superficial, the experiential components of the city that had provided the strongest identifying characteristics were translated but maintained. Just as importantly we must consider the many churches which replaced a partially or wholly destroyed temple while preserving its predecessor's architectural context. Most people's experience of a temple was from the outside, whether during sacred time or otherwise and the urban temples were often the focus of expansive architectural ensembles that may have included a precinct wall, propylea, approach streets and neighbouring structures. The effect of these conversion scenarios was that urban vistas were perpetuated and sacred localities preserved under a Christian guise. So the grand architectural devices of entrance that had provoked and stirred emotions of expectancy on approach to the holy place were appropriately re-employed. Churches that occupied the sites of temples in this way were re-inventing exactly the same visual vitality for a new urban liturgy.

Aphrodisias

To extract meaning from these changes in the built environment we must appreciate the city as an articulated whole and consider the impact of Christianized buildings beyond the limits of the individual monument. Recent excavation and survey at Aphrodisias in Caria has aimed at clarifying the organisation and planning of the urban topography and in particular the relationship between the buildings and the street system (Smith & Ratté 1995:42; 1996:16; 1997:10–16, fig. 1; 1998:225–30, fig. 1). This has led to a much clearer understanding of the Christian impact on the city, a subject previously explored in an article by Cormack (Cormack 1990a). In this section of my paper I will attempt to build on his work in the light of more recent research at the site and will also suggest that the various Christianized elements appear to have been connected in a more intimate way than may initially have been suspected (Figure 5).

The temple of Aphrodite, patron goddess of the city, was converted into a church dedicated to St Michael sometime after the middle of the fifth century (Smith & Ratté 1995:44–6). The temple complex, including an elaborate *temenos* and forecourt, occupied an extensive area between two major north-south streets. The principal approach was from the east side through a *tetrapylon* that projected into the main street (Paul 1996: figs.1–2; Smith & Ratté 1998:228; Figure 5). The space between the *tetrapylon* and the *temenos* appears to have been occupied by a forecourt, with the main access to the precinct itself afforded by a 3 metre wide doorway in the centre of the monumental and highly articulated east *temenos* wall (Doruk 1990).

However, when the temple was converted the principal approach was shifted to the church atrium on the west side and at some point the eastern *temenos* doorway was blocked by the insertion of a west-facing brick apse. This implies that the Christian liturgical usage of the site extended beyond the bounds of the church proper, but how far and for what purpose is difficult to ascertain. It is also not clear whether any approach route was maintained from the east. Limited excavation in the forecourt appears to indicate that at least a portion of this area was given over to high status domestic residences (Smith & Ratté 1996:8–9). However, the *tetrapylon* was restored sometime after the turn of the fifth century and at some point a relief bust of Aphrodite on its west tympanum was defaced and replaced with a cross (Smith 1996:11–3) perhaps indicating that this monument was still considered to be part of the Christianized complex. Whether the conversion of the temple area, therefore, effectively severed the pre-existing communication between the two major north-south streets of the city is not yet clear.

Figure 5. Aphrodisias, city plan (after Smith & Ratté 1997)

Abutting the outside of the *temenos* wall to the north was an elaborate structure that has been tentatively identified as the residence of the bishop (Campbell 1996:188–92; Smith & Ratté 1998:230–2). Two other structures in the southern sector of the city also appear to have been significant nodes in the urban liturgy of Byzantine Aphrodisias. The first is a four-columned monument identified as a *tetrakionion*, which served to monumentalise the junction of the main street running south from the church atrium with an east-west street running past the theatre baths. It was probably built in the fifth or sixth century and was structurally similar to a monument on the Arcadiane at Ephesos (Smith & Ratté 1995; 48–51, figs. 22–3; 1996:13–6, figs. 7–9). It has been argued that the columns of the Ephesian example held statues of the evangelists (Foss 1979:57–8, fig. 16; Yegül 1994:100)[4], and I would suggest that the symbolic nature of the Aphrodisian example was equally if not more overt.

This interpretation of what might normally be perceived as a 'secular' monument is based on the Byzantine history of this junction after the early seventh century when a small *triconch* church was built, which entirely encased the monument, but apparently without employing it structurally within its fabric (C.Ratté, pers. comm.)[5]. This implies that the church was recognising the *tetrakionion* as the marker of a meaningful intersection in the Christian city, which may well have some reflection on the original significance of the *tetrakionion* itself. Much like the *tetrapylon* at the east end of the temple court, it acknowledged and emphasised a focal point at an intersection of special importance within the city plan .

The second Christianized monument I will mention is the theatre, which probably remained in use until the early seventh century. It is located on the main street running south from the temple *tetrapylon* and close to its junction with the street running east from the *tetrakionion*. The theatre in antiquity was the scene of ritual as well as entertainment and at Ephesos formed the sole stopping place on the Salutaris procession (Rogers 1991:102–103). Theatres, in general, appear to continue to provide a focus for public activity in the Christian period, although it often seems that their usage underwent some change (Roueché 1991). With the decline of 'immoral' public displays in the Christian city, the theatre of Aphrodisias may indeed have taken on more responsibility for ritual, as sometime in the middle of the sixth century, large images of the archangels were painted on the walls of a room in the stage building (Cormack 1991). One of these paintings, of particularly high quality, is identified as St. Michael, Aphrodite's usurper as the new patron of the city.

Thus the inter-relationship of Christian elements within the topography of Aphrodisias becomes clearer. The restoration and Christianization of the *tetrapylon* at the east end of the temple court suggests that it may have functioned as a part of the church complex as it had with the temple. However there was a shift in emphasis towards the major street on the west side that linked the bishop's residence, the church atrium and the monumentalized intersection to the south. The other major node of the early Byzantine city was the theatre, which lay on the same major street as the *tetrapylon*, and which also may have become a focus for Christian ritual. From the evidence of the dominating new church and the other Christianized monuments, as well as the connecting streets, we can begin to see the emergence of a symbolic map of the Christian city, based entirely on the existing armatures and landmarks. It does not take much extension of the imagination to envisage the scope for ritual procession within this interconnected framework of meaningful monuments.

Gerasa

We finally return to Gerasa, where we have already witnessed the processional organisation of the Artemis complex. The Christian usurpation of Gerasa focused primarily on the urban centre in the vicinity of the temple. From the late fourth to sixth century churches sprang up around this old pagan focus, yet without advancing into the sacred *temenos* itself (Wharton 1995:64–74). One particular church, built within the *propyleon* of the temple, served to breach what would have been the major processional route from the east (Figure 2). The initial reaction of the excavators and more recent interpretations of the site is that the church symbolises the severance of this major artery of the city, and perhaps therefore symptomatic of the collapse of the bridge to the east (Kraeling 1938; Browning 1982:147–52). This interpretation fails to explain the presence of eastern entrances to this church, which in other contexts, most notably Constantinople and Cilicia, have been associated with a processional liturgy (Mathews 1971:105–7; Hill 1996:28–37). Rather than ultimately nullifying this architectural scheme, the construction of this church may therefore have effectively restored meaning to it via a revived emphasis on procession which, moreover, rendered the street through the *propyleon* obsolete for any purpose other than a ritual one.

Conclusions

In this paper I have attempted to take the perspective of the observer and participant in urban ritual and procession in order ascribe more subtle meaning to the impact of church building on perceptions of the urban ritual topography. It has not been possible here to consider the implications for the many cities in this region where the symbolic map *does* appear to undergo a dramatic transformation in the fourth to sixth centuries, for example at Ephesos, Sardis and Corycos. Certainly the fact that few common threads can be drawn between the fate of temples in different cities reflects the great diversity in Christian attitudes towards the monuments themselves (Saradi-Mendelovici 1990:47).

The reasons and motivations for temple conversions, from a symbolic 'victory of the cross', through the eradication of pagan demons, to pure expediency, have been discussed extensively elsewhere and are not the subject of this paper [see Bayliss in preparation]. I merely wish to suggest that the implantation of a church within an existing and aggrandised architectural scheme quite probably had far-reaching implications and may have achieved a subtle coercive effect, even if it was done so unwittingly. In terms of visual impact the exposed remains of a temple would moreover set one of these churches apart from others as something special or different. Many would surely recognise the ancient sanctity of the place and the attitude toward the building must on the whole have been a positive one [6]. For the generation or two who had witnessed or participated in urban ritual and procession before the closure or destruction of their cities' temples there would be a certain familiarity in the urban manifestation and context of Christianity, which presented itself as the natural and inevitable successor to worship of the old gods. There is perhaps a lesson we should learn from recent studies in the art of this period; that scholars who have long sought to find explanations for the pell-mell of pagan and Christian symbolism appearing in late antique contexts, perhaps missed the point that to the fourth century viewer the distinction was not so clear (Elsner 1995:251–270).

Pope Gregory the Great apparently advised Augustine of Canterbury to purify the standing temples of the Angli so that they might be put to use as churches:

> that when the people themselves see that these temples are not destroyed, they may put away error from their heart, and, knowing and adoring the true God, may have recourse with the more familiarity to the places they have been accustomed to.
>
> (Epistles 76)

Although these instructions were given at a time when the Christianization of the eastern cities was considered by most to be complete, they nevertheless reveal an attitude that almost certainly had a longer pedigree. In this sense it was the *familiarity* of the sacred topography that may have been instrumental to the Christianization of many late antique cities. The perpetuation of the symbolic map with a Christian veneer was befitting to the Christian ethos to convert, not destroy, the Other in society. The archaeology has demonstrated that in many cases more than the temples were preserved. Also the approaches, vistas and outward appearance of the site are maintained, which to a degree perhaps even mystified the usurpation of a sacred place.

Many churches built from temples re-employed the architectural composition and urban imagery that had made the temples such a visual force in the urban landscape. Thus symbolic maps of cities were translated and given Christian meanings, expressed and re-enforced through procession. So in many cities and for many people, the individual and communal experience of sacred time and place remained remarkably unchanged despite dramatic social upheaval and a period of great dynamism in the built environment.

Department of Archaeology, University of Newcastle upon Tyne

Although a significant proportion of research into pilgrimage has concentrated on the motivations of the pilgrim and the concept of the Holy Place (MacCormack 1990), the analysis of the archaeology of pilgrimage has concentrated predominantly on the monumental architecture of the surviving pilgrimage centres, their layout, and the activities that took place in them (Ousterhout 1990:108; Stopford 1994:59).

Archaeological work on pilgrimage centres has traditionally tended to concentrate either on describing the activities performed by pilgrims around sites, or on detailed descriptions of their monumental architecture and layouts, focusing on building designs and decoration, and although acknowledging symbolism, interpretations have often followed typological, functional and historical approaches (Mango 1978:7–9). It has been considered, for example, that the layout of these sites facilitated the organisation of the large numbers of people who visited them (Stopford 1994:66). An example of this tradition of interpretation may be found in a discussion of split-level Crusader churches; the design of these buildings may have allowed the religious communities to continue worshipping on the floor above without being disturbed by pilgrims (Pringle 1987:351). But how did this arrangement affect the pilgrim's experience? Though he or she could not see the liturgy taking place - could it be heard? How might the combination of this architectural layout and liturgical actions have effected their experience? The architecture did far more than present large numbers of people with the opportunity to take part in ritual at specific places as they processed around a pilgrimage centre. We must not dehumanise our interpretations of these pilgrimage centres where emotions and senses would have played such a part.

In order to understand the experience of the pilgrim at these places we also need to appreciate the role of his or her own background and motivations for being there, as well as the architecture of the place (Lang 1994:318). The architecture alone cannot have determined behaviour, although it may have 'afforded' certain actions; the experience itself will have depended greatly upon the background and motivation of the visitor (Lang 1987:103–4). In spite of the fact that pilgrims may come from very different backgrounds, bringing and imposing a diversity of perceptions and meaning to the shrine (Eade & Sallnow 1991:10), pilgrims' motivations in general will be different from those of other tourists (Leyerle 1996:121); since although each visitor to a pilgrimage site has a different background, a sizeable proportion of pilgrims, as 'religious tourists', have a similar motivation. Whether they have travelled a long and arduous, or a much shorter journey to the site, they come prepared to arrive at a sacred place. Even before they arrive, they are in many cases open to accept the sacred nature of the site and are therefore more susceptible to the sacred experience than an ambivalent and uninformed visitor. It is the motivation behind the journey to the sacred place that differentiates the pilgrim from other tourists. Theirs' was spiritual journey complete with additional expectations and an agenda that goes beyond most travel experience. For many there was an expectation not just of the new and the exciting but of the sacred and the supernatural.

Smith explains, the idea of the *loca sancta*, the holy place, was seen as powerful, awe-inspiring, dangerous, important, precious and to be approached with due seriousness and gravity, setting it apart from the profane (Smith 1992:240). He remarks that 'The Holy can be approached only with due preparation' (Smith 1992:240). The holy place was, for the early medieval pilgrim, the object of yearning: *desiderum*, a journey not merely in space but of the soul (MacCormack 1990:22).

The study of the architectural layout of the sixth century pilgrimage centre at Mount Sinai by Finkelstein (1981:81) noted a series of prayer niches lining the approach to Jebel Musa, the summit of the mountain. Coleman & Elsner (1994:78) interpreted these as 'mini-goals' marking the ascent up Mount Sinai. Finkelstein (1985:56) also noted that paths facilitated movement towards the focus at Mount Sinai, via these opportunities for stationary liturgy. McKevitt also identified the movement of pilgrims towards the most sacred part of a shrine in an anthropological study of the pilgrimage site of Padre Pio in Italy. His observations recognised movement towards the tomb of Padre Pio via other places on the site, associated with Pio's life, which became the foci of attention of pilgrims (McKevitt 1991:90). Points of significance, often offering the opportunity for ritual activity, are a common feature of the architecture of pilgrimage centres.

Finkelstein (1981:81) describes how some of the locations of prayer niches on the approach to the summit of Mount Sinai were places where there was a 'magnificent' view, and from some the peak was visible. These structures were places where pilgrims prayed and monks it is argued, provided an 'interpretative and liturgical form for pilgrim-experience' (Coleman & Elsner 1994:78). Those pilgrims who sought a particular experience would have been more receptive to the symbols than those coming loaded with indifference or scepticism.

These niches, like similar devices used elsewhere (see below), can be understood to be not just mini-goals to the pilgrim, neither were they just 'staging posts' or 'markers' on the way to the main goal. For, as well as being places to aim for while on the journey and places of activity, these structures had an experiential quality. As places for prayer, these niches became an integral part of the experience of the sacred site, since prayer may be both a personal and public activity. The position of the niches at places of significance within the site means that the liturgy practised there may have been given meaning by monks (Coleman & Elsner 1994:78) or may have been conducted with extra symbolism, but the experience itself belonged to the pilgrim.

Coleman & Elsner (1994:74) highlighted the failure of anthropologists to examine how the 'physical characteristics of pilgrimage sites can provide a religious topography designed to impose – or at least suggest behavioural and ideological conformity'. They concluded that the pilgrimage to Sinai incorporated at least two levels of transformation, one on the level of theology, and one on the level of self:

> Through liturgy, images, the constant reading of scripture, and personal prayer, the pilgrim would have been associated with the biblical events which actually took place at the site

(Coleman & Elsner 1994:85)

In this study I hope to demonstrate that these paths that are typical of Pilgrimage centres, vary in physical appearance: they may be simple or monumentalised, colonnaded or covered, curved or straight, they may have run uphill or descended into tunnels, they may have provided and prevented lines of sight to final destinations. Whatever the nature of the path, its effect was to keep the pilgrim moving between the points of stationary liturgy, by stimulating anticipation for what was to come.

This investigation aims to explore the relationship between the architectural devices, physical characteristics and the pilgrims themselves by concentrating on examples of pilgrimage centres from the late Roman period in southern Turkey. The religious background of pilgrims and their expectation provide motivation for the activities they perform within the pilgrimage centre, which are of critical importance for their experience. It can be suggested that the more motivation the pilgrim has, the more meaningful the liturgy at each station will be for the individual and therefore the more fulfilling the experience. The fact that the pilgrim is given the opportunity to undertake a whole succession of such activities means that each fulfilling experience will add to the cumulative experience at the site.

The cumulative effect of undertaking a succession of liturgical activities, each with its own meaning, would have prepared the pilgrim for the final focus of the site mentally: full of expectation and excitement, nervousness and apprehension in order that the final encounter with the focus, perhaps a sacred relic, might be an experience of heightened emotional significance.

The succession of potential experiences featured along the linear layout of pilgrimage centres, and the architectural and striking natural environment of many centres would have afforded the opportunity to create feelings of anticipation and suspense as approach was made towards the final destination. The momentum behind this movement at the pilgrimage centre is provided by the desire to approach the most sacred part of the site. These feelings could have been increased by facilitating or depriving sight of the goal while still at a distance (Coleman & Elsner 1994:78); by the behaviour and actions of other people; the location of elements of surprise and distraction, e.g. touts selling trinkets, monks, shrines, tombs, baptisteries or baths and other rituals peculiar to the place; and images in the form of paintings, mosaics and sculptures, which would have held symbolism and meaning for their viewers.

> Christians are concerned with the invisible one beyond all sense perception, and yet, paradoxically, they communicate with the Deity, normally, in and through sensory forms. Their religious life is expressed through the world of the body, its glance, its word and its gesture. Even their spiritual concepts are derived from the impressions received through the senses.

> (McKenzie 1988:15)

Sensations could also be aroused through the use of light, colours, temperature, sounds and smells and by causing pilgrims to undergo physical exertion prior to their arrival; these devices afford the potential for a heightened experience at the final goal. The cumulative effect of the sensory properties of the environment was to afford an experience worthy of the sacred place, but only if the visitor was open and receptive to these properties.

The veneration of sacred places was a very important aspect of the early Medieval World. *Loca Sancta,* or sacred places, which were the objects of these journeys have been the focus of much research but little work seems to have concentrated on the way in which the sacred place is actually created in the mind of the medieval pilgrim. For a place to be appreciated as sacred it must convince; McKevitt explains how twentieth century pilgrims visiting San Giovanni Rotundo come familiar with the myths of Padre Pio and ready for a spiritual experience: 'One or other of these is always granted because the pilgrimage facilitates intimate contact with the divine in the form of the special powers felt to reside in this sacred place' (McKevitt 1991:93).

Through hearing information about holy places before arriving and personal preparation on the pilgrimage (McKevitt 1991:92), the pilgrim thus comes to the site anticipating the Holy. The place must be able to afford an experience that will maintain this preconception in order to perpetuate its reputation. McKevitt says, 'The sacred is not something given or something fixed, but must be constantly created and recreated. A conscious effort is needed on the part of the pilgrim to use and appropriate symbols, myths and rituals in order to vivify the experience of the pilgrimage and to make real the sacredness of the place' (McKevitt 1991:79).

In order to understand the success of the medieval *loca sancta* we need to be aware of the potential for the pilgrimage centre to enable the pilgrim to vivify the notion of the sacred place that they bring with them. The sacred place must not be a disappointment. Relics or tombs were often the focus of the *loca sancta*. What is of interest here is how the pilgrim came to associate for example an old bone, whether in an elaborate case or not, with divine power. If we acknowledge that architecture is not enough to determine behaviour, then neither is material culture: in this case a reliquary with its contents. In this study I will list briefly evidence from three pilgrimage centres which are examples of *loca sancta*; following this, I will attempt to show how devices at these sites would have worked with the motivation of the pilgrim and contributed to the sacred experience.

Figure 1 Line of four arcosolia situated after the baptistery at the West end of the colonnaded walkway.

Alahan

Alahan, dated from the fifth century AD, is built on a huge rock-cut ledge on the side of the Göksu Valley, in southern Turkey (Gough 1985; Hill 1996:68–83; Figure 5). Archaeological and epigraphic evidence from the site have been used to suggest its function as a pilgrimage centre (Hill 1998, 317); there is a church at either end of the site joined by a colonnaded walkway. The route from west to east between these two structures passes a baptistery, a shrine, and four tombs in arcosolia (Figure 1); then follows a colonnaded walkway before arriving at the 'East Church' (Figure 2), beyond the 'East Church' was a steep path to a spring complex, bath and well (Gough 1985:10–16). This is a monumentalized environment, built in a very impressive geographical position:

> ...by whatever means this ascent is made, the impression on a visitor when he reaches the top is likely to be one of wonder. Wonder at the grandeur and extent of the buildings which stretch away to the right, and wonder, as he turns back towards the road up which he has come, at the magnificence of the wide views over the valley of the Göksu, to Mahras Dag on its far side and to the ranges of the blue Isaurian hills beyond. A moment or two is needed to catch breath

> (Gough 1985:12)

Excavation suggests that initial construction, although not in a single phase, took place in a short space of time, with the colonnaded walkway and baptistery being the last to be built (Gough 1963:114). The site offers the pilgrim the opportunity, at specific points, to seek personal involvement in this sacred place: to venerate saints, to witness and obtain baptism and to follow a well defined route via these points between the churches at either end of the complex. At the far end of the site, the sacred spring, like the cistern near the end of the path at Mount Sinai (Finkelstein 1985:60) would have enabled pilgrims to quench their 'thirst'. As well as archaeological evidence for figural mosaics there is also imposing architectural sculpture full of imagery and symbolism that would have held messages for the pilgrims (Gough 1962:180).

Figure 2 Shrine (foreground right), situated on the southern side of the colonnaded walkway, with East Church in background

Gemile Ada

At Gemile Ada, an island off the coast of Lycia, thought to be a pilgrimage site, there were five churches dedicated to St. Nicholas, patron saint of sailors, travellers and pilgrims (Tsuji 1995). The settlement lay around the outside of the island, surrounding the interior, where the funerary monuments and the ecclesiastical monuments were situated.

The route from 'Church 4' up the hill to 'Church 3' is made via a long and vaulted passageway (Foss 1994:74), which has niches along its way, lined with tombs. At particular points where two vaulted passageways join, one encounters small centrally planned areas built with domed roofs (Tsuji 1995:Figure 6). Further procession is facilitated around the churches by additional passageways. Tombs positioned in the niches along the lines of these vaulted corridors provide a role as objects for veneration, but also the passages themselves monumentalise the path, encompassing the tombs and linking the churches. Their gradients, orientation, line, sensory properties, sounds and smells afford and prevent opportunities to take part in a variety of potential activities and lend themselves to a variety of experiences.

Meryemlik

Another of these pilgrimage places was the site of Meryemlik or St. Thecla (Herzfeld· & Guyer 1930; Hill 1996:208–234; Figure 6) situated on a hill a couple of kilometres outside Silifke, the ancient city of Seleucia, on the shores of the Mediterranean (Ferguson 1990:887). Though the site has been planned, it is largely unexcavated. There are two main literary sources relating to this site: the Miracles of St Thecla (Dagron 1978) and the account of a visit to the site by the fourth Century pilgrim, Egeria (Wilkinson 1971, 121).

Having known about Meryemlik for some months and studied it in published material, I was finally able to make my own trip to this last site late one afternoon last August. After a 20 minute

Figure 3 The cutting at Meryemlik, view along the cutting from the entrance.

Figure 4 The cutting at Meryemlik, emerging from the mouth of the cutting, view of the site (Courtesy of Richard Bayliss).

walk from Silifke the final approach was up a relatively steep hillside. Near the crest of the hill the final approach is guided through a rock-cut passage. This passage is *c.* 4m wide, cut into the rock to a depth of *c.* 3 to 4m and faced with ashlar masonry. Even when I was halfway along the passage – because it is rising to pass over the crest of the hill and because it is on a slight bend – I was unable to see the site (Figure 3).

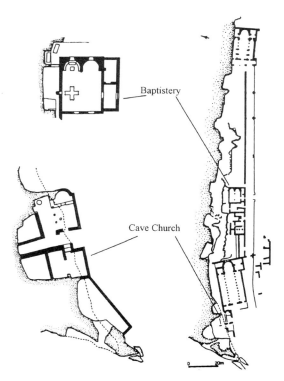

Baptistery

Cave Church

Figure 5 Plan of Alahan (Courtesy of Dr. Stephen Hill (1996)).

It was only when I emerged from the mouth of this passage that the plateau on the top of the hill, where the pilgrimage centre was once situated, became visible. I experienced a feeling of anticipation and excitement as my eyes were drawn to the end of the cutting, and I came closer to its mouth. The path continues forward; but what you see today is an almost barren plateau, in the distance the remains of the apse of the Basilica of St. Thecla, underneath which is the sacred cave (Figure 4).

From piles of rocks and rubble, my plan revealed information about the site, traces of which could be made out on the ground. As an archaeology student, I had decided before arriving that the place was important, that was my motivation, these insubstantial remains were proof enough. For the early Christian pilgrim, motivation for visiting St. Thecla's and recognition of the importance of the place would have been based on different criteria, but the passageway would have performed a similar role.

The Miracles of St. Thecla provide more vivid information about the site. They describe gardens at the sanctuary (Miracle 36:17–21, Dagron 1978), which had live birds: signets, cranes, geese, doves and birds from Egypt (Miracle 24, Dagron 1978). Dagron suggests that these birds would have brought joy to the visitors for aesthetic reasons (Dagron 1978:69–70); but these birds were also Christian symbols: as a group they symbolised paradise, individual birds were frequently used in Christian art to symbolise themes such as eternal life. These symbols had often been appropriated by Christianity from earlier religions but came to represent an important part of Christian iconography, occurring frequently in mosaics, paintings, and sculptures: for example: in the mosaic from the apse of St. Appolinare in Classe in Ravenna (Deichmann 1958, 385). The garden at Meryemlik was all that was represented and symbolised in these 2–D images of paradise, but alive and real.

Further along the path were two enormous rock-cut cisterns on the right of the road, a bath building on the left and a huge domed basilica similar to the East Church at Alahan – known as the Cupola Church – and the remains of a splendid fifth century basilica, where now just the apse is standing. This building was rebuilt in the fifth century in place of an earlier structure and although very little is immediately visible above ground today, the crypt or cave itself, which was the shrine to St Thecla, still exists.

The gate to the crypt, the most sacred part of the site, was unlocked for me and two others by the guard; as I went down the steps the temperature dropped dramatically and once inside the cave, I was struck by the way I could hear nothing but our footsteps. As we walked around inside I carefully examined the cave in my attempt to be a diligent student of such buildings. Suddenly, the silence was broken by literally twenty-five fourteen year olds who had also come to experience the cave, but who did so by scrambling over every corner of it laughing and shouting. The breaking of the silence and their behaviour changed the atmosphere for me totally. However, this change in atmosphere and their behaviour did not remove my motivation for visiting the place; what struck me was their apparent lack of understanding of the archaeology, the architecture, religious history and significance of the place. I later accepted that they were simply behaving in a way that the architecture allowed but very probably not for which it was intended. But I was interested to notice that my own sense of the importance for the place did not seem to be appreciated by them.

A few weeks later, I spent a day at Konya on the central Anatolian plateau, where I wandered around the mosque at Mevlana, a place of Moslem pilgrimage. I looked at early copies of the Koran and the beautiful decoration of the interior, treating it more like a museum than a sacred site. As I approached the tomb of the Mevlana I noticed two young women standing just in front of it; the emotion in their facial expressions, the tears running down their cheeks and their postures challenged me to re-examine how they could have felt so much emotion when I was feeling so little.

In both situations I found that my own reaction to the place had been different to that of others. This is hardly surprising, and bears out Lang's assertion that although the architecture of a place may facilitate a particular experience there, it may 'afford' other behaviours and experiences as well (Lang 1987:103), to a large extent it is the motivation and background of the person that determines the experience. Importantly also, the behaviour and reactions of people in such a place may contribute to the experience of others there, but will not always have a discernible impact on them.

Evidence why pilgrims visited St Thecla's is not conclusive. According to Egeria, a pilgrim who was on her way back to western Europe from the Holy Land, she visited the site because it was not far out of her way (Egeria 22.2, Wilkinson 1971:121). The sources identify another motivation for visiting the site, Miracle 39 describes those 'without particular piety' who came to the site to relax because it was a calm place (Miracle 39) (Dagron 1978:77). This special quality was appreciated by more than just pilgrims and gives a clear impression that the site was viewed by its visitors to be different from the profane, that it was sacred.

The motivation and preparation to a large extent came from the pilgrim; but the architecture and environment of the site could work with that motivation to carry it along in the same way as a film uses a sequence of devices to afford reactions. A sizeable proportion of a film's audience might be crying as other individuals in the same cinema find a scene over sentimentalised and rather 'nauseous'. Different people will exhibit varying behaviour in responses to the same film, but through leading a whole audience through a sequence of devices similar reactions can be provoked in a significant proportion of viewers. Through examining the archaeology of pilgrimage centres it

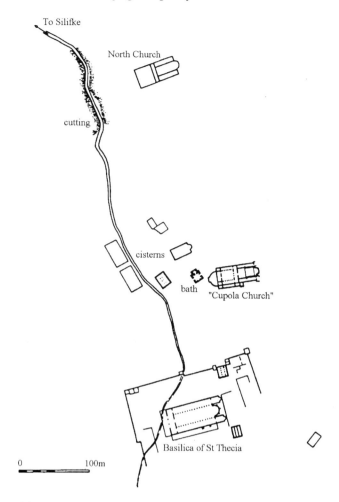

Figure 6 Plan of Meryemlik (Courtesy of Dr. Stephen Hill (1996)).

has been identified that movement is facilitated along simple, or monumentalised paths in the form of colonnades or vaulted passageways, via a sequence of 'stations'.

The sensory properties of the architecture however, afford different subconscious perceptions. In particular, noise and light affect our subconscious subjective perceptions of the quality of any behavioural setting (Lang 1987:130–1). Such changes in perception would be afforded by moving from a long vaulted passageway into a domed space as at Gemile Ada – the change in architecture would represent a change in acoustic properties so that the behaviour of sound would have changed; the behaviour of light would also have changed. The recreation of the sensory impact of these architectural features is difficult for us as archaeologists. We will need to predict the nature of the architecture itself with certainty in order to begin to approach problems of sounds and lighting and we need to understand these and the motivations of the pilgrims to understand the experience.

The expansion and development of sites is represented by an increase in the number of opportunities for stationary liturgy and the monumentalisation of the paths linking those points of activity. Features that would have offered additional opportunities to take part in ritual would have reinforced the potential of the site to create feelings of anticipation and suspense. The colonnaded walkway was the last part of Alahan to be built, the path was being used already and the building of the colonnade simply reinforced it. The shrine of St. Thecla was there when Egeria visited Meryemlik; by the time the Miracles were written the sacred garden with the birds existed. There was an organic development at these places that reinforced the sequential experience.

The opportunities for participation offered at particular points, involved potentially emotional activities. Baptism, signifying death and rebirth to eternal life would only be undertaken once. The baptistery in the early Church was seen as a womb for that rebirth (Underwood 1950:50). Clearly to be baptised or watch a baptismal ceremony was potentially a very emotional activity. These sites also offered the opportunity to pray at particular places; prayer may be defined as, 'the expression of one's desires to, or communication with a god or some spiritual power' (Macdonald 1981:1054); but a place of prayer alone cannot demand prayer. Motivation for prayer, especially sincere prayer, must come from the one who prays. Clearly the depth of prayerfulness depends upon the mental attitude of the one who prays. Preparation of this mental attitude is thus critical, and it is in this preparation that the environment may contribute.

Icons were the visual counterpart to hymns and sermons. We can understand something of the way that the people related to the icons in the medieval period from the testimonies of those who defended them during the period of their destruction known as iconoclasm. These relics were seen by John of Damascus (ca. 675–753/4) as 'Receptacles of divine energy' (Hahn 1990:91). Matthews cites the poet Agathias from whom we learn the importance of reciprocal eye contact between the image and the worshipper as a means for transmitting prayers (Matthews 1997, 26).

Icons were seen by some as appearing to be living beings, speaking to those who looked at them. This demonstrates something of the mindset of these people–they were prepared for spiritual experience. In today's Western World the majority of people, though not all (Middlemiss 1996) seem less able to expect a spiritual experience. Ancient sources and anthropology seem to suggest that people in the Medieval World were much more open to the concept of a spirit world, saints, omens and demons (Whittow 1996:134–5). The medieval pilgrim saw the icons through different eyes; when we study icons we do not have this medieval background. The pilgrim saw icons in their original context, not photographed for study in a book or lit by electric light in the church. Flickering candles lit the icon, so that every aspect of every single tessera of the mosaic reflected the light slightly differently. The icons might have seemed to be moving, many pilgrims willed these images to be alive. Egeria writes that the Church of the Anastasis was ablaze with lamps and filled with smells from the censors (Egeria 24.10; Wilkinson 1971:125). The icons were in a sensual environment and visited by people full of expectation, they demanded and received a sensual response.

The final goal of the pilgrim at each site was to reach its focus, where the experience was most strong. This focus was often a sacred relic or tomb. Holy objects such as this took on great significance in the Early Christian period. They could be used to invoke a spiritual presence, for protection, healing and salvation (Ousterhout 1990:115). People explained how, in their devotion, they sought sensual experiences with these relics through loving and kissing the icons. Relics were a link to the supernatural; after the sequential preparation at the site, pilgrims were ready to receive the relics' power.

The experience need not have ended at the relic since the scent contained in pilgrim bottles would have helped the pilgrims to relive their experience of the sacred site, even though they may be hundreds of miles away, by stimulating their memories through smell (van Driel-Murray pers. comm.)

Conclusions

Ousterhout and Mango have highlighted the problem of trying to understand liturgy from church types (Mango 1974:9–10; Ousterhout 1990:108). It would be highly speculative to place too much interpretation on the fact that domed basilicas occur at a number of pilgrimage sites in southern Turkey (Myra, Germia, Alahan, Meryemlik) but it may be useful to explore briefly the acoustic effect of the change from basilical design to domed basilical design. Hill (1996) has discussed the appearance of the domed and transept basilicas in Cilicia and Isauria and has suggested that these provincial buildings, found at Alahan and Meryemlik, predated those at Constantinople such as Hagia Sophia (Hill 1996:60–61).

As a final point, I wish to stress that the acoustic properties of the new structures would have been different from the earlier basilical ones. The dome is acknowledged to be a particularly difficult architectural component to work with acoustically because it has a very distinct sound reverberation and echo characteristics (Mikeska & Lane 1959:862); however, we know that acoustic qualities were understood by ancient architects (Vitruvius 5:108). The use of the dome in church architecture in the East came to be very common in subsequent years, thus we may consider the adoption of the domed basilica to have been a successful innovation. Whether the change in acoustic and light properties of these new buildings was a consequence or a motivation for the change, is largely irrelevant to the point that for the visitor inside one of these newly designed churches, not only would the building look different, but also sound different to a basilical church. It is clear that something very unique was taking place at those sites where a change was first implemented from the basilica to the domed basilica.

Thus, it is tempting to believe that the successful adoption of the dome for important structures, at southern Anatolian pilgrimage centres, before its subsequent use in churches elsewhere, may have been due partly to the sensory properties of this new type of built space. Such properties may have afforded an environment suitable for a significant sensory experience for the visitors, particularly since these structures are found at sites where the sequential experience would have been so important [1]. The particularly well preserved example from Alahan would provide the ideal material to model one of these buildings and to explore the way in which sound and lighting behaved.

Pilgrimage centres were places of religious devotion and emotion. The social and religious background of the pilgrim played a vital part in the pilgrimage experience, but also critical were the pilgrimage centres and their role as sacred places. They had to confirm the pilgrims' expectations. They did this by providing the opportunity for the pilgrim to join in through a gradual succession of potential experiences, afforded by the sequential layout of the pilgrimage centres. Through the opportunity to take part in potentially emotive ritual, actively or passively at specific places and to move between these points via sacred paths whilst surrounded by a sensual environment full of music and smells, symbolism and mystery, the pilgrims' expectation and anticipation grew until the final encounter with a sacred object was one which might well provoke great emotion. This was a very unique environment and one which is not easily experienced through forms of representation used in archaeological publication to date.

Department of Archaeology, University of Newcastle upon Tyne

Endnote
[1] The building of a twentieth century domed church for its shape without contemplating the effect the structure would have on the behaviour of sound produced by the required liturgical activity, necessitated the provision of buffers and absorbent wall coatings in order to achieve more satisfactory acoustics (Mikeska & Lane 1959).

Bibliography
Bayliss, R.A. 1997a. The Alacami in Kadirli: transformations of a sacred monument. *Anatolian Studies*, 47:57–87.
Bayliss, R.A. 1997b. Alacami Kadirli. *Anatolian Archaeology* 3:14 & backcover.
Bayliss, R.A. 1998. *The Alacami; excavation, survey and three-dimensional reconstruction of a late Roman basilica in Cilicia (Southern Turkey).* http://museums.ncl.ac.uk/alacami/alacami.htm.
Coleman, S. & Elsner, J. 1994. The pilgrim's progress: art, architecture and movement at Sinai. *World Archaeology*, 26(1):73–90.
Dagron, G. 1978. *Vie et Miracles de Sainte Thècle texte grec, traduction et commentaire.* Bruxelles: Société des Bollandistes.
Deichmann, F.W. 1958. *Ravenna Hauptstadt des Spätantiken Abendlandes Band 3 Frühchristliche Bauten und Mosaiken von Ravenna.* Wiesbaden: Franz Steiner Verlag GMBH.
Eade, J. & Sallnow, M.J. 1991. *Contesting the sacred: the anthropology of Christian pilgrimage.* London: Routledge.
Ferguson, E. 1990. (ed.) *Encyclopaedia of early Christianity.* London: Garland Publishing.
Finkelstein, I. 1981. Byzantine prayer niches in southern Sinai. *Israel Exploration Journal*, 31:81–91.
Finkelstein, I. 1985. Byzantine monastic remains in southern Sinai. *Dumbarton Oaks Papers*, 39:39–81.
Foss, C. 1994. The Lycian coast. *Dumbarton Oaks Papers*, 48:1–52.
Gillings, M. & Goodrick, G.T. 1996. *Sensuous and reflexive GIS: exploring visualisation and VRML.* http://intarch.ac.uk/journal/issue1/gillings_index.html.
Gough, M. 1962 The Church of the Evangelists at Alahan: a preliminary report. *Anatolian Studies*, 12:173–84.
Gough, M. 1963. Excavations at Alahan monastery. *Anatolian Studies*, 13:105–16.
Gough, M. 1985. Alahan monastery and its setting in the Isaurian countryside. In M. Gough (ed.) *Alahan An early Christian monastery in southern Turkey.* Toronto: Pontifical Institute of Medieval Studies, pp.3–21.
Hahn, C. 1990. Loca Sancta souvenirs: sealing the pilgrim's experience In R. Ousterhout (ed.) *The blessings of pilgrimage.* Illinois: University of Illinois Press, pp.85–97.
Herzfeld, E. & Guyer, S. 1930. *Meriamlik und Korykos.* Monumenta Asiae Minoris Antiqua 2. Manchester: Manchester University Press.
Hill, S. 1996. *The early Byzantine churches of Cilicia and Isauria.* Birmingham Byzantine and Ottoman Monograph 1 Aldershot: Variorum.
Hill, S. 1998. Alahan and Dag Pazari. In R. Matthews (ed.) *Ancient Anatolia: fifty years' work by the British Institute of Archaeology at Ankara.* British Institute of Archaeology at Ankara: Oxford, pp.315–339.
Lang, J. 1987. *Creating architectural theory: the role of the behavioural sciences in environmental design.* New York: Van Nostrand Reinhold.
Lang, J. 1994. *Urban design. the American experience.* New York: Van Nostrand Reinhold.
Leyerle, B. 1996. Landscape as cartography in early Christian pilgrimage narratives. *Journal of the American Academy of Religion*, 64:119–143.
MacCormack, S. 1990. Loca Sancta: the organization of sacred topography in late antiquity. In R. Ousterhout (ed.) *The blessings of pilgrimage.* Illinois: University of Illinois Press, pp.7–41.
Macdonald, A. M. 1981. (ed.) *Chambers twentieth century dictionary.* Edinburgh: Chambers.
Mango, C. 1978 *Byzantine Architecture.* London: Faber and Faber.
Matthews, T.F. 1997. Religious organization and church architecture In H.C. Evans & W.D. Wixom (eds.) 1997. *The glory of Byzantium art and culture of the middle Byzantine era, AD 843–1261.* New York: Metropolitan Museum of Art, pp.20–82.
McKevitt, C. 1991. San Giovanni Rotundo and the Shrine of Padre Pio. In J. Eade & M.J. Sallnow (eds.) *Contesting the sacred: the anthropology of Christian pilgrimage.* London: Routledge, pp.77–95.

McKenzie, P. 1988. *The Christians: their practices and beliefs. An adaptation of Friedrich Heiler's phenomenology of religion.* Nashville: Abingdon Press.

Middlemiss, D. 1996. *Interpreting charismatic experience.* London: SCM Press.

Mikeska, E.E. & Lane, R.N. 1959. Acoustical problems in two round churches. *The Journal of the Acoustical Society of America,* 31(vii) July:857–865.

Ousterhout, R. 1990. Loca Sancta and the architectural response to pilgrimage In R. Ousterhout (ed.) *The blessings of pilgrimage.* Illinois: University of Illinois Press, pp.108–125.

Pringle, D. 1987. The planning of some pilgrimage churches in Crusader Palestine. *World Archaeology,* 18 (3):341–362.

Reilly, P. & Rahtz, S.P.Q. 1992. *Archaeology and the information age: a global perspective.* One World Archaeology 21 London: Routledge.

Smith, J. E. 1992. The experience of the holy and the idea of God. In S.B. Twiss & H.C. Walter (eds.) *Experience of the sacred readings in the phenomenology of religion.* London: Brown University Press, pp.238–247.

Stopford, J. 1994. The archaeology of Christian pilgrimage *World. Archaeology,* 26(1) June:57–72.

Tsuji, S. (ed.) 1995. *The survey of early Byzantine sites in Ölüdeniz Area (Lycia, Turkey).* Japan: Osaka University.

Underwood, P. A. 1950. The fountain of life in manuscripts of the Gospels. *Dumbarton Oaks Papers,* 5:43–138.

Whittow, M. 1996. *The making of Orthodox Byzantium, 600–1025.* London: Macmillan.

Wilkinson, J. 1971. *Egeria's travels.* London: SPCK.

Christianity and the End of Roman Britain

by David Petts

Although an early fifth century date is accepted by most as the end of Roman political control of the diocese of Britannia, it is clear that there were continued links into the early medieval period, particularly in the West of the country. The study of Western or Celtic Britain is dominated by the study of early Christianity and its archaeology, yet in the Roman period it is often suggested that Britain was barely Christianised. In this paper I want to suggest some reasons why this contrast should exist, and explore the relationship between *Romanitas* and Christianity in Late Antiquity.

The end of Roman Britain has been a subject of much debate in recent years, though there is very little agreement to be found. Arguments for long-term continuity (Dark 1994a) compete with those for an end that was 'nasty, brutish and short' (Esmonde Cleary 1989:161). It seems that the end of Roman Britain can be as complicated or as simple as we want it to be. It is possible to take a minimalist approach, and place the end of Roman Britain in AD 410, with the Honorian Rescript. The exact events of this year are unclear, but it is seems that at this point official Roman political control of the diocese of Britain ceased (Salway 1981:443–4).

This simple model for the end of Roman Britain has the advantage of providing a clean divorce between Britain and the Western Empire, and all that follows are merely sub-Roman successor states. But we know things were not that simple, today we cannot interpret the end of Roman Britain in strictly political terms.

For the last twenty years another approach has been to look at the economic end of Roman Britain. An emphasis has been put on the importance of the cessation of the Roman coin supply, and the taxation cycle which this coinage enabled (e.g. Esmonde Cleary 1989:139; Millett 1992:224–7). Thus the end of Roman Britain has been placed in the mid-fifth century with the catastrophic collapse of the 'Roman Economy', reverberations echoing throughout British society, leaving a collapsed and enervated society which easily fell victim to the minimal number of Germanic immigrants who are now seen to be the orthodox interpretation of the *adventus saxonum*. Thus, in many ways, it could be argued that Britain underwent the same social processes as found in mainland Europe, following Chris Wickham's model of a move from 'taxation modes' to 'tributary modes', but in a period of 20–30 years rather than 200 (Wickham 1984).

However now with the advent of post-processual, structural and symbolic modes of thought in archaeology, we are encouraged to see the end of Roman Britain, as being a symbolic shift. The end of Roman Britain is now the end of a cultural construct: in the words of the historian Ian Woods 'Ultimately the end of Roman Britain is the history of fifth and sixth-century opinion' (Woods 1984:2). This leads to the obvious question: whose opinions?

We are faced with many players on the Late Roman scene, all with valid opinions about the end of Roman Britain. There will inevitably be a disjunction between the opinions of Roman bureaucrats in Cirencester or Trier, Scots and Irish raiders, settling Saxons, Romanized Britons living in Somerset, or Hibernicized Cornish in Dumnonia. Following AD 410, it can quite easily be seen that we could potentially have a series of 'imagined Roman Britains' dying out over a period of two hundred years. There is also the disjunction between what people say and what people mean: when Charlemagne had himself crowned Holy Roman Emperor by Leo III on Christmas Day AD 800 in Saint Peter's Basilica in Rome he undoubtedly made a claim to be the heir of the Roman Empire, but did he really think he was a Roman? It seems highly unlikely that by this time there would be a conscious harking back to a former era of greatness. Any consideration of the end of the Roman world from a symbolic stand point, should aim to outline this slow transition from Roman to Romanesque.

It is clear that even in the minds of the Romans themselves the nature of being Romanized was complex and multi-faceted. Around AD 477 in Sidonius Apollinaris' letter to Arbogast, Count of Trier, a descendant of the Frankish *magister militem* of the AD 390s, this ambiguity can be seen:

> You have drunk deep from the spring of Roman eloquence and dwelling by the Moselle, you speak the true Latin of the Tiber. The splendour of the Roman speech, if it exists anywhere, has survived in you, though it has long been wiped out from the Belgian and Rhenish lands: with you and your eloquence surviving, even though Roman law has perished at our border, the Roman speech does not falter.

Ep IV.17

So can we categorize Arbogast as a Roman? Linguistically, he is a Latin speaker, genetically he's of German origin; as for his own self-perception, we cannot know. So is Arbogast a Roman?: politically? no; linguistically? yes; genetically? no; in his own perception? maybe. This ambiguity can equally be seen in Olympiodorus' description of the wedding of Visigothic federate King Ataulf to Galla Placidia, the sister of the Emperor Honorius at Narbonne.

> There Placidia, dressed in royal raiment, sat in a hall decorated in the Roman manner, and by her side sat Ataulf, wearing a Roman generals cloak and other manner of Roman clothing.

Olympiodorus frg. 24

This description of Ataulf's Roman military garb appears to be very Roman, whereas this combination of military regalia with secular power is fundamentally non-Roman: the Romans tried to keep the upper military ranks clearly distinguished from the upper civic ranks (Barnish 1991:72).

Does the archaeology and history of the late Roman period, become impossible? Can we characterise these changes, and how do we recognise them in the archaeological record? If the Roman Empire only existed in the head, how do we recognise its end in the archaeological record? To start with, it is clear that it is crucial to incorporate historical documents into the picture. This is not to say that the documentary record must be privileged, but in the Roman Empire, and especially with the growth of Christianity, texts become an increasingly important means of social and cultural reproduction (Brown 1971). The use of the textual model for reading material culture is common in archaeology (Hodder 1986:122–4), but amongst archaeologists there often seems to be a reluctance to use the same critical approaches to reading the texts themselves. Whilst early medieval historians seem happy to engage with the theoretical issues associated with text based archaeology such approaches remain untheorized amongst those working in Roman Britain (Dark 1994b:1–5; Driscoll 1984, 1988; Rahtz 1984).

But we still face the problem of how we recognise in the archaeological record, something that cannot be effectively conceptualised on paper. It is clear that it is impossible to reach an 'essentialist' definition of what characterises Roman Britain, and it is equally clear that the concept of *Romanitas* is both contextually specific and dynamic.

We have to make choices, we can either become stuck in a relativistic mess with discussions of what marks the end of Roman Britain, and reach an impasse caused by conflicting definitions, or we must make clear and explicit which definitions we are using and argue with reference to these specific criteria. I suspect that many of the disagreements, which characterise the scholastic discussion of late and sub-Roman Britain, are partly due to this definitional misalignment.

Britain and Rome: AD 400–600

I hope to consider here just one aspect of sub-Roman Britain: what may be termed the 'poetics of power' (Geertz 1980:123). I am not so much interested in the mechanics and practical administrative elements of fifth century Britain, but the metaphors, models and terms of reference mobilised in the political life of the British regions of the Diocese.

First there are some practical issues to consider: namely the date at which Britain become independent from the Roman empire, to which we must turn to the documentary and historical evidence. The Honorian Rescript of AD 410 suggests that at this point the Roman Empire released the Diocese, though it is unclear whether this was intended to be a permanent decision or an act of temporary *realpolitik*. However, from Gildas' *De Excidio* we know of the 'Groans of Britain', a plea to the Roman *magister militem*, for help against the raiding Picts and Scots, written sometime between *c.* AD 428 and AD 454 (*DE* 20). This plea is typical of the type of the petition sent to Roman emperors by cities and *civitates* within the Empire (Barnish 1991:8) and suggests that until the mid-fifth century the British were prepared to accept some level of participation and integration with the Western Roman Empire. Beyond this point we have very little direct insular textual evidence.

The external textual evidence is far from clear. If we jump to the fifth century, it is clear that Byzantium's knowledge of Britain is poor (Cameron 1996:213–6). Although Procopius records Belisarius offering Britain to the Goths, it is clear that this was anything but a serious offer (*Gothic Wars* 2:6:28), Belisarius explicitly says that Britain is very shaky, and he seems to think that there are two islands, one name Brettia, and one named Britannia (*Gothic Wars* 4:20). He also recounts a hazy legend about the souls of the dead being ferried to the islands by locals. The one thing he is clear about, though, is that Roman rule of the island ended with the revolt of Constantine III, and it was henceforth ruled by tyrants (*Vandal Wars* 1:2:38). This contrasts with Byzantium's attitudes to other old parts of the Empire: it is clear from Justinian's reconquests of Africa and Italy that he was interested in reclaiming at least part of the old Western Empire, even though North Africa had been under Vandalic occupation for at least one hundred years (Cameron 1993:104–28). Rather than seeing the British as rebels it is clear that by the end of the fifth century, the Romans were actively courting British military help in Gaul against King Euric of the Goths. The Roman general Arvandus is condemned for treason for persuading Euric to attack the British, north of the Loire, instead of making peace with the 'Greek Emperor' (Sid. *Ep.* 1:7). This is the last external reference to British rather than Saxon leaders for a considerable period, and in a context that suggests an alliance between two independent powers, rather than any form of subordination. Whilst the Frankish King Theudebert writes to Justinian in the mid-sixth century claiming hegemony over the Jutes, probably in Kent, and, later, Angles who appear in Frankish embassies (*Gothic Wars* 5:20), British leaders seem to disappear from the continental scene. Meanwhile the Eastern Empire was busy courting the Franks and their Saxon allies, during the Byzantine reconquest of Italy (Wallace-Hadrill 1985:75–6). It is clear that by the end of the fifth century the British successor kingdoms had become politically isolated from the Continent. The Byzantine Empire made no claim to the Diocese, and were more interested in wooing the Frankish kingdoms in France, who in turn had political links with the Saxons, rather than the British. Britain was not seen as politically part of the Roman Empire, nor indeed within its immediate political ambit. It is clear from the British textual evidence that by the mid-fifth century when St Patrick was probably writing that he too believed that Britain to be politically distinct from the Roman Empire. In his *Letter to Coroticus*, a Scottish warlord, he wrote 'I do not say to my fellow citizens, nor to fellow citizens of the Roman Empire, but to fellow-citizens of the Demons, because of their evil actions' (*Epistola* 2). He distinguishes clearly between the British (his own citizens) and the Romans: though he utilises the language of civic belonging (*cives*) rather than of ethnic belonging (*gens*).

New world views such as those promoted by Christianity would have had a major impact. In the same way that early Roman concepts of empire and imperialism were as significant in the creation of the Empire, as simple economic motives, so the rhetoric of Christianity led to new avenues and approaches in the late Roman discourse of Empire. Christian doctrines of the universality of the church opened up alternative symbolic resources to draw on, beyond that of Empire (Cameron 1991). With the decline of the Imperial cult and the rise of Christianity there was no longer a simple equation between the state religion and state (Fowden 1993:80–100). Indeed Rome was not the first Christian kingdom, that honour goes to either Edessa or Armenia (Fowden 1993:76–9), and by the end of the fourth century there were other Christian kingdoms, outside the bounds of the Empire, such as Axum in Ethiopia (Phillipson 1997:111–8).

Whilst it is difficult to argue that the Eastern empire was 'caesaropapist', with the church being under the absolute control of the Emperor, he had the authority to appoint and dismiss patriarchs, legislate on church affairs and summon ecumenical councils, in a manner without parallel in the West, where both political and religious authority was much more dispersed (Cameron 1993:67–8). With lack of a centralized Roman authority in the West, there was no absolute measure of what it meant to be Roman; the only unifying ideology being Christianity. This is not to say that it was compulsory to be Christian to partake in the legacy of the Empire, as is attested by the use of Roman coin designs on pagan German bracteates (Magnus 1997), but it is clear that once kingdoms began to have designs on wider territorial power Christianity was quickly perceived to be a powerful ideological tool.

The period from AD 400–600 in the West of Europe is the story of the struggle between church and secular power, a struggle to find a new metaphor to describe their relationship. It is only in the late sixth and seventh century, with the rise of the papacy under Gregory the Great and, in Britain, the Synod of Whitby, that a new balance between church and state evolved. These two centuries of turmoil were ultimately the period when the issue of who were the true heirs of the Roman empire was fought out, in battles, books and material culture.

Department of Archaeology, University of Reading

Bibliography

Alkemade, M. 1997. Elite lifestyle and the transformation of the Roman world. In L. Webster & M. Brown (eds.) *The transformation of the Roman world: AD400–900.* London: British Museum Press, pp.180–5

Barnish, P. 1991. *Emperor, prefects and kings: the Roman West AD395–566.* London: Duckworth.

Barrett, J. 1995. *Fragments from antiquity: an archaeology of social life in Britain 2900–1200BC.* Oxford: Blackwell.

Brown, P.J. 1971. *The world of Late Antiquity.* London: Thames & Hudson.

Brown, P.J. 1981. *The cult of the saints.* Chicago: University of Chicago Press.

Brown, P.J. 1988. *The body and society: men, women and sexual renunciation in early Christianity.* London: Faber & Faber.

Cameron, A. 1991. *Christianity and the rhetoric of Empire: the development of Christian discourse.* Berkeley: University of California Press.

Cameron, A. 1993. *The Mediterranean world in Late Antiquity, AD 395–600.* London: Routledge.

Cameron, A. 1996. *Procopius and the sixth century.* London: Routledge.

Collins, R. 1995. *Early Medieval Spain: unity in diversity.* London: MacMillan.

Curchin, L. 1990. *The local magistracies of Roman Spain.* Toronto: University of Toronto Press.

Dark, K.R. 1994a. *Civitas to kingdom: British political continuity, AD 300–800.* Leicester: Leicester University Press.

Dark, K.R. 1994b *Discovery by design: the identification of secular élite settlements in western Britain: AD 400–700* Oxford: BAR British Series 237.

Driscoll, S. 1984. The New Medieval Archaeology: theory versus history. *Scottish Archaeological Review,* 3(2): 104–8.

Driscoll, S. 1988. The relationship between history and archaeology : artefacts, documents and power. In S. Driscoll. & M. Nieke (eds.) 1988. *Power and politics in early medieval Britain and Ireland.* Edinburgh: Edinburgh University Press, pp.162–188.

Dumville, D. 1995. The idea of governance in sub-Roman Britain. In G. Ausenda (ed.) *After Empire: towards an ethnology of Europe's Barbarians.* Woodbridge: Boydell & Brewer, pp.177–216.

Esmonde Cleary, A.S. 1989. *The ending of Roman Britain.* London: Batsford.

Forcey, C. 1998. Whatever happened to the heroes? Ancestral cults and the enigma of Romano-Celtic temples. In C. Forcey, J. Hawthorne, & R. Witcher (eds.) *TRAC97: proceedings of the seventh annual Theoretical Roman Archaeology Conference* Oxford: Oxbow, pp.87–98.

Fowden, G. 1993. *Empire to Commonwealth: consequences of monotheism in late antiquity.* Princeton: Princeton University Press.

Frend, W.H.C. 1982. Romano-British Christianity and the West: comparison and contrast. In S. N. Pearce (ed.) *The early Church in Western Britain and Ireland* Oxford: BAR British Series 102, pp.5–16.

Geertz, C. 1980. *Negara: theatre state in nineteenth century Bali.* Princeton: Princeton University Press.

Gildas. *The ruin of Britain and other documents.* (ed. & trans M. Winterbottom 1978). London: Phillimore.

Hamp, E.L. 1996. Vortiporis Protictoris. *Studia Celtica,* 30: 293

Harhiou, R. 1977. *The fifth century AD treasure from Pietroasa, Romania in the light of recent research.* Oxford: BAR International Series 24.

Hawkes, S.C. & Dunning, G. 1961. Soldiers and settlers in Britain in the fourth and fifth century, with a catalogue of animal ornamented buckles and related belt-fittings. *Medieval Archaeology,* 5: 1–70.

Henig, M. 1995. *The art of Roman Britain.* London: Batsford.

Hodder, I. 1986. *Reading the past.* Cambridge: Cambridge University Press.

Howgego, C. 1995. *Ancient history from coins.* London: Routledge.

Howlett, D. 1995. *The Celtic Latin tradition of Biblical style.* Blackrock: Four Courts.

Howlett, D. 1998. Literate culture in 'Dark Age' Britain. *British Archaeological News,* 33: 10–11.

James, E. 1988. *The Franks.* Oxford: Blackwell.

Janes, D. 1996 The golden clasp of the Roman state. *Early Medieval Europe,* 5(2): 127–153.

Johns. C. 1996. *The jewellery of Roman Britain: Celtic and Classical Traditions.* London: UCL Press.

King, C. 1992. Roman, local and barbarian coinages in fifth century Gaul. In J.F. Drinkwater & H. Elton (eds.) 1992. *Fifth century Gaul: a crisis of identity* Cambridge: University Press, pp.184–195.

Krautheimer, R. 1965. *Early Christian and Byzantine architecture.* Harmondsworth: Penguin.

Lewit, T. 1991. *Agricultural production in the Roman economy AD 200–400.* Oxford: BAR International Series 568.

Magnus, B.1997. The firebed of the serpent: myth and religion in the migration period mirrored through some golden objects. In L. Webster & M. Brown (eds.) 1997 *The transformation of the Roman World: AD 400–900.* London: British Museum Press, pp.194–202.

Mawer, F. 1995. *Evidence for Christianity in Roman Britain.* Oxford: BAR British series 243.

Millett, M. 1992. *The Romanization of Britain: an essay in archaeological interpretation.* Cambridge: Cambridge University Press.

Millett, M. 1995. An early Christian community at Colchester. *Archaeological Journal,* 152: 451–4.

Nash-Williams, V. 1950. *The early Christian monuments of Wales.* Cardiff: University of Wales Press.

Olympiodorus *The Fragmentising Classicising Historians of the Later Roman Empire.* (ed. & trans. R.C. Blockley, 1981–3). Liverpool: Liverpool University Press.

Patrick. *His Writings and Muirchu's Life.* (ed. & trans. A.B. Hood, 1978). London: Phillimore

Phillipson, D.W. 1997. *Ancient Ethiopia.* London: British Museum Press.

Procopius. *History of the Wars (Vols 1-3)* (trans. H.B.Dewing) Harvard: Harvard University Press.

Rahtz, P. 1984. The Nuer Medieval Archaeology – some comments on theory versus history. *Scottish Archaeological Review,* 3(2): 109–112.

Salway, P. 1981. *Roman Britain.* Oxford: Clarendon Press.

Schaffer, P. 1984. Britain's *Iudeces.* In M. Lapidge & D. Dumville (eds.) *Gildas: new approaches.* Woodbridge: Boydell & Brewer, pp.151–157.

Sidonius Apollinaris *Lettres: Tome II-III* (trans. A. Loyer, 1970) Paris: Sociétés d'édition Les Belles Lettres.

Thomas, C. 1981. *Christianity in Roman Britain to AD 500.* London: Batsford.

Thompson, E.A. 1984. *Saint Germanus of Auxerre and the end of Roman Britain.* Woodbridge: Boydell & Brewer.

Van Dam, R. 1985. *Leadership & community in Late Antique Gaul.* Berkeley: Uni. of California Press

Wallace-Hadrill, J.M. 1985. *The Barbarian West 400–1000.* Oxford: Blackwell.

Watts, D. 1991. *Christians and pagans in Roman Britain.* London: Routledge.

Wickham, C. 1984. The other transitions: from the ancient world to feudalism. *Past & Present,* 103: 3–360.

Wood, I. 1984. The end of Roman Britain: the Continental evidence reviewed. In M. Lapidge & D. Dumville (eds.) *Gildas: new approaches.* Woodbridge: Boydell & Brewer, pp. 1-9.

Identities and Cemeteries in Roman and Early Medieval Britain

by Howard M. R. Williams

Introduction

How can we reconstruct the cultural significance of cemeteries from past societies? It is often assumed that cemeteries discovered by archaeologists in some way reflect homogeneous communities that had once lived in the locality. In turn, burial rites directly or indirectly reflect the beliefs, ideologies and social organisation of these communities (e.g. Morris 1992) and it is often stated that burial customs reflect the priorities and strategies of mourners rather than the deceased (e.g. Barrett 1994). For many periods and places in the past, these are reasonable and logical assumptions. However, it is the purpose of this paper to suggest that such a view severely restricts our understanding of the social and cultural significance of funerals and burial places in the complex, plural and heterogeneous societies found in southern and eastern Britain during the first millennium AD. Case studies from social anthropology and sociology will be used to illustrate the ways in which a variety of groups, many not related to the deceased, can become involved in the same funerals and the uses of the same burial space. At one level these studies act as 'cautionary tales', suggesting the danger of trying to understand the archaeological evidence from cemeteries in terms of the ideologies and practices of any single group. Yet, more importantly, they provide us with a new starting point for understanding the social role of burial places in past societies. By becoming foci for engagements and interactions between different groups, cemeteries can become central to the definition, reproduction and transformation of group identities including those based on class, religion and ethnicity. The use of material culture, monumentality, space and place in funerary rituals and subsequent social practices focused on burial sites might all be implicated in processes of group definition and re-evaluation. Such cases of inter-group relations during funerals and at cemeteries are probably more frequent than are often assumed. Indeed it can be argued that cases where cemeteries served homogeneous social and cultural groups without the intervention of others, are likely to be exceptions rather than the rule in many past societies.

This new perspective can be followed through to provide new preliminary interpretations of cemeteries and their context during the late Roman and early medieval periods. It is suggested that inter-group relations focused upon burial sites were fundamental in the construction and reproduction of group identities since death rituals required groups to deal with the discourses and beliefs of other groups and define their distinctive place in the world. The character and frequency of inter-group engagements during funerals and at burial sites contributed towards the emergence of new cultural identities in both the later Roman and early medieval world.

Anthropological and sociological studies of mortuary practices

In the disciplines of sociology, anthropology, history and the use of data from these subjects by archaeologists, there is a long tradition for studies of funerary practices and cemeteries to investigate single ethnic, tribal or religious communities in isolation. Any comparisons are between distinctive cultures and any influences and interactions between groups in the mortuary context are either under-played or left unexamined (Binford 1972; Bloch & Parry 1982; Carr 1995; Huntingdon & Metcalf 1991; Irish et al. 1993; O'Shea 1984; Parkes, et al. 1997; Ucko 1969). However, there are increasing numbers of studies that address the role of funerals and burial sites in terms of inter-group relations rarely considered by archaeologists but with striking implications for archaeological studies, interpretations of funerary rituals and cemeteries.

Chinese rituals and cemeteries in Thailand

Overseas Chinese communities represent a useful starting point for such discussions because recent anthropological work has explicitly discussed the importance of death rituals and burial places in their relations with other cultural groups. Firstly, let us discuss the importance of funerary rites and seasonal ceremonies of the Chinese ethnic minority in Thailand. Funerals are public displays central to the social life of the Chinese minority and highly visible to the Thai majority. Hill (1992) demonstrates the means, by which Chinese funerals incorporate a range of Thai religious practices, even including Thai Buddhist monks into their funerals. What appears syncretistic in fact emphasises the distinctiveness of the Thai and Chinese communities. Funerals are said to symbolise a 'Chinese' identity and links to a Chinese past (Hill 1992: 325, 328). Indeed, it appears that these interactions with the wider society through public funerals serve to sustain the Chinese community's distinctive cultural identity (Hill 1992).

This expression of identity is not only articulated through the burial of the dead, but through rituals that involve appropriating the dead of other groups. Through the *Hsui-kou-kou* festival ('festival to refine the restless ghosts' bones), the Chinese community takes responsibility of Thai 'bad deaths' through a series of elaborate and public rituals. Formoso (1996) argues that many Thai people regard these ceremonies as evidence of the successful acculturation of the Chinese into their social and political life while perceiving the Chinese community as tainted and polluted through their intimate links with bad deaths. On the other hand, Chinese groups also perceive these rituals as potentially polluting and dangerous and see their treatment of Thai bad deaths as a worthy act, a symbol of the socio-economic, moral superiority and distinctive identity (Formoso 1996).

This case study provides a fascinating example of inter-group relations and co-operation through funerals and burial sites by which each group perceives the rituals in different ways. It appears that these public and formalised mortuary interactions help define and reproduce ethnic identities and socio-economic status of Chinese communities within Thai society (ibid. 1996).

Chinese cemeteries in Singapore

An important lesson for archaeologists is the way that burial space can be incorporated into relations between the Chinese communities, other groups and political authorities. The example of Chinese burial grounds in Singapore suggests ways in which multiple discourses, sometimes in conflict, can surround the burial places and mortuary practices of one ethnic group. Cemeteries are the focus for ancestor worship, yet the Chinese communities have had to adapt and negotiate with the authorities of Singapore who hold very different attitudes towards Chinese cemeteries. State discourses focus upon the large amount of valuable space taken up by Chinese graves, public health and hygiene concerns, and an awareness that the kinship-based focus of ancestor worship is dangerous to nationalist ideologies (Yeoh & Hui 1995). Consequently, political tensions surround the use and maintenance of these burial sites, supporting the view that:

> Far from being the product of a monolithic culture, burial space as a social product is often construed in a plurality of ways and invested with diverse if not antithetical meanings by different individuals and social groups

> (Yeoh & Hui 1995:184)

Yeoh & Hui (1995) demonstrate the nature of Chinese discourses, focusing upon *fen shui* and ancestor worship that incorporate funerary rituals and burial space in the negotiation of their power relations and ethnic identities in a plural society (see also Barley 1995:114–5). Therefore, archaeologically identifiable aspects of funerary practices and burial spaces are central to these processes of identity construction and reproduction.

Bali – religious affiliation and village solidarity

Similar themes are applicable to Bali where funerals are often interpreted in terms of élite power and ritual display (e.g. Geertz 1980). However, political and cultural identities can often be played out in terms of conflict and co-operation in almost every stage of mortuary practices, even the manner of mourning a death and the expression of emotion. Linda Connor (1995) discusses differences in mourning patterns between Balinese Hindus and Muslims during the pre-cremation ceremony surrounding the washing of a corpse. The ceremony is an important part of funerary procedures; while Balinese Hindus display a stoic reaction to the ceremony, Muslim relatives attending the same ritual express their sadness and shed tears. Connor suggests that these differences in mourning practices and the expression of grief are observed by mourners and embody wider political and cultural tensions in Bali. These concern religious differences between Islam and Hinduism and the nature of a separate Hindu-Balinese identity in a largely Muslim state. She describes how one ceremony following the death of an elderly male caused consternation among relatives who were married to Muslims: 'The corpse-washing brought into high relief the conflicting allegiances of the deceased's two daughters' (Connor 1995:552), demonstrating that in Bali: '...experiences of death and bereavement may be constituted through multiple and contested discourses in shifting contexts of sociality' (Connor 1995:538).

Funerals and access to burial sites can define village solidarities and relations between élite groups and village communities. Carol Warren's (1993) discussion of disrupted death ceremonies illustrates the ways by which inter-group tensions become manifest during funerary rites. Village identity can be expressed through their burial sites and by excluding individuals and sections of society from burial at these locations; sometimes funerals of unpopular individuals are disrupted and occasionally their coffin broken open and the corpse mutilated. Therefore, the treatment of the body and the location of the grave become heavily contested events in which different groups attempt to assert their rights and identities in relation to others. While the funerals of powerful individuals have been discussed in terms of élite power, competition and elaborate displays and cosmologies (Geertz 1980), there is the potential for their disruption as an expression of popular protests and alternative readings of the events. Once again, funerals and burial places cannot be fully understood in terms of the ideas and practices of one group.

Java – the role of funerary specialists

The above examples illustrate the ways in which participation in rituals, access to, and use of, burial space as well as the treatment of the corpse together with many other aspects of death and burial can be central to the ways that groups interact and define their identities. On Java, Clifford Geertz describes another example of co-operation and inter-dependence over death rituals between cultural groups in a plural society. Geertz describes the dependence of a rural non-Muslim community upon Muslim ritual specialists and secular authorities for the organisation and proper transformation of the deceased and mourners through the rites of passage. This co-operation breaks down at a time of political unrest and Government agents advise Muslim authorities not to participate in non-Muslim rural funerals. Rather than diffusing tensions, this appears to create and enhance inter-group animosity. When a boy died in a non-Muslim village community and there was no one to preside over the funeral and deal with the pollution and danger of the corpse, the scenario threatened the fabric of inter-group relations. Clearly, mutual co-operation and funerals can maintain social stability, inequalities and relations between groups, but when these relations break down the friction caused might increase awareness of group distinctions based upon political affiliation, religious practices and beliefs (Geertz 1973).

In addition to the relatives of the deceased, a variety of funeral specialists including coffin makers, priests, musicians, hired mourners, corpse handlers and gravediggers aid in the organisation of funerals. On many occasions such as the Java example, these specialists come from outside the local community and sometimes they may derive from completely distinctive religious, ethnic or cultural groups. For example, Jonathan Parry's study of the ritual specialists associated with the holy city of Benaras in northern India seems to demonstrate the role of ritual specialists in controlling and interpreting funerary rites (Parry 1994:75–148, see also Watson 1982:157). Funerary specialists can be an important medium for co-operation between groups, the negotiation of group identities. There is the potential for such interactions to go one step further, leading to the dependence of groups upon funerary specialists and eventually their acceptance of these specialists' attitudes and practices towards death and burial. Group interactions surrounding death can define and emphasise differences, but on other occasions they might lead to the active transformation of group identities and relations between groups.

Ethnicity, class and cemetery space: Britain, Ireland & America

Let us now focus more on the ways that burial space can incorporate multiple discourses or the use of numerous groups. Local authority centuries in Britain and Northern Ireland during the last two cemeteries provide a further example of group interaction and conflicting values surrounding funerals and burial sites. The very origin of these cemeteries can be traced to a variety of motivations and ideologies; from middle class concerns over public health to dissenting Christian denominations wishing to be buried in consecrated ground outside the control of the Anglican church (Rugg 1997). Once in use, the spatial organisation of the cemetery and monumentality of graves emphasised the ideologies and class divisions of the rapidly transforming and industrialising society. In particular, the ordering of graves, the patterns of movement through the cemetery and the symbolism of elaborate funerary monuments created a distinctive environment for different groups to experience élite discourses on death and dying. Concerning the Undercliffe cemetery at Bradford it has been stated that:

> In the urban cemetery of the new industrial town, even more precisely than in the new industrial town itself, the class state which was developing could be neatly demonstrated by the lines on a map or plan

> (Rawnsley & Reynolds 1977:220)

In addition to class divisions, spatial distinctions and grave monuments in nineteenth and twentieth century cemeteries can embody distinctions in cultural and religious identities, as discussed by Lindsay Prior for Belfast cemeteries.

> ...the cemetery inscribes in spatial terms the social cleavages which afflict the living and the distinctions which order the latter are very often evident in the intimate details of the gravestone inscriptions.

> (Prior 1989:117)

Similar practices seem to take place in some American cemeteries. In a review of the evidence, Davies (1997) illustrates the close relationships between public funeral rites, patterns of remembrances and the reproduction of ethnic identities in the United States. A variety of ethnic groups from Italians to Ukrainians and Gypsies maintained separate cemeteries or burial plots, acting as anchors for their distinctive identities and cultural origins. Conversely, he observes the ideological functions of large communal cemeteries in linking members of a culturally diverse population into a symbolic unity in death (Davies 1997:98). In a variety of ways, funerals and cemeteries clearly hold an active part in the reproduction and transformation of ethnic identities. We should not underestimate the overtly political nature of many funerals for ethnic groups in a plural society, establishing links with a homeland, symbolising group unity, articulating political demands and evoking injustices done to them by others. For example, this is evident in the funerals of Chilean exiles in parts of Europe (Eastwood 1989) and the funerals of Black communities in America before and after emancipation from slavery (Perry 1993).

As a last case study, Judith Okely's work on the Traveller Gypsies provides an important example of the mechanisms by which death rituals and cemeteries reproduce ethnic group distinctions. British Gypsies use local authority cemeteries and churchyards for burial. In doing so they associate their dead with non-Gypsies. In a situation with close parallels with the Chinese communities of Thailand, by giving up their dead to local authorities and the Church, Gypsies associate death pollution and the ghosts of the dead with the wider British population. Okely argues that death is regarded as analogous to assimilation into the rest of British society and that the dead are associated with similar qualities to non-Gypsy people: sedentary in their graves and dangerous to Gypsies (Okely 1983:220, 228). Therefore, the apparent assimilation of Gypsy groups into the rest of society upon death masks a central way by which Gypsies mark and reproduce a cultural distinctiveness. The separation of the living and the dead acting as a metaphor for ethnic divisions even though Gypsies and non-Gypsies are not divided in death (Okely 1983:217–30). This example is not alone among cases where a group or tribe may take on the practices of other groups at funerals and the treatment of the dead that appears to help maintain rather than diffuse distinctions between groups (Barley 1995; Parker Pearson 1982).

Summary – inter-group relations in death rituals
We cannot expect these examples to encapsulate all of the possible ways that groups interact during funerals, although they incorporate some common themes that are very important for our understanding of archaeological data.

* Funerals and burial sites in 'complex' and 'plural' societies can involve a variety of different groups who bring with them their own ideologies, expectations and practices.
* Even if a single group exclusively uses a burial site, other groups may become involved in funerary rites in a variety of roles from ritual specialists to merely onlookers. Even when other groups are absent or deliberately excluded their ideologies can still permeate and influence funerals and the use of burial space.
* Therefore, funerals and cemeteries can become the focus of multiple and conflicting attitudes and beliefs surrounding death and burial.
* Inter-group relations during rituals and the use of burial sites can perpetuate and emphasise the differences between groups. Alternatively, interactions during funerals and at burial sites, can lead to the transformation of existing identities and social arrangements into novel collective identities involving disparate cultural groups through the shared experiences of ritual practices and relations with ancestors.
* These interactions are likely to take place between groups of unequal standing, wealth and authority, facilitating the control of rituals and funerals by one group over numerous peoples with different religious or ethnic affiliations.
* Only some of the complex inter-group mortuary relations will be archaeologically visible and many may be obscured or hidden by the very nature of the inter-relations. Despite this the treatment of the corpse, use of cemetery space, material culture and monuments, in other words all those aspects that are archaeologically visible, can hold central importance in relations between groups and the expression and negotiation of their identities.

Some implications for the interpretation of late Roman cemeteries
We can now attempt to demonstrate the significance of these themes in addressing the archaeological evidence for late Roman and sub-Roman cemeteries in southern and eastern Britain between the third and sixth centuries AD. For the late Roman period, the anthropology and sociology generate a background from which to explore relations between groups of different ethnic, religious, social and political backgrounds attending funerals and using burial sites. In particular, they suggest a re-consideration of the socio-political significance of the standardization, relative homogeneity and 'managed' character of late Roman extra-mural cemeteries (Esmonde Cleary 1992; Philpott 1991:226; Thomas 1981).

Firstly let us consider the significance of cemeteries and the population they served. Cemeteries were an important part of the topography of the late Roman town and its hinterland. Burial places would have been the final destination for funerary processions but also contexts for graveside rituals. A wide variety of social activities could have taken place at cemeteries in addition to burial rites and they may leave archaeological traces (e.g. Flower 1996:98; Toynbee 1971:49–54; Watts 1991; Whytehead 1986:65–7). The ordering of graves into rows and lines with individual plots, often respected, would have encouraged the use of graves and cemeteries as a whole as important and enduring places for relatives to visit and contact the dead. Furthermore, under the influence of Christian ideas and practices, certain cemeteries became foci for public worship at chapels, baptisteries and churches. In Britain there is some tentative evidence for such practices including the possible cemetery church from Butt Road, Colchester (Crummy *et al.* 1993:187, 189) and the chapel and baptistery at Icklingham, Suffolk (Biddle & Kjolbye-Biddle 1996; Harries 1992:56, 59; Thomas 1981:170; Watts 1991:63; West 1976). Cemeteries were not only used for burial of the dead and ancestor rites but also could have incorporated religious worship, public and civic rituals during the fourth and fifth century AD. Placed alongside major roads leading out of towns, cemeteries would be constantly encountered by local people and travellers during daily life as well as ritual occasions. Therefore rituals and processions en route to the cemetery or taking place at cemeteries would have been highly visible, public affairs within clear sight of all manner of groups and individuals living in the environs.

Against this background we must consider the highly stratified nature of late Roman society as well as the cultural and religious diversity of the population of lowland Britain. At the late Roman cemetery of Poundbury outside Dorchester in Dorset, there seems to be evidence that the cemetery served a population drawn from Dorchester's rural hinterland as well as the town itself. Once again this appears to emphasise the substantial region that extra-mural cemeteries served, and the variety of groups drawn to these sites. At Lankhills and Poundbury there are subtle hints from grave goods, ritual practices and lead isotope evidence of groups from other parts of the Empire being buried in the cemetery and/or influencing burial rites (Clark 1979:383–5; Molleson 1992:46). The burial populations of extra-mural cemeteries are likely to have been drawn from a multitude of religious groups with discrete or varying beliefs but with similar practices surrounding death. Not only did this include distinctions between 'élite' and 'popular' religious traditions and the myriad of pagan cults that existed in Roman Britain, but also possible divisions amongst Christian groups known to have existed in the late Roman West. Of course, late Roman Britain was a highly stratified society and burial space around towns is likely to have incorporated plots and cemeteries for groups of different status. Occasionally the status of families or households demarcated by the use of mausolea, stone and lead coffins (Clark 1979:190–1; Farwell & Molleson 1993:237; Philpott 1991:53). Certain plots would have been owned by families as suggested at Poundbury and Butt Road, Colchester (Crummy *et al.* 1993:158; Molleson 1992:44) or burial clubs for poorer people as suggested by the excavator for Trentholme Drive (Wenham 1968:46).

Clearly, extra-mural cemeteries served a multitude of social, cultural and religious groups even when they did not employ distinctive burial rites that archaeologist's can confidently identify. This leads us to the question; why cannot we clearly see this diversity in the funerary record? Perhaps we should not expect to identify all these groups clearly and unambiguously in the archaeological record since burial rites are influenced by élite groups, civic authorities and funerary specialists as well as the wishes of the deceased and his/her immediate kin and friends (Naumann-Steckner 1997:146–7; Toynbee 1971). The relative regularity and uniformity of funerary rites may also be related to their public nature. With so many different groups involved in funerals or acting as audience for the rituals, the practices and symbolism of burial rites might have had to be regularised and simplistic in order to achieve meaning and significance to as many groups as possible. The symbolism of the rites may have been directed by those authorities able to influence the public presentation of the funeral and the manner of burial.

Consequently the extra-mural zone of cemeteries around Roman towns in the fourth and early fifth centuries represented important arenas for social interaction. Engagements between groups and individuals at funerals and burial sites and the roles performed by representatives of groups held important implications for the way different groups perceived others and legitimated, naturalised and objectified their identities. Access to cemeteries, and the organisation of burial rites may have been carefully restricted by those controlling cemetery space through kinship structures, burial clubs, social, religious or cultural identities or networks of patronage (Patterson 1992). Control and uses of cemeteries may have helped legitimate élite ideologies and culture onto the wider population in death. For example, in areas where Christianity pervaded élite culture, managed cemeteries may have embodied an idealised vision of the dead in terms of spiritual kinship (Harries 1992:60). These processes might lead to burial sites incorporating a range of different groups and encouraging a 'collective' and 'idealised' community of the dead that provided a contrastive commentary upon the pluralistic and stratified society of the living. Extra-mural cemeteries reflect a new emphasis upon the organisation and orchestration of funerals by authorities and funerary specialists and consequently promoting their ideologies and political strategies. For burial sites such as Queenford Farm, Dorchester-upon-Thames, their 'managed' nature reflects the 'administrative machinery' of towns, the strategies of élites and ritual specialists rather than the religious beliefs of the buried population (Chambers 1987:66; Thomas 1981:232).

While the degree of control over late Roman burial sites may have suppressed and rendered invisible the distinctive beliefs and practices of many groups, we should not overstate the influence of authorities over death rituals. Burial sites are difficult to control and may have become foci for conflicting discourses surrounding death and burial. For example, in Rome during the fourth century, martyr's tombs became the focus for meetings by heretic groups in addition to their place in the 'orthodox' cult of saints sanctioned by the Church (Maider 1995). In late Roman Britain where Christianity had a much weaker hold, we might expect tensions and conflict between groups to be embodied in burial space and funerary ritual. One practice that may represent some of these tensions is decapitation: possibly a response to the perceived danger and pollution of the dead (Harman *et al.* 1981; Philpott 1991). Such practices are found in both rural and urban contexts and perhaps they flourished in areas and times, when civic authorities and priests could not preside over funerals and burial rites. This appears supported by sites such as Ashton where decapitation took place among the backyard burials and was absent from the formal, organised cemetery (Watts 1991:64). Poundbury cemetery 1 stands in contrast to the cemeteries 2 and 3 but also with other cemeteries around Dorchester such as Allington Avenue. Where cemetery 1 appears more formalised with a large number of 'Christian' burial traits, the others sites display more 'pagan' practices including decapitation rites (Farwell & Molleson 1993:236–9). Other examples of pronounced distinctions in funerary rites between adjacent cemeteries include burial plots at Shepton Mallet, Somerset (Leach 1990). Watts has argued, this may represent distinctions between the burial sites of pagan and Christian communities (Watts 1991:64–5), yet this could represent the varying degrees of control and organisation over burial space by ritual specialists and élite authorities. At some sites there was more flexibility for alternative social statements and religious practices expressed by mourners at the graveside.

The socio-political significance of extra-mural cemeteries in late Roman Britain did not lie solely in their identification as 'pagan' or 'Christian' (pace Watts 1991). Some fourth century cemeteries might be regarded as Christian and others as pagan, yet the evidence suggests that many incorporated a range of different religious and social groups living and dying in close proximity. This approach is in sharp contrast to those that try to objectively identify religious and ethnic affiliation from the burial evidence without considering the social and landscape context of cemeteries around Romano-British towns. Such approaches are not naïve because they assume that ethnicity and religion are important in death rituals, but because they fail to address the ways in which the interaction of diverse groups might affect the organisation of funerals and burial places. If we can assume that groups existed in hermetically sealed units both in life and in death, without interaction or dependence on others, we might expect their religious, social and ethnic identities to be clearly expressed in the archaeological record of cemeteries. Otherwise, we must accept that the archaeological manifestations of death and burial embody a complex network of exchanges and influences of different ideas and practices from frequent inter-group relations. Perhaps we might consider the significance of cemeteries to reside in the very diversity of groups drawn together in public funerals and the numerous discourses that these groups brought to such gatherings. It may have been the ability of cemeteries to incorporate this diversity of ideologies and practices into a relatively uniform and controlled framework of burial practice that is at the basis of their importance for understanding later Roman death, society and the reproduction of identities at numerous levels. From this perspective it is possible for us to appreciate the value of the anthropological and sociological case studies presented above; since they re-configure our basic assumptions and premises concerning the archaeology of cemeteries in Roman Britain.

Some implications for cemeteries of the fifth and sixth centuries AD

In many ways, 'Anglo-Saxon' communal cemeteries of the late fifth and sixth centuries AD appear to be very different from those found in the same regions in the fourth century AD. Despite attempts to identify continuities with late Roman graves, artefact styles and burial practices show an overwhelming debt to Continental Germanic rites. Both inhumation and cremation rites are practised; inhumation graves being accompanied by jewellery and weapons, cremated remains usually placed in ceramic containers (Welch 1992). Cemeteries vary greatly in size but larger inhumation cemeteries such as Dover Buckland (Evison 1987) and mixed rite cemeteries such as Abingdon Saxon Road (Leeds & Harden 1936) can contain several hundred graves, while cremation cemeteries such as Spong Hill in Norfolk contained several thousand burials (McKinley 1994). Many burial sites were placed in prominent locations, reusing prehistoric and Roman monuments and close to contemporary settlements. In some cases they were probably serving numerous households and communities spread over a substantial territory (see McKinley 1994:66–71). Many authors have suggested that 'Anglo-Saxon' cemeteries may have incorporated both native groups and the descendants of immigrants from northern Germany and southern Scandinavia (e.g. Härke 1990).

Therefore, some of the broad theoretical themes concerning inter-group relations at funerals and burial sites derived from anthropology and sociology may have significance for our understanding of these sites as well. It seems reasonable to assume that immigrant Germanic and native British groups would have come into direct and frequent contact throughout this period in many regions of southern and eastern England. As times and places for communal gatherings of substantial numbers of people, mortuary practices and burial sites might have been one of the contexts in which groups of different origin, custom and language came into frequent contact (Williams 1998). Consequently, we can consider 'Anglo-Saxon' cemeteries in the light of relations between heterogeneous immigrant and indigenous social groupings rather than solely in terms of the traditional debates concerning population replacement or insular culture change (see Arnold 1997:19–32; Higham 1992:168–88; Welch 1992:97–107). By analogy with some of the anthropological and sociological case studies presented above, it might be possible to argue that such structured interactions in the funerary context may have provided a catalyst for the construction and transformation of group identities and social relations between groups. Germanic groups that held sway over funerary space and the rituals conducted there could have made a disproportionate contribution to the organisation of mortuary practices. In turn, such control could have actively influenced social arrangements, attitudes towards the dead and concepts of ancestry and identity.

It seems surprising that traditional Anglo-Saxon scholarship has discussed only some of the possible interactions between 'British' and immigrant 'Germanic' groups through mortuary practices and cemeteries. These might have included:

- The burial of Germanic individuals and their kin in communal cemeteries as an expression of their distinctive cultural identity and to symbolise boundaries with native groups.
- The burial of native individuals and groups living alongside or integral to Germanic households and communities in 'Anglo-Saxon' cemeteries. This might include slaves, servants, friends, guests, spiritual kin, marriage partners and their families. These groups would be subsumed into Germanic identities in death and their graves may appear 'Anglo-Saxon'.
- Either through coercion or reciprocal relations, culturally independent native groups in Anglo-Saxon territories may give up their dead to Germanic groups for burial in 'Anglo-Saxon' cemeteries.
- Germanic groups might secure the participation of native individuals and groups in Germanic funerals and burial rites in other capacities:
  a) Observing/attending Germanic mortuary practices and observing/attending other communal gatherings at burial sites.
  b) Providing labour and performing non-specialist roles in funerals.
  c) Giving gifts, contributing animals (e.g. for sacrifice) and materials (i.e. pyre wood, grave goods) at the funeral.
  d) Providing funerary specialist services: priests, other rituals specialists, grave diggers, musicians, mourners etc.
- The emulation of Germanic mortuary practices by native groups following frequent and long-term exposure and influence from immigrant groups.
- The exclusion of native groups from Germanic mortuary practices or rejection of Germanic mortuary practices by native groups. Native groups in these instances may have followed 'sub-Roman' mortuary practices (i.e. west-east burial without grave goods, a visibly different rite from those in Anglo-Saxon cemeteries. For sub-Roman sites, see Petts 1997).

Perhaps 'British' groups initially maintained their cultural identities in some areas because their interactions at funerals emphasised their distinctiveness and separateness from Germanic groups. There continues to be limited archaeological evidence for British survival, and this might reflect the inability of indigenous British groups to control and communicate identities in death rituals rather than the absence of such groups. By participating in Germanic mortuary rituals and burying their dead in 'Anglo-Saxon' cemeteries (perhaps effectively giving up their dead to a different set of traditions and cultural values), funerals and the use of cemeteries may have been a central process in the gradual acculturation of British communities into Germanic social arrangements. Rituals were therefore inculcating British groups with the 'mytho-symbolic' ideals of Germanic communities (see Smith 1986:52–3; Härke 1997, Williams 1998). Inter-group relations during death rituals could have been an important agent for social change and identity negotiation in this period.

Conclusions

We have seen a preliminary attempt to address the potential complexities in social relations behind the cemeteries of the fourth, fifth and sixth centuries AD. These themes are often left undiscussed by archaeologists, yet are central to the kinds of interpretation we wish to make from the archaeological evidence for death and burial in the first millennium AD – burial sites not only concern those being buried and their kin, but funerary specialists, political authorities and a multiplicity of other groups influencing and participating in funerary rituals.

For late Roman cemeteries this allows us to appreciate that the social significance of burial sites may have resided in their *inclusive* nature, drawing together a range of disparate religious and cultural groups for communal rituals and links with ancestors and the supernatural. These practices could have emphasised distinctions between groups, but perhaps also served to bring about a construction of common identities in death beyond the identities of kin groups.

For early Anglo-Saxon cemeteries this perspective helps us to explain the relative invisibility of distinctively indigenous mortuary practices in many parts of southern and eastern England. British communities may have initially retained their identities and culture yet were rendered archaeologically invisible by practising unaccompanied west-east burial rites even in the 'Germanic regions' of southern and eastern England. Others still may be rendered archaeologically invisible by the complexity of their interactions with Germanic groups. Over the long term, mortuary practices could have been one of the ways which British people living within Anglo-Saxon territories were incorporated into Germanic social organisations and ideologies.

It might be considered that these themes are somehow irrelevant for archaeological studies of burial sites given the fact that many of the processes of inter-group interaction and competing discourses might be regarded as archaeologically invisible. Yet, I would argue that it is only by understanding the complexities of group interactions can we begin to adequately appreciate and interpret the formation of the archaeological record of cemeteries; the treatment of the body, the use of material culture and monuments, and the landscape setting of cemeteries. In both the Roman and post-Roman studies, these perspectives force us to reappraise the traditional approaches to cemeteries and mortuary practices and their social significance. From these perspectives, it might be legitimate to regard southern and eastern England during the fourth, fifth and sixth centuries as contested landscapes in which mortuary practices and cemeteries provided important symbolic resources for groups to structure and transform their identities and social relations.

Department of Archaeology, University of Reading

Acknowledgements

Many thanks to Ken Dark, Bruce Eagles, Hella Eckardt, Heinrich Härke, David Petts, John Pearce, Thea Politis, Aaron Watson, Rob Witcher and the anonymous referee for commenting on earlier drafts of this paper. I would also like to thank Philip and Susan Williams for their support and kindness.

Bibliography
Arnold, C. 1997. *An archaeology of the early Anglo-Saxon kingdoms.* London: Routledge.
Barley, N. 1995. *Dancing on the grave – encounters with death.* London: Abacus.
Barrett, J. 1994. *Fragments from antiquity. An archaeology of social life in Britain, 2900–1200BC.* Oxford: Blackwell.
Bloch, M. & Parry, J. 1982. *Death and the regeneration of life.* Cambridge: Cambridge University Press.
Biddle, M. & Kjolbye-Biddle, B. 1996. The quest for St Alban continues. *The Alban Link,* 45:10–22.
Binford, L. 1972. Mortuary practices: their study and their potential. In L. Binford (ed.) *An archaeological perspective.* London: Seminar, pp.208–243.
Carr, C. 1995. Mortuary practices: their social, philosophical-religious, circumstantial and physical determinants. *Journal of Archaeological Method and Theory,* 2 (2): 105–200.
Chambers, R. A. 1987. The late- and sub-Roman cemetery at Queensford Farm, Dorchester-upon-Thames, Oxford. *Oxoniensia,* 52:35–69.
Clarke, G. 1979. *The Roman Cemetery at Lankhills.* Oxford: Clarendon.
Connor, L.H. 1995. The action of the body on society: washing a corpse in Bali. *Journal of the Royal Anthropological Institute,* 1 (3):537–559.
Crummy, N. Crummy, P. & Crossan, C. 1993. *Colchester Archaeological Report 9: excavations of Roman and later cemeteries.* Colchester: Colchester Archaeological Trust.
Davies, D.J. 1997. *Death, ritual and belief – the rhetoric of funerary rites.* London: Cassell.
Eastwood, M. 1989. The politics of death – rituals of protest in a Chilean exile community. In. S. Cederroth, C. Corlin & J. Lindström (eds.) *On the meaning of death: essays on mortuary ritual and eschatological belief.* Uppsala: Uppsala University Press, pp.77–94.
Esmonde Cleary, S. 1992. Town and country in Roman Britain? In. S. Bassett (ed.) *Death in towns.* Leicester: Leicester University Press, pp.28–42.

Evison, V.I. 1987. *Dover: the Buckland Anglo-Saxon cemetery.* London: HBMC Archaeological Report 3.

Farwell, D.E. & Molleson, T.L. 1993. *Excavations at Poundbury 1966–1980. Volume 2: the cemeteries.* Dorchester: Dorset Natural History and Archaeology Society Monograph Series 11.

Flower, H.I. 1996. *Ancestor masks & aristocratic power in Roman culture.* Oxford: Clarendon Press.

Formoso, B. 1996. Hsiu-Kou-Ku: The ritual refining of restless ghosts among the Chinese of Thailand. *Journal of the Royal Anthropological Institute,* 2(2):217–234.

Geertz, C. 1973. *The interpretation of culture.* London: Hutchison.

Geertz, C. 1980. *Negara: the theatre state in nineteenth-century Bali.* Princeton: University Press.

Härke, H. 1990. 'Warrior Graves'? The background of the Anglo-Saxon weapon burial rite. *Past and Present,* 126: 22–43

Härke, H. 1997. Material culture as myth: weapons in Anglo-Saxon graves In. C.K. Jensen & K.H. Nielsen (eds.) *Burial and society: the chronological and social analysis of archaeological burial data.* Aarhus: Aarhus University Press, pp.119–127

Harmen, M., Molleson, T.I. & Price, J.L. 1981. Burials, bodies and beheadings in Romano-British and Anglo-Saxon cemeteries. *Bulletin of the British Museum of Natural History,* 35:145–188.

Harries, J. 1992. Death and the dead in the late Roman West. In. S. Bassett (ed) *Death in towns.* Leicester: Leicester University Press, pp.56–67

Higham, N. 1992. *Rome, Britain and the Anglo-Saxons.* London: Seaby.

Hill, A.M. 1992. Chinese funerals and Chinese ethnicity in Chiang Mai, Thailand. *Ethnology,* 31:315–330.

Huntingdon, R. & Metcalf, D. 1991. *Celebrations of death.* Cambridge: Cambridge University Press.

Irish, P., Lundquist, K.F. & Nelson, V.J. (eds.) 1993. *Ethnic variations in dying, death & grief: diversity in universality.* Washington: Taylor & Francis

Leach, P.J. 1990. The Roman site at Fosse Lane, Shepton Mallet. An interim report of the 1990 archaeological investigations. *Somerset Archaeology and Natural History,* 134: 47–56.

Leeds, E.T. & Harden, D. 1936. *The Anglo-Saxon cemetery at Abingdon, Berkshire.* Oxford: Ashmolean.

Maider, H. 1995. The topography of heresy and dissent in late fourth century Rome. *Historia,* 44: 232–249

McKinley, J. 1994. *Spong Hill Part 8: the cremations.* East Anglian Archaeology 69. Norfolk: Norfolk Museums Service.

Molleson, T. 1992. Mortality patterns in the Romano-British cemetery at Poundbury Camp near Dorchester. In. S. Bassett (ed.) *Death in towns.* Leicester: Leicester University Press, pp.43–55.

Morris, I. 1992. *Death-ritual and social structure in Classical Antiquity.* Cambridge: University Press.

Naumann-Steckner, F. 1997. Death on the Rhine; changing burial customs in Cologne, third to seventh century. In L. Webster & M. Brown (eds.) *The transformation of the Roman world AD 400–900.* London: British Museum Press, pp.143–157.

Okely, J. 1983. *The Traveller Gypsies.* Cambridge: Cambridge University Press.

O'Shea, J. 1984. *Mortuary variability.* New York: Plenum.

Parker Pearson, M. 1982. Mortuary practices, society and ideology: an ethno-archaeological study. In I. Hodder (ed.) *Symbolic and structural archaeology.* Cambridge: University Press, pp.99–113.

Parkes, C.M., Laungani, P. & Young, B. (eds.) 1997. *Death and bereavement across cultures.* London: Routledge.

Parry, J. 1994. *Death in Benaras.* Cambridge: Cambridge University Press.

Patterson, J.R. 1992. Patronage, collegia and burial in Imperial Rome. In. S. Bassett (ed.) *Death in towns.* Leicester: Leicester University Press, pp.15–27.

Perry, H.L. 1993. Mourning and funeral customs of African Americans. In D.P. Irish, K.F. Lundquist & V.J. Nelson (ed.) *Ethnic variations in dying, death and grief: diversity in universality.* Washington: Taylor & Francis: pp. 51–66.

Petts, D. 1997. Burial and gender in late- and sub-Roman Britain In. C. Forcey, J. Hawthorne & R. Witcher (eds.) *TRAC97: proceedings of the seventh annual Theoretical Roman Archaeology Conference Nottingham 1997.* Oxford: Oxbow, pp.112–124.

Philpott, R. 1991. *Burial practices in Roman Britain – a survey of grave treatment and furnishing AD 43–410.* Oxford: BAR British Series 219.

Prior, L. 1989. *The social organisation of death – medical discourse and social practice in Belfast.* London: MacMillan.

Rawnsley, S. & Reynolds, J. 1977. *The Undercliffe Cemetery, Bradford.* History Workshop 4: 215–221.

Rugg, J. 1997. The origins and progress of cemetery establishment in Britain. In. P. Jupp & G. Howarth (eds.) *The changing face of death.* London: MacMillan Press, pp. 105–119.

Smith, A.D. 1986. *The ethnic origins of nations.* Oxford: Blackwell.

Thomas, C. 1981. *Christianity in Roman Britain to AD 500*. London: Batsford.

Toynbee, J.M.C. 1971. *Death and burial in the Roman world*. Baltimore: John Hopkins University Press.

Ucko, P. 1969. Ethnography and the archaeological interpretation of funerary remains, *World Archaeology*, 1: 262–290.

Warren, C. 1993. Disrupted death ceremonies: popular culture and the ethnography of Bali. *Oceania*, 64: 36–56.

Watson, J. 1982. Of flesh and bones: the management of death pollution in Cantonese society. In M. Bloch & J. Parry (eds.) *Death and the regeneration of life*. Cambridge: University Press, pp. 155–186.

Watts, D. 1991. *Christians and pagans in Roman Britain*. London: Routledge.

Welch, M. 1992. *Anglo-Saxon England*. London: Batsford.

Wenham, L. 1968. *The Romano-British Cemetery at Trentholme Drive, York*. London: HMSO.

West, S. 1976. The Roman Site at Icklingham. In. S. West (ed.) *Suffolk: East Anglian Archaeology 3*. Suffolk County Planning Department. pp. 63–126.

Whytehead, R. 1986. The excavation of an area within a Roman cemetery at West Tenter Street, London E1. *London & Middlesex Archaeological Society*, 37: 23–236.

Williams, H.M.R. 1998. Monuments and the past in Anglo-Saxon England. *World Archaeology*, 30(1): 90–108.

Yeoh, B.S.A. & Hui, T.B. 1995. The politics of space: changing discourses on Chinese burial grounds in post-war Singapore. *Journal of Historical Geography*, 21(2): 184–201.

Quoit Brooches and the Roman-Medieval Transition

by Geoff Harrison

Introduction

Research has shown that there are marked material differences in the archaeology of 'Roman Britain' and 'Anglo-Saxon England'. Explanations for the transition between these two periods in the fifth century regularly refer to the movements and interactions of defined ethnic groups, such as 'Angles', 'Saxons' and the 'native' population. The aim of this paper is to highlight why these ideas have become explanations for archaeological change in the fifth century and why such approaches might be due for reconsideration. Additionally, alternative explanations for material culture change, which do not rely on assumptions about material culture and its relationship to ethnic groups and their movements, will be proposed.

These issues will be addressed through a case study using an annular brooch type known as the 'quoit brooch'. These brooches will be examined for two reasons. Firstly, they are usually dated to the mid-fifth century, the time at which, according to interpretations of documentary sources, changes caused by the migration of ethnic groups from the continent to eastern England occurred. Secondly, they have been interpreted as both native 'British' brooches, and also 'Germanic' artefacts occurring in England due to the migration of people(s) from the continent. This conflict of interpretation raises issues related to how archaeologists understand material culture and the Roman-Medieval transition in general.

Quoit brooches and their interpretation

Quoit brooches are decorated annular brooches found as grave goods in cemeteries in southern and eastern England (Figure 1). Functionally, they are assumed to have been for holding together garments at the shoulder (Owen-Crocker 1986:28). The brooch classification used here was devised by Barry Ager (1985), who in turn based his work on that of E.T. Leeds (1945:46–8). The debates refer mainly to annular Types B, C (Figure 2, 3) and D1 (Figure 4) along with the penannular Type A (Figure 5). Types D2–4 are not discussed as Ager (1990:154) claims they have 'no demonstrable connection with the Quoit Brooch Style', nor are Type E brooches which have been labelled 'Broad-banded Annulars' as opposed to quoit brooches (Ager 1985). These types are mainly differentiated by size and the arrangement of the pin-stop (see Ager 1985; 1990 for full discussion of forms). Only one Type A brooch and nineteen Types B-D1 are known (or eighteen and a half, one Type B brooch is fragmentary).

A majority of the known brooches were found in the late nineteenth and early twentieth centuries. In their reports, excavators recorded the brooches using a variety of terms, such as 'circular bronze brooch' (Read 1895:372) or 'bronze annular' (Griffith & Salzman 1914:22). Furthermore, the reports of these initial discoveries made no direct inferences about the ethnic identity of those who were buried with the brooches, other than that they were found in cemeteries broadly referred to as 'Saxon' (Read 1895) or 'Anglo-Saxon' (Griffith & Salzman 1914).

E.T. Leeds (1936) was the first person to discuss the brooches as a defined and significant type, and to apply the term quoit brooch. In *Early Anglo-Saxon Art and Archaeology* he also stated his concern with native survival (Leeds 1936:1). Leeds believed that up to that time, archaeologists had paid too much attention to the role of the Germanic migrants into England, no doubt influenced by the historical account of Gildas; a late fifth or sixth century monk who told of the death, destruction and complete population replacement caused by the Germanic invasions. This had led to minimal consideration by archaeologists of the fate of native Britons after the Germanic influx. With this in mind, Leeds sought to identify indigenous people through the archaeological evidence, and hence achieve a better understanding of how the two groups of people interacted (Leeds 1936:1–2). His concern for the 'native' population may have been influenced by the political climate in late 1930s Europe and what has been called the 'anti-German backlash' within archaeology (Lucy 1998:14).

An important aspect of this research was Leeds' (1945:44) belief that the penannular brooch was a relic of 'the older native culture', one which would demonstrate the presence of indigenous people and population continuity. He believed penannular brooches could be traced back to types known from the pre-Roman Iron Age which continued in use through the Roman period (Leeds 1936:3; 1945:44). Thus, for Leeds, the Type A brooch provided a crucial link in his argument about the relationship between quoit brooches and indigenous populations. Its native origins were confirmed by the penannular form, while its decorative styles and the penannular inner ring of the Type B brooch (Figure 3) linked it to the other annular quoit brooches (Types B-D: Leeds 1945:46). Furthermore, all known Type A-D brooches were found in 'Anglo-Saxon' cemeteries, that is to say, in the same cemeteries as a range of distinctively 'Germanic' artefacts and burial rites. Hence, Leeds believed quoit brooches demonstrated the presence of 'native' people in 'Germanic' cemeteries. They could therefore be used to infer a degree of native survival despite the influx of Germanic people(s) which archaeologists had often previously asserted all but wiped out the indigenous population. Leeds concluded:

> There is every reason to believe that they [quoit brooches] are objects antedating the invasion, and if it is desired to know what the native women were wearing before or at the time of Hengest's landing, this group supplies the information.
>
> (Leeds 1936:7)

Egil Bakka (1958) and Sonia Chadwick Hawkes (1961) refuted this view. They believed the brooches were entirely Germanic (as they had animal motifs (Bakka 1958:13)) and were the predecessors of later metalwork styles. For example, Hawkes called the ornamentation on Type A-C brooches (as well as other artefacts) the 'Jutish Style A'. She concluded that:

> The origins of this [quoit brooch] animal style appear to have been in southern Scandinavia in the fifth century...It is also the earliest expression of Anglo-Saxon zoomorphic ornament and the precursor of mature Style I in England.
>
> (Hawkes 1961:71)

Roman stylistic influences, such as 'fur' on animal bodies (Leeds 1936:4; Hawkes 1961:53–4), were attributed to trade between northern Gaul and southern Scandinavia (Hawkes 1961:61). The brooches were dated to c. AD 450 (Bakka 1958:13), broadly when archaeologists believe the historical sources describe the beginning of Germanic incursions into eastern England. Further contributions to the debate were made by Evison (1965), Haseloff (1974), and Ager (1985; 1990), who refined the existing chronologies and cultural affiliations of the brooches, so as to better understand their place in fifth-century history.

This outline of research on quoit brooches shows that, to a certain extent, concern for the brooches was instigated by Leeds' research interests in 1936. Yet, throughout the subsequent contributions, the central theme has remained the same; did the brooches represent 'native' people surviving in the post-migration context, or did they have continental, 'Germanic' antecedents and thus support the migration hypothesis?

Reassessments

Having identified this as the main theme of the debates involving quoit brooches, it is worth making a more detailed and critical examination of the theory that underlies the discussion. The aim is to make explicit the assumptions and conceptual frameworks that have been used by archaeologists in interpreting both quoit brooches and the Roman-Medieval transition itself.

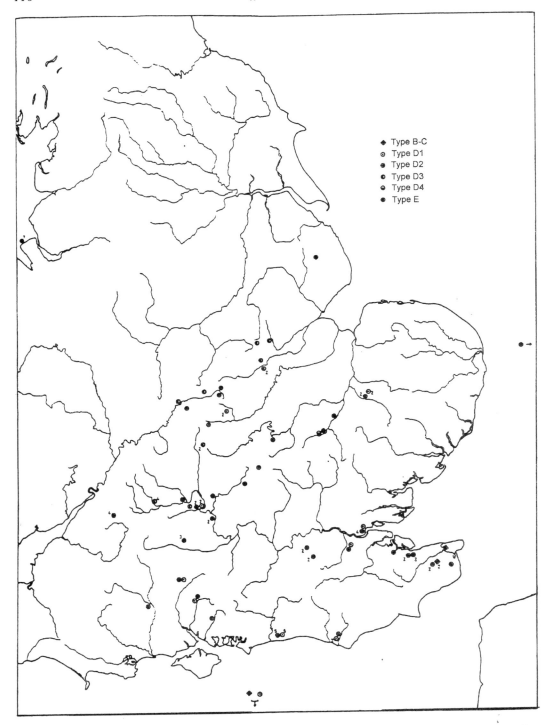

Figure 1. Distribution map of quoit brooches (Types B-D) and Broad-banded Annular brooches (Type E)
(After Ager 1985:33. Reproduced with permission).

Figure 2. Type B quoit brooch (British Museum).   *Figure 3. Type C quoit brooch (British Museum)*

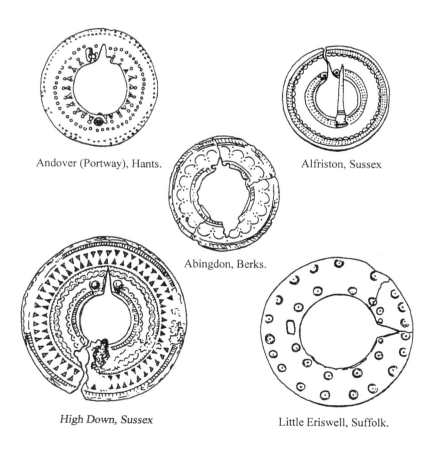

Andover (Portway), Hants.   Alfriston, Sussex

Abingdon, Berks.

High Down, Sussex   Little Eriswell, Suffolk.

Figure 4. Type D1 quoit brooches (After Ager 1985. Reproduced with permission).

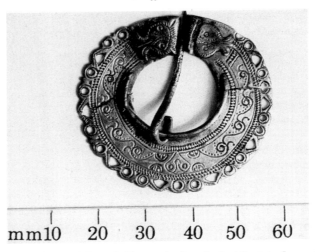

Figure 5. Type A penannular quoit brooch (Sussex Archaeological Society, Lewes Museum).

As noted above, the main emphasis of this debate has been the use of quoit brooches to identify the presence of certain ethnic groups in a particular cemetery, be they 'Germanic' people or 'natives'. Furthermore, because the brooches were linked so closely to these social/ethnic groups it was assumed that in the case of Germanic brooches/motifs, when they are found in a previously non-Germanic area (i.e. south-eastern England) people must also have moved or migrated into that region. Historical sources undoubtedly influenced this model for explaining the distribution of quoit brooches, and their role will be discussed further below.

These assumptions have, of course, not been exclusive to the interpretation of quoit brooches. From the beginnings of 'Anglo-Saxon' archaeology certain types of material culture, such as pottery and brooches, were used to infer the migrations of ethnic groups from north-western Europe and southern Scandinavia to eastern England (e.g. Kemble 1855). The debate has not been static. Initially, complete population replacement by a mass migration/invasion was generally envisaged (e.g. Freeman 1903), whereas now many scholars acknowledge the potential complexity of the transition and prefer the idea of small scale migrations, perhaps by a Germanic elite whose distinctive material culture became widely acculturated (e.g. Härke 1990; Higham 1994). Despite these developments, the idea that ethnic change (be that of a whole population or only the elite) was a fundamental catalyst for the formation of 'Anglo-Saxon England' has remained part of the academic debate. As Jones has stated:

> The question of the scale and significance of the Anglo-Saxon immigrations forms the marrow in the historical bone of contention regarding the nature of the transition between Roman Britain and Anglo-Saxon England.

> (Jones 1996:39)

Quoit brooches have been part of the debate surrounding the transition. However, it should be asked why they have been the subjects of so many detailed studies when there are only twenty such brooches. Their significance may be attributed to the fact that there are relatively few diagnostic types of material dated specifically to the mid-fifth century (e.g. Equal-armed brooches, Cruciform brooches (Böhme 1986) and certain pottery types (Myres 1969)). Thus, they have become significant for understanding changes at a time when the documents might lead us to believe ethnic groups were migrating. Being relatively rare yet significant items, their definition is contentious and becomes polarised between 'native' or 'Germanic' explanations.

It is these polarised interpretations which make quoit brooches a revealing medium through which to re-examine the Roman-Medieval transition. However, this contradictory position is not inherent in the brooches; the objects themselves have not changed. Rather, the debate empha- sises the subjectivity of artefactual categorisation and demonstrates that it must be the assump- tions, interpretations and conceptual frameworks used by scholars that are at issue.

As stated above, an important aspect of the quoit brooch debate has been the assumption that artefacts reflect certain ethnic identities. The aim of the next section is to highlight why archae- ologists have assumed that this relationship exists and to show how this has influenced transition period archaeology.

Material culture and ethnic identities

The perceived correlation between material culture and ethnic identities has been funda- mental to Anglo-Saxon archaeology since its inception in the nineteenth century (e.g. Kemble 1855. For a full discussion of the appearance of this methodology and how it differed from pre- vious discussions of material and identities see Hannaford 1996; Hides 1996). However, re- searchers have noted that the 'culture = people equation' (Shennan 1991:31) also had its origins in the specific academic and socio-political milieu which existed in Europe at this time (e.g. Jones 1997; Shennan 1989).

An important element of this context was the emergence of racial theory as a means of dis- cussing human social groupings, both in academic and popular literature. Ethnicity appears to have long been integral to human social interaction (although the extent to which it may be con- sidered an essential part of human behaviour is a moot point (Bentley 1987), as is the relation- ship between ethnicity and other types of grouping, such as by religion or politics (Hannaford 1996:58)). However, the specifically racial view of ethnicity (whereby ethnicity is a sub-division of race (Hannaford 1996:3)) arose from developments in the natural sciences and the application of Darwin's theories on biological evolution to human societies and the social sciences (Hanna- ford 1996:275; Hides 1996:40). In this way, aspects of human existence, such as language and culture (including material culture), became integral to the biological/blood relations that were said to unite members of what thus became a bounded racial or ethnic group.

Additionally, the study of biological evolution was concerned with the origins and develop- ment of 'Man' [*sic.*] (Hides 1996:37). Thus, in the human/social sciences, the historical devel- opment of cultural and linguistic racial features was also investigated (Hides 1996:37). This historical component in the definition of racial/ethnic groups was particularly important for an- other significant motivating force in nineteenth-century thought - that of nationalism. Indeed, racialism helped define national identities and was itself promoted by the emergence of nation states (Diaz-Andreu & Champion 1996:5–6). It was in this context of national/ethnic histories that identifying the past by archaeological means became a powerful tool. Archaeological evi- dence by its very nature can be interpreted in a number of ways. Also, it may have great antiq- uity and is not restricted to documentary sources (Diaz-Andreu & Champion 1996:19–21). Fur- thermore, with the application of theories linking culture and identity, archaeological evidence provided a means of demonstrating the origins, continuity and movements of 'nations' through time and space. The emerging nations were thus given a sense of timelessness and legitimisation through their antiquity (Austin 1990:15).

Although overt racialism and nationalism is generally no longer present in early medieval ar- chaeology, the quoit brooch debates demonstrate the perpetuation of theories linking material culture directly to ethnic groups. In highlighting the development of thinking on quoit brooches it is clear that they became significant at a certain time and in response to particular questions being asked by archaeologists about the nature of the transition and the relationship between 'native' and 'Germanic' people(s). Furthermore, concepts used to interpret the brooches, in- volving bounded, immutable ethnic groups and archaeological cultures, derive from the specific context of nineteenth-century racial theory and nationalism.

Despite the fact that links between culture and racially-influenced views of social identity were first made in the nineteenth century (Hides 1996:41), the identities ascribed by scholars to the users of quoit brooches were derived from much earlier historical sources, such as Gildas, Bede, Procopius and the Gallic Chronicle of 452. These sources have been interpreted by the same scholars as referring to bounded ethnic groups and thus support the approaches to the transition period used in archaeology from the nineteenth century onwards. Indeed the longevity of the traditional model may be attributed to the seemingly close relationship found between archaeological and historical evidence. For example, the pottery types found in both north-western Germany and East Anglia may be seen to echo Bede's narrative about the movements of the Angles and Saxons (*HE.* 1:15). However, some historians have taken a more critical approach to these documents. They have demonstrated the problems of using the texts as sources of objective historical record, as the authors composed them for specific reasons. It has been said that Gildas wrote a 'sermon' (Yorke 1993:45), while Bede composed a religious history dedicated to King Ceolwulf (Hanning 1966:75; Bede *HE.* preface). Furthermore, the references to ethnic identities need not be taken at face value.

Using continental sources as a starting point, a number of historians have demonstrated that early medieval ethnicity was not an immutable, bounded social categorisation for a specific group of people. Rather, it has been shown that ethnic labels were subjective and fluid (e.g. Geary 1983; Pohl 1991; 1997). They were assigned to, or used by groups and individuals on the basis of, for example, origins, customs, laws and language (Geary 1983:19). Ethnicity has also been called a 'situational construct' (Geary 1983:16), drawing attention to the fact that it is:

> a subjective process by which individuals and groups identified themselves or others within specific situations and for specific reasons.

(Geary 1983:16)

Furthermore, it has been pointed out that we only really know about ethnicity in elite and literate contexts; hence, the identities created and maintained by a majority of the population are unknown (Amory 1994:4; Pohl 1991:41; 1997:9).

These conclusions have important implications for how archaeologists categorise material culture and the people(s) to whom it may be linked. To call a quoit brooch either Germanic or native (or indeed Angle or Saxon) may well be limiting our understanding of the early medieval usage of ethnic identities. The notion of fixed and bounded ethnic groups contradicts the view of ethnicity as a fluid and situational social practice (see also Bentley 1987; Jones 1997 for more detailed considerations) in which a number of identities may be held by an individual, being expressed to greater or lesser extents depending on the context of interaction. These approaches to ethnicity have led some to doubt the existence of defined, bounded, perhaps territorial ethnic groups as 'real' entities (Shennan 1989:11), although they may become powerful and influential ideas to groups or individuals in specific contexts (cf. Jenkins 1997:168). We might instead think of overlapping social networks of varying scales (Shennan 1989:11).

Additionally, archaeological research has produced results which may again lead us to question the general applicability of broad, perhaps regional, ethnic groupings, as derived from historical sources such as Bede. Research by Pader (1982) and Lucy (1998) has identified localised patterning in mortuary practice. We cannot ignore broader patterns (e.g. brooch distributions or the occurrence of cremations and inhumations), but we might ask if these have diverted archaeological research from investigating local identities and the contexts in which quoit brooches were found. Being found in graves means the brooches must primarily be interpreted as a constituent of a burial costume, placed with the deceased by mourners. Thus, a direct relationship between the 'dress' and identities ascribed to the deceased in death and the clothes worn or identities used by an individual in life can not be assumed (Thomas 1991:104). Furthermore, there are identities other than ethnicity with which the mourners could have been concerned, such as age or gender, and if ethnicity was a factor, did they actually recognise the 'native'/'Germanic' dichotomy, or were more local identities important to them? Unfortunately, detailed evidence about the graves in which a majority of quoit brooches, especially types A-C, were found does not survive, so a detailed contextual comparison is not possible. However, where the evidence does exist, the brooches were associated with material, (such as finger rings and four or more beads) usually found in (biologically sexed) 'female' graves (Brush 1993).

The problems associated with linking material culture directly to ethnicity are further highlighted by ethnographic studies made in Africa. These studies (e.g. Hodder 1982; De Corse 1989) show that this relationship cannot be taken for granted. De Corse found that out of all material culture in his study area in Sierra Leone, only shrines were implicated in the negotiation of ethnicity and these were highly variable in style and not present at every site (1989:138). Thus, for archaeologists who cannot talk to the users of the artefacts, it is even more difficult to discern which material may or may not be used specifically to negotiate ethnicity. Were quoit brooches used to represent a particular ethnic identity, or was this done through material and/or practices that do not survive archaeologically? De Corse concluded that his research:

> ...demonstrated the difficulty in using material culture to ascribe ethnicity or even to define broader cultural groups

> (De Corse 1989:138)

This is equally true in archaeology.

Migrations

Quoit brooches have not only been used as evidence for certain ethnic groups, but as noted above, owing to perceived close associations between material culture and ethnic groups, they have also been used to infer migrations of people (Bakka 1958; Hawkes 1961). The strength of the migration hypothesis throughout the course of 'Anglo-Saxon' archaeology may be attributed to the seemingly complementary nature of historical and archaeological evidence. However, a number of historians have asked why the early medieval sources refer to migrations in the first place.

Firstly, it is important to note that none of the authors who refer to the movements of peoples in the fifth century around the North Sea were eyewitnesses. Both Bede and Gildas, the two most influential insular sources for archaeologists, saw the events of the mid-fifth century as significant episodes in the past. Additionally, it is notable that both these authors were writing as Christians. Hanning has asserted the importance of Christianity in shaping the 'historical imagination' (1966:2) of the authors; the Bible influenced how they conceptualised, explained and expressed the past. Gildas was explicit about this influence:

> And I could see that in our time too, just as Jeremiah had lamented, 'the city' (that is, the church) 'sat solitary, bereaved'...I gazed on these things and many others in the Old Testament as though on a mirror reflecting our own life

> (*DEB*. 1.5–7)

In the Bible (especially the Old Testament), narrated events are commonly explained as Divine interventions in the human world (Howe 1989:45). The prosperity of God's people(s) was assured while His laws were obeyed, and disasters seen as a sign of His displeasure with the nation's immorality (Hanning 1966:46). Disasters, which served to alter the established order, were regularly brought about by external groups of people who caused death and destruction and thus became God's agents on earth (Howe 1989:59; e.g. Jeremiah, Lamentations, Isaiah 9 and 10). For Gildas, this was an influential model. He used the Old Testament as 'a storehouse of historical *exempla*' (Hanning 1966:58), such that:

The aim of the historical chapters of *De Excidio* can be said to be the establishment of the British past firmly within the context of the history of salvation, i.e. of the guidance of history by divine providence

(Hanning 1966:57)

Hence, the English origin myth was also strongly influenced by a Biblically inspired rhetorical and narrative device:

The coming of the Saxons is less significant as an event in itself than as the climax to a series of punishments meted out by God to the British

(Howe 1989:41)

The work of Gildas was fundamental in the creation of the English origin myth, and it certainly influenced Bede (Hanning 1966:73). However, the aims of the *Historia Ecclesiastica* were somewhat different to Gildas' work (see above). There was also a shift in emphasis between the two accounts. Gildas presented the Britons as a 'latter-day Israel' (*DEB.* 26.1) being tested by God, while Bede presented the English as the 'new Israel' (Hanning 1966:70) inheriting England from the sinful Britons. Despite these differences, the model was flexible enough to allow both authors to write specifically Christian accounts, in terms of eschatology and salvation history referring to groups of peoples, (rarely individuals) in the same narrative context:

For Bede, as for Gildas, history [in Britain] is a drama played out on an island stage by those who cross the sea

(Howe 1989:51)

Thus, descriptions of invasions/migrations by external peoples may be seen as rhetorical, narrative devices, appropriated from Judeo-Christian texts whose writers also used migrations as a key explanatory framework. To a late antique/early medieval devout Christian writer, the Old Testament may have been both the origin and justification for expressing the past in this way, creating a powerful and influential origin myth. The narratives were 'credible in their claims to ancient origins, which does not mean that they are factual accounts of actual origins' (Pohl 1997:9). Similar ideas may be applied to continental sources of this period (e.g. the Gallic Chronicle of AD 452, Muhlberger 1990). These narrative methods were adopted by archaeologists through their use of sources such as Bede and Gildas, yet it must be accepted that the sources do not necessarily record the actual occurrence of migrations. Thus, a direct relationship between these texts and archaeological evidence from the fifth century (such as quoit brooches) cannot be assumed.

The above observations about ethnicity, migrations and historical sources have important implications for the study of quoit brooches and as a result of these critiques we might question the general applicability of the prevailing discourse within which these interpretations have taken place. It may also be asked if these are the only means to interpret quoit brooches?

Alternative approaches

If previous approaches to the interpretation of quoit brooches, referring to ethnic change and migrations, can be challenged, it is necessary to seek alternative understandings. Firstly, however, it is important to stress that, despite the critical approaches outlined above an entirely negative view of the evidence need not be adopted.

Highlighting why the narratives may have taken the form that they did, forces us to question the applicability of the historical model to the archaeological evidence of the mid-fifth century. Yet we cannot simply dismiss the idea that there may have been migrations of people which were recorded by later authors (albeit for specific reasons and narrated through certain rhetorical conventions); this was clearly a strong tradition in early medieval literate circles. We also cannot dismiss migrations as a potential explanation for material culture patterning, even if the historical and archaeological basis on which they have been 'proven' is questionable. However, if migrations are considered as a stimulus for change, Anthony (1990) has suggested that they should not be discussed as simple, uni-directional movements of entire populations. Rather, more complex, sometimes two-way movements by sections of a population for specific purposes might be envisaged. Finally, despite the observation that material culture is not a reliable means of inferring ethnic identities, we cannot simply dismiss or explain away recognised material culture patterns, such as the similarity of artefact types found across north-western Europe and around the North Sea littoral.

The aim therefore is to interpret material culture patterns and changes without relying on potentially problematic assumptions. To turn to the possible alternative explanations, the occurrence of exchange/trade networks has been discussed in the quoit brooch debate. Hawkes (1961:61) and Evison (1965:77) refer to a flourishing trade between northern Gaul and Scandinavia during the late Roman period, which accounted for the perceived 'Roman' influences on 'Germanic' quoit brooches. Additionally, it is interesting to note that decorative influences for quoit brooches have been found from around the North Sea periphery; from Jutland (Hawkes 1961), northern Gaul/Frankia (Evison 1965) and even from the late Roman Mildenhall Treasure in East Anglia (Evison 1965). It might therefore be hypothesised that the North Sea was a unifying geographical feature around which people and material culture could circulate, rather than a divide across which migrations or invasions must take place. Carver (1990:117) has suggested the existence of a North Sea 'zone of interaction'. He does, however, believe it to be only a post-migration phenomenon of the seventh and eighth centuries as the settlement of eastern England by Germanic immigrants in the fifth century is 'well documented' (Carver 1990:117). If the migration model is based on the aggregation of questionable assumptions, it might be asked if such a 'zone of interaction' was also operating in the fifth century?

Building on this idea, it is too simplistic to say that because quoit brooches (or their decorative motifs) were known and available around the North Sea littoral, they would automatically have been used by those who came into contact with them through some form of passive acculturation. 'Post-Processual' studies have described material culture as 'active' and integral to the social practices of groups/institutions and the individuals of which they are constituted. Material can be used to structure, express and maintain certain practices and identities (e.g. Barrett 1991:6). As such, when seeking to explain material culture change, it is important to consider the possibility that material is not used arbitrarily. Rather, it may be (consciously or subconsciously) appropriated into social practice (cf. Niles 1997) by groups or individuals to mark a range of identities and affiliations in certain contexts; be they identities used in life or ascribed in death. Material need not only be imposed from an external source, as when migrations are seen as the primary catalyst in archaeological transitions, or even imposed and acculturated more widely, as with the idea of an elite migration (Härke 1990; Higham 1994).

This can be briefly illustrated with a modern analogy. In 1997 the most rapidly expanding market for the quintessentially 'English' Barbour wax-cotton jacket was Asia. This was not as a result of English people moving to that region. Rather, it implies that a type of material culture, which people know to have a very defined set of social connotations, was being appropriated into a different context to that in which it was originally conceived. Hence, it is not simply the jackets themselves which are desirable, but the associated identity (i.e. rural 'Englishness') which goes along with them. Yet because the material is not used in its original context, the meaning and the identities it helps create will be subtly different. It is an identity of association that is being appropriated through Barbour jackets in places like Japan, not one of actual membership of a particular identity group. Therefore, the same material types cannot be assumed to represent the same identities wherever they are found and understanding contexts of use is a vital part of interpreting the role of material culture in social practice.

To summarise, the traditional assumptions implicating migrations in fifth-century material change have been highly influential. However, it is argued here that a variety of factors may have produced the known fifth-century artefact distributions around the North Sea (Shennan 1989:12) and it is important to explore these other means by which material becomes dispersed, and how and why it was appropriated.

It may in fact be questionable to use quoit brooches as evidence for migration. The continental parallels used to demonstrate this are purely decorative (e.g. Hawkes 1961). The 'Quoit Brooch Style' of ornamentation is only found in combination with the quoit form of brooch in England (apart from the single Type B brooch from Bénouville, France). Yet despite this, it may be significant that scholars have perceived in these brooches both 'native/Roman', as well as 'Germanic' decorative elements. Quoit brooches may represent not physical processes of population movement, but the emerging influence of new decorative styles from around the North Sea periphery on pre-existing metalworking techniques and decoration. They may have been appropriated by groups and individuals to signify new social practices or identities (or at least new material conditions through which these were conducted), perhaps associated with the specifically 'Germanic' identity recorded in later historical and poetic texts. Alternatively, these records may be later constructions with 'Germanic' metalwork styles available in the North Sea region being appropriated more as an alternative to the established and understood symbols of 'Romanitas' in the context of declining Imperial influence, or undermining, what might be called, 'Romanized' practices in eastern Britain. More specifically this process may have overlapped with the construction of some form of 'female' identity in the burial context (see above).

Conclusions

The preceding discussion has demonstrated that Leeds initiated the debates surrounding quoit brooches, possibly as a means of pursuing his specific research interest in 1936. Similarly, the theoretical framework within which the brooches have been interpreted (involving defined ethnic groups and the Biblically and historically derived notion of migrations) have shown to be rooted in assumptions produced by nineteenth-century racial theory and nationalism.

To avoid using these assumptions in explaining the distribution of quoit brooches and their related decorative styles, alternatives have been outlined. It was concluded that, although migrations (in some form) cannot be ruled out, it is also important to consider the potential role of exchange and especially the idea that material can be appropriated into social practices by groups and individuals for a variety of reasons. Thus, quoit brooches may be interpreted as evidence for changing social practice and material culture usage in the context of late Roman/early medieval burial rites.

While this is only one hypothesis and one artefact type, this study has important implications for the Roman-Medieval transition. If it is accepted that the notion of ethnic group migrations is, to some extent a construct, then for archaeologists to continue to consider these issues (however complex the interaction between groups is seen to be or on whatever scale the migrations) is in effect maintaining the development of 'paradigms to explain that which they themselves have created' (Bond & Gilliam 1994:13).

The alternative interpretation of quoit brooches presented above, which stresses the importance of social practice and the possibility of material appropriations, leads to a very different view of the transitions; one in which the process is not simple, clear-cut or reliant on migrations as the only catalyst. Furthermore, social practice is context-specific. In the case of quoit brooches being found in cemeteries, it is the mortuary context and its associated practices that are important. Indeed, notwithstanding studies of settlements and economics, fifth-century archaeology is still dominated by cemetery evidence, which is also commonly used to demonstrate ethnic change and the effect of migrations. Yet this was only one context of social practice and it must be asked if changes here, which are believed to mark the transition, were reflected equally in other areas of social practice which constituted people's lives. This approach should draw attention to the complex dynamics of social change, recognising the importance of both individuals and their wider context, showing that migrations and the movements of ethnic groups are not the only means by which to understand the material culture changes through which archaeologists study the transition from Roman Britain to early medieval England.

Department of Archaeology, University of Durham

Acknowledgements

I would like to thank Howard Williams and David Petts for arranging the TRAC session at which this paper was originally presented and Barry Ager, the British Museum and Sussex Archaeological Society/Lewes Museum for sending me photographs and allowing me to use their illustrations. I am also very grateful to Sam Lucy, Martin Millett and the anonymous referee for their comments on drafts of this paper. Any faults, however, remain my own responsibility.

Bibliography

Ager, B. 1985. The smaller variants of the Anglo-Saxon quoit brooch. *Anglo-Saxon studies in archaeology and history*, 4:1–35.

Ager, B. 1990. The alternative quoit brooch: an update. In E. Southworth (ed.) *Anglo-Saxon cemeteries: a reappraisal*. Stroud: Sutton Publishing, pp.153–161.

Amory, P. 1994. Names, ethnic identity and community in fifth century Burgundy. *Viator*, 25:1–30.

Anthony, D. 1990. Migration in archaeology: the baby and the bathwater. *American Anthropologist*, 92:895–914.

Austin, D. 1990. The 'proper' study of Medieval archaeology. In D. Austin & L. Alcock (eds.) *From the Baltic to the Black Sea: studies in Medieval archaeology*. London: Unwin Hyman, pp.9–42.

Bakka, E. 1958. On the beginning of Salin's Style I in England. *Universitetet i Bergen Abok, Historisk-Antikvarist rekke*, 3:1–83.

Barrett, J. 1991. Towards an archaeology of ritual. In P. Garwood, D. Jennings, R. Skeates & J. Toms (eds.) *Sacred and profane: proceedings of a conference on archaeology, ritual and religion*. Oxford: Oxford University Committee for Archaeology Monograph 32, pp.1–9.

Bede *Ecclesiastical history of the English people*. (eds. B. Colgrave & R. Mynors, 1969). Oxford: Clarendon Press.

Bentley, G.C. 1987. Ethnicity and practice. *Comparative studies in society and history*, 29:24–55.

Böhme, H.W. 1986. Das ende der Römerherrschaft in Britannien und die Angelsächsische Besiedlung Englands im 5. Jahrhundert. *Jahrbuch des Römisch-Germanischen Zentralmuseums Mainz*, 33 (2):469–575.

Bond, G.C. & Gilliam, A. 1994. Introduction. In G.C. Bond & A. Gilliam (eds.) *Social construction of the past*. London: Routledge, pp.1–22.

Brush, K. 1993. *Adorning the dead – the social significance of early Anglo-Saxon funerary dress in England (fifth to sixth century AD)*. Cambridge: Unpublished Ph.D Thesis.

Carver, M. 1990. Pre-Viking traffic in the North Sea. In S. McGrail (ed.) *Maritime Celts, Frisians and Saxons*. York: CBA Research Report 71, pp.117–125.

De Corse, C. 1989. Material aspects of Limba, Yalunka and Kuranko ethnicity: archaeological research in northeastern Sierra Leone. In S. Shennan (ed.) *Archaeological approaches to cultural identity*. London: Unwin Hyman, One World Archaeology 10, pp.125–140.

Diaz-Andreu, M. & Champion, T. 1996. Nationalism and archaeology in Europe: an introduction. In M. Diaz-Andreu & T. Champion (eds.) *Nationalism and archaeology in Europe*. London: University College London Press, pp.1–23.

Evison, V. 1965. *The fifth century invasions south of the Thames*. London: University of London & Athlane Press.

Freeman, E. 1903. *The historical geography of Europe*. London: Longmans, Green & Co.

Geary, P. 1983. Ethnic identity as a situational construct in the early middle ages. *Mitteilungen der Anthropologischen Gesellschaft in Wien*, 113:15–26.

Gildas *The ruin of Britain and other works*. (ed. & trans. by M. Winterbottom, 1978.). London: Phillimore.

Griffith, A.F. & Salzman, L.F. 1914. An Anglo-Saxon cemetery at Alfriston, Sussex. *Sussex Archaeological Collections*, 56:16–53.

Hannaford, I. 1996. *Race: the history of an idea in the West*. Baltimore: Johns Hopkins University Press.

Hanning, R. 1966. *The vision of history in early Britain: from Gildas to Geoffrey of Monmouth.* New York & London: Columbia University Press.

Härke, H. 1990. 'Warrior Graves?' The background of the Anglo-Saxon weapon burial rite. *Past and Present,* 126:22–43.

Haseloff, G. 1974. Salin's Style I. *Medieval Archaeology,* 18:1–15.

Hawkes, S.C. 1961. The Jutish Style A: a study of Germanic animal art in southern England in the fifth century AD. *Archaeologia,* 98:29–75.

Hides, S. 1996. The genealogy of material culture and cultural identity. In P. Graves-Brown, S. Jones & C. Gamble (eds.) *Cultural identity and archaeology: the construction of European communities.* London: Routledge, pp.25–47.

Higham, N.J. 1994. *The English conquest: Gildas and Britain in the fifth century.* Manchester: Manchester University Press.

Hodder, I. 1982. *Symbols in action.* Cambridge: Cambridge University Press.

Howe, N. 1989. *Migration and mythmaking in Anglo-Saxon England.* New Haven & London: Yale University Press.

Jenkins, R. 1997. *Rethinking ethnicity: arguments and explorations.* London: Sage Publications.

Jones, M. 1996. *The end of Roman Britain.* Ithaca: Cornell University Press.

Jones, S. 1997. *The archaeology of ethnicity: constructing identities in the past and present.* London: Routledge.

Kemble, J.M. 1855. On mortuary urns found at Stade-on-the-Elbe, and other parts of northern Germany. *Archaeologia,* 36:270–283.

Leeds, E.T. 1936. *Early Anglo-Saxon art and archaeology.* Oxford: Clarendon Press.

Leeds, E.T. 1945. The distribution of Angles and Saxons archaeologically considered. *Archaeologia,* 91:1–106.

Lucy, S. 1998. *The Anglo-Saxon cemeteries of East Yorkshire.* Oxford: British Archaeological Report British Series 272.

Muhlberger, S. 1990. *The fifth century Chroniclers: Prosper, Hydatius and the Gallic Chronicler of 452.* Leeds: Francis Cairns.

Myres, J.N.L. 1969. *Anglo-Saxon pottery and the settlement of England.* Oxford: Clarendon Press.

Niles, J. 1997. Appropriations: a concept of culture. In A. Frantzen & J. Niles (eds.) *Anglo-Saxonism and the construction of social identity.* Gainesville: University Press of Florida, pp.202–228.

Owen-Crocker, G. 1986. *Dress in Anglo-Saxon England.* Manchester: Manchester University Press.

Pader, E-J. 1982. *Symbolism, social relations and the interpretation of mortuary remains.* Oxford: BAR International Series 130.

Pohl, W. 1991. Conceptions of ethnicity in early Medieval studies. *Archaeologia Polona,* 29:39–49.

Pohl, W. 1997. Ethnic names and identities in the British Isles: a comparative perspective. In J. Hines (ed.) *The Anglo-Saxons from the Migration period to the eighth century: an ethnographic perspective.* Woodbridge: Boydell Press, pp.7–32.

Read, C.H. 1895. On excavations in a cemetery of South Saxons on High Down, Sussex. *Archaeologia,* 54:369–382.

Shennan, S. 1989. Introduction: archaeological approaches to cultural identity. In S. Shennan (ed.) *Archaeological approaches to cultural identity.* London: Unwin Hyman, One World Archaeology 10, pp.1–32.

Shennan, S. 1991. Some current issues in the archaeological identification of past peoples. *Archaeologia Polona,* 29:29–37.

Thomas, J. 1991. *Rethinking the Neolithic.* Cambridge: Cambridge University Press.

Yorke, B. 1993. Fact or fiction? The written evidence for the fifth and sixth centuries AD. *Anglo-Saxon Studies in Archaeology and History,* 6:45–49.

as a decline (Brogiolo 1987), or sometimes as a complete disappearance of the urban life (Carandini 1993). The latter, on the other hand, takes a more optimistic view and sees continuity of town life characterised by transformation and reuse of different classical buildings (La Rocca Hudson 1986; Wickham 1981). These opposed ideas have been connected with national cultural influence by Ward Perkins (1996). An intermediate approach has been recently suggested by Lepelley (1996:5): in late Antiquity we see both an evident breakdown and yet a surprising continuity of life. These transitions are connected with historical events. The weakening of the Roman Empire obviously prompted a new balance between social organisation and economic systems (Thébert 1983). In this process, classical towns were firstly 'de-constructed' and then 'reconstructed' in a new form (Ermini Pani 1998:214; Wataghin 1996).

In fact, it is necessary to point out that the 'classical city' was a particular type of town, characterised by a close involvement of the aristocracies in civic politics and urban culture. In considering the structure of power of the Roman Empire, towns were its most important expression, displaying in their public areas and buildings, a connection with the model of Rome (Luiselli 1992; Storoni Mazzolani 1967). The destiny of these towns reflects the evolution and the life of the Roman Empire. In this period it is possible to speak of a Roman urban organisation and of a starting point, provided by the model of Rome. We can also say that life in most towns during the expansion and apex of the Roman Empire had certain visible traits in common, especially related to public architecture, and, for this reason, it is legitimate to analyse and compare some elements of the different urban areas of this period. But, after the collapse of Rome, when the universal imperial model fails, their subsequent evolution is different. In the late antique period the lack of an all-embracing political and cultural structure leads to much greater regional diversity. For this reason, it is sometimes possible to compare towns within the same geographical areas, where the historical context is similar and where urban trajectories may be alike (cf. papers in Christie & Loseby 1996). Notwithstanding, as already shown in the case of Carthage, it is possible to single out characteristics that we can consider common to all late antique towns, despite the chronology and the geographical area. This is the effect of similarity in human character and human necessities, sometimes modified by different cultures (Blacking 1970:229).

The character of a late antique town: a review of some aspects.

Reviewing the archaeological evidence for the late antique town, we can identify common elements, which are characterised principally by the reuse and transformation of buildings belonging to the classical town (Caniggia 1973–4). Some aspects may be pointed out.

In considering the changing use of classical public buildings it is necessary to bear in mind that they usually had a specific function and this character shows that each of them was in use until a given moment, that is, as long as society needed that space. This means that the life of a public building tends to be shorter than the life of housing space, which is always necessary to a community; instead the changing of the public spaces is connected with the transformation of a key social group and its requirements. In considering the different types of classical public buildings in imperial towns we can enumerate; *fora*, baths, buildings for games and spectacles, temples. All of these were transformed and reused in different ways, always determined by the needs of the new society, resulting from the waning of Roman power and the emergence and diffusion of the Christian religion. For example, in Carthage the principal *forum,* the theatre and the odeon of the town (Picard & Baillon 1992) were partially occupied by private houses, during the sixth century. In these cases, we have a record of the transformation of public spaces into private ones, which is a common phenomenon of urban decay (Medhurst & Parry Lewis 1969:27–8, 55). But sometimes public spaces preserved their original public function as foci for the urban community. In fact, the diffusion of a new religion directs the reuse of some public buildings (especially baths, judicial *basilicae,* and, later, temples) as churches. We can cite the examples of *Tipasa, Sabratha, Leptis Magna,* in Northern Africa, where the judicial *basilicae*

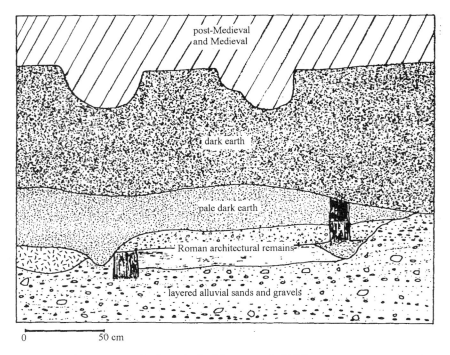

Figure 2 Hypothetical section at a dark earth site (Courty et al. 1989)

were transformed into churches (Caillet 1996:192); or the case of *Maktar*, where a church (Basilica IV) reused part of the bath (Thermes de l'Ouest) complex (Duval 1971:305–17). In addition there was a transformation of temples into ecclesiastical structures, as in *Thuburbo Maius*, where the *cella* was used as a baptistery (Caillet 1996:195), and *Oratoria* were built in the theatre and amphitheatre, as indeed at Carthage (Picard & Baillon 1992). Theatres and amphitheatres, as well as open areas, such as the *fora* were also often transformed into military and defensive structures. This reuse of public space points out, once more, that most of the areas that had been expressions of the power of Rome were given the new function of protecting the inhabitants. These new towns, where we can identify on one hand, the natural disappearance or rather decay of the monumental symbols of Rome, and on the other, the reuse of the same monuments for the needs of the inhabitants, are still organised as living spaces and so should be considered as such.

Another important element is the identification of meeting places, besides churches. In the countryside there were rural markets and we should imagine similar areas in towns, devoted to commercial exchange and social life, even if these areas were no longer monumentalised. In Carthage the north sector of the circular harbour in the sixth century was restored with an organisation very similar to the *soukh* of later Islamic towns (Hurst 1994:63, 81). The traditional fashion of considering religious buildings as the only meeting places in this period might be reassessed – the example of Carthage shows that there were probably also other areas connected with such social activity in these towns.

The presence of graves inside the urban area can also be reconsidered. They show a new relationship between death/dead and life/living rather than simply decay; in fact the particular bond with the dead, the *cura animarun* clearly determined the necessity of closer proximity between houses and tombs. Significantly, especially in the earlier period we can recognise a planned intramural distribution of the tombs; as claimed, for instance at Rome, where fifth century tombs inside the city are spatially organised around cultural areas and always in proximity to streets, rather than randomly across the town (Meneghini & Santangeli Valenzani 1993).

Recent research also requires us to re-assess the so-called 'dark earth', that is, dark-coloured and seemingly homogeneous urban occupation deposits (Courty *et al.* 1989:261). In the past, this archaeological evidence was considered to be connected with cultivated areas inside the city. Recently the same deposits have been interpreted alternatively as the decayed remains of poor structures, built of wood and mud brick (Courty *et al.* 1989:261–8). This modified perspective, (Figure 2) allows us to explore the relationship between the environment and the distribution of poor housing inside the town (Motta 1997:264). There has been a tendency to consider the continuity of use of principally Roman buildings, even if transformed according to new situations; but it should kept in mind that there was also much poor housing. Further, many of these structures were connected with production areas, indicating self-sufficiency, in contrast with the earlier integrated Roman imperial system.

Conclusions

Considering all of these elements – the use of public buildings in new contexts, change connected with the reuse of private buildings, the construction of poorer quality housing and burial within the town – it is evident that the general image of the town is radically different from the imperial predecessor. This means that our approach to the evidence of late antique towns should be different from that used by classical archaeologists. Traces of human presence and their relationship with the environment are the main elements to interpret and understand urban life in late Antiquity (Carver 1981).

Borrowing the words of Parker Pearson & Richards (1994:3), 'our environment exists in terms of our actions and meanings'. This is even more appropriate after the decay of the Roman Empire, with its models and ways of expression, when the local inhabitants become the principal protagonists of the life of their town. The latter is now a space organised and controlled by the needs of individuals, and no longer the requirements of Rome. For this reason, even greater attention must be paid to social organisation, population and subsistence (Leech 1981:57–60). In approaching the study of any late antique town we should abandon our classical perspective; we should not consider the decay of Roman urbanism as a dramatic and final moment in urban history; but rather should value the late antique town in its own terms, considering its own particular economic and social character, its new meeting places, its relationship with the environment and its ties with relations of power.

School of Archaeological Studies, University of Leicester

Acknowledgements

D.J. Mattingly , N. Christie, Y. Thébert, F. Zevi and N. Terrenato offered useful stimuli and suggestions. Thanks are also due to I. Lana for his directions on historical sources. L. Stirling, R. Kipling, L. Farr, R. Witcher and M. Brizzi kindly read and commented on the manuscript. The remaining errors are my responsibility.

Bibliography

Bairam-Ben Osman, W. & Ennabli L. 1982. Notes sur la topographie chrétienne de Carthage: les mosaïques du Monastère de Bigua. *Revue des Etudes Augustiniennes*, 28 (1–2):3–18.

Balmelle, C., Ben Abed, A., Ben Mansour. S., Ben Osman, W., Darmon, J.P., Ennaifer, M., Gozlan, S., Hanoune, R., Jeddi, N. & Raynaud, M. P. 1990. Recherches franco-tunisiennes dans la maison de criptoportique. Centre d'Etudes et de Documentation Archéologique de la Conservation de Carthage 11, pp:11–18.

Basham R.1978. *Urban anthropology. The cross-cultural study of complex society.* Palo Alto, California: Mayfield Publishing Company.

Ben Abdallah Benzina, Z.B. 1990. Aperçu sur la fouille menée à Carthage, le long de la berge occidental du port marchand. Une hypothèse de topographie. *Bulletin des travaux de l'Institue National du Patrimoine*, 5:135–144.

Blacking, J. 1970. The myth of urban man. In H. L. Watts (ed.) *Focus on cities. Proceedings of conference organised by the Institute of Social Research at the University of Natal Durban* (July 1968). Natal Durban: Natal Durban University, pp.228–238.

Brogiolo, P. 1987. A proposito dell'organizzazione urbana nell'alto medioevo. *Archeologia Medievale*, 14:48–56.

Caillet, J. P. 1996. La transformation en Eglise d'édifices publics et de temples à la fin de l'antiquité. In C. Lepelley (ed.) *La fin de la cité antique et le début de la cité Medievale*. Bari: Edipuglia/Galliard, pp.191–211.

Cameron, A. 1996. *Changing cultures in early Byzantium*. Variorum Collected Studies 536. Great Yarmouth: Galliard Ltd.

Caniggia, G. 1973–4. Lettura delle persistenze antiche nei tessuti urbani medievali. In *Atti del Convegno Internazionale sui metodi di studio della città antica*. Centro studi e documentazione sull'Italia romana, 5:327–357.

Carandini, A. 1993. L'ultima civiltà sepolta o del massimo oggetto desueto, secondo un archeologo. In *Storia di Roma. 3. L'età tardoantica. 2. I luoghi e le culture*. Torino: Einaudi, pp.11–38.

Carandini, A., Anselmino, L., Panella, C., Pavolini, C. & Caciagli, R. 1983. Rapporto preliminare delle campagne 1973–1977. *Quaderni di Archeologia della Libia*, 13:9–61.

Carver, M. O. H. 1981. Sampling towns: an optimistic strategy. In P. Clark & S. Haselgrove, *Approaches to the urban past, Occasional Paper 2*. Durham: Durham University Press, pp.65–90.

Carver, M.O.H. 1993. *Arguments in stone*. Exeter: Oxbow

Christie, N. & Loseby, S.T. 1996. *Towns in transition: urban evolution in late Antiquity and the early Middle Ages*. Aldershot: Scolar Press.

Cicero, *De Re Publica. De Legibus*. (trans. C. Walker Keyes, 1928). London: William Heinemann.

Courty, M. A., Goldberg, P. & Macphail, R. 1989. *Soils and micromorphology in archaeology*. Cambridge: Cambridge University Press.

Cyprianus (Sancti Cypriani Episcopi Opera). *Corpus Christianorum*, IIIA pars II. (ed. M. Simonetti, 1976). Brepols: Editores Pontificii.

De Robertis, F. 1974. *Storia delle corporazioni e del regime associativo nel mondo romano 2*. Bari: Tipografia del Sud.

De Robertis, F. 1981. Il fenomeno associativo nel mondo romano. Dai collegi della Repubblica alle corporazioni del basso Impero. Roma: L'ERMA di Bretschneider.

Deneauve, J. & Villedieu, F. 1977. Le Cardo Maximus et les édifices situés à l'est de la voie. *Antiquités Africaines*, 11:95–130.

Deneauve, J. & Villedieu, F.1979. Le Cardo Maximus et les édifices situés à l'est de la voie. In S. Lancel (ed.) *BYRSA 1. Rapports preliminaires des fouilles*. Rome: L'ERMA di Bretschneider, pp.143–176.

Duval, N. 1971. Eglise et thermes en Afrique du Nord. Notes sur les installations chrétiennes dans les constructions thermales, à propose de Madaure et de Mactar. *Bulletin Archéologique du Comité des Travaux Historiques et Scientifiques*, nouvelle série 7:297–305.

Duval, N. 1972. Etudes d'Architecture chretienne nord-africaine 1. Les monuments Chrétiens de Carthage. *Mélanges de l'Ecole Française de Rome. Antiquité*, 84:1071–1172.

Duval, N. & Lézine, A. 1959. Nécropole chrétienne et Baptistére souterrain à Carthage. *Cahiers Archéologiques*, 10:71–147.

Ellis, S.P. 1988. *Carthage Sewers Project*. Centre d'Etudes et de Documentation Archéologique de la Conservation de Carthage 9: 22–37.

Ennabli, L. 1997. *Carthage. Une métropole chrétienne du IV à la fin du VII siècle*. Paris: CNRS Editions.

Ermini Pani, L. 1998. La 'città di pietra': forme, spazi, strutture. In *Europa fra tarda Antichità e alto Medioevo. Settimane di studio del Centro Italiano di Studi sull'Alto Medioevo* (3–9 aprile 1997), 45, 1. Spoleto: Tipografia Artigiana Tuderte, pp.211–255.

Hammond, M. 1972. *The city in the ancient world*. Cambridge, Massachusetts: Harvard University Press.

Humphrey, J.H. 1980. Vandal and Byzantine Carthage: some new archaeological evidence. In J. Griffiths Pedley (ed.) *New light on ancient Carthage*. Ann Arbor: University of Michigan Press, pp.85–120.

Hurst, H. & Roskams, S. 1984. *Excavations at Carthage. The British Mission 1.1. The Avenue du President Habib Bourguiba Salammbo: the site and finds other than pottery*. Sheffield: Charlesworth.

Hurst, H. 1994. *The Circular Harbour North side 2.1. The site and finds other than pottery.* Oxford: OUP

Iciek, A., Jagodzinski, A. & Kolendo, J. 1974. *Carthage. Cirque–Colline dite de Junon–Douar Chott. Recherches archéologiques et geographiques polonaise effectuées en 1972.* Wroclav, Warszawa, Krakow & Gdansk: ZakPond Narodowy Imienia Ossolinskisch Wydawnictwo Polskiej Akademii Nauk.

La Rocca Hudson, C. 1986. 'Dark Ages' a Verona. Edilizia privata, aree aperte e strutture pubbliche in una città dell'Italia Settentrionale. *Archeologia Medievale*, 13:31–78.

Labate, M. 1991. Città morte, città future un tema della poesia augustea. In *MAIA. Rivista di letterature Classiche*, 43:167–184.

Lana, I. 1961. *Rutilio Namaziano.* Torino: Università di Torino-Facoltà di lettere e Filosofia/ Fondazione Parini Chirio.

Leech, R. 1981. Medieval urban archaeology in the north west: problems and response. In P. Clark and S. Haselgrove (eds.) *Approaches to the urban past.* Durham: Durham University Press, pp.55–64.

Lepelley, C. 1996. De la cité classique à la cité tardive: continuités et ruptures. In C. Lepelley (ed.) *La fin de la cité antique et le début de la cité Medievale.* Bari: Edipuglia/Galliard, pp.5–13.

Lézine, A. 1968. *Carthage–Utique. Etudes d'architecture et d'urbanisme.* Paris: CNRS Editions.

Lézine, A. 1969. *Les Thermes d'Antonin.* Tunis: Société Tunisienne de Diffusion.

Lucretius *De Rerum Natura.* (trans. W.H. D. Rouse, 1924). London: William Heinemann.

Luiselli, B. 1992 *Storia culturale dei rapporti fra mondo romano e mondo germanico.* Roma: Herder.

Medhurst, F. & Parry Lewis, J. 1969. *Urban decay. An analysis and policy.* London: Hazell Watson & Viney.

Meneghini, R. & Santangeli Valenzani, R. 1993. Sepolture intramuranee e paesaggio a Roma tra IV e VII secolo d.C. In L. Paroli and P. Delogu (eds.) *La storia economica di Roma nell'Alto Medioevo alla luce dei recenti scavi archeologici.* Firenze: All'Insegna del Giglio, pp.89–111.

Morrill, R.L. 1974. *The spatial organisation of society.* Second edition. Belmont: Duxbury Press.

Motta, L. 1997. I paesaggi di Volterra nel tardoantico. *Archeologia Medievale*, 24:245–267.

Ovid, *Metamorphoses.* (trans. F.J. Miller, 1931), 2 vols. London: William Heinemann.

Panella, C. 1993. Merci e scambi nel Mediterraneo tardoantico. In *Storia di Roma. 3. L'età tardoantica. 2. I luoghi e le culture.* Torino: Einaudi, pp.613–702.

Parker Pearson, M. & Richards, C. 1994. Ordering the world: perceptions of architecture space and time. In Iidem (eds.) *Architecture and orders. Approaches to social space.* London & New York: Routledge, pp.1–37.

Picard, G.C. & Baillon, M. 1992. Le théâtre Romain de Carthage. In *Actes du Ve Colloque International d'Histoire et Archéologie de l'Afrique du Nord. Spectacles, vie Portuaire, Religions* (Avignon 1990). Paris: Editions du Comité des Travaux Historiques et Scientifiques, pp.11–27.

Rakob, F. 1991. Die Römischen Bauperioden. In J. Holst, T. Kraus, M. Mackensen, F. Rakob, K. Rheidt, O. Teschauer, M. Vegas, I. Wiblé & A. Wolff, *Karthago 1. Die Deutschen Ausgrabungen in Karthago.* Mainz: Philipp Von Zabern, pp.242–251.

Roncajolo, M. 1988. La città. Storia e problemi della dimensione urbana. Torino: Einaudi.

Roskams, S. 1996. Urban transition in North Africa: Roman and Medieval towns of the Maghreb. In N. Christie & T. Loseby (eds.), *Towns in transition: urban evolution in late Antiquity and early Middle Ages.* Aldershot: Scolar Press, pp.159–183.

Rutilius Namatianus *De Reditu.* (trans. E. Castorina, 1967). Firenze: Sansoni Editore.

Senay, P. 1992. Le Monument Circulaire. In L. Ennabli (ed.), *Pour Sauver Carthage.* Tunis: UNESCO/INAA, pp.105–113.

Stager, L.E. 1978. Excavations at Carthage 1975. The Punic Project: first interim report. *The Annual of the American Schools of Oriental Research,* 43:151–178.

Stevens, S. T. 1993. *Bir el Knissia at Carthage: a rediscovered cemetery church. Report 1.* Ann Arbor: University of Michigan.

Stevens, S.T. 1995. Sépultures tardives intra-muros. In *Monuments funéraires. Institutions autoctones. Actes du VIe Colloque International sur l'Histoire et l'Archéologie de l'Afrique du nord (Pau 1993).* Paris: Editions du Comité des Travaux Historiques et Scientifiques, pp.207–217.

Storoni Mazzolani, L 1967. *L'idea di città nel mondo romano.* Milano & Napoli: Ricciardi edizioni.

Strabo *The Geography.* (trans. H.L. Jones, 1928). London: William Heinemann.

Styrenius, C.G. and Sander B. 1992. Byrsa: la villa aux bains. In L. Ennabli (ed.) *Pour Sauver Carthage.* Tunis: UNESCO/ INAA, pp.151–154.

Thébert, Y. 1983. L'évolution urbaine dans les Provinces orientales de l'afrique Romaine Tardive. *Opus*, 2:99–130.

Victor Vitensis Historia Persecutionis Africanae Proviniciae. In M. Petschenig, 1881. *Corpus Scriptorum Ecclesiasticorum Latinorum*, 7. Vindobonae: Geroldi Filium Bibliopolan Academiae.

Ward Perkins, B. 1996. Urban continuity? In N. Christie & T. Loseby (eds.), *Towns in transition: urban evolution in late Antiquity and early Middle Ages*. Aldershot: Scolar Press, pp.4–15.

Ward Perkins, B. 1997. Continuists, catastrophists and the towns of post-roman northern Italy. *Papers of the British School at Rome*, 65:157–167.

Wataghin Cantino, G.1996. Quadri urbani nell'Italia settentrionale fra tarda Antichità e alto Medioevo. In C. Lepelley (ed.) *La fin de la cité antique et le début de la cité Medievale*. Bari: Edipuglia/ Galliard, pp.239–279.

Wells, C. 1992. Le mur de Théodose et le Secteur nord-est de la ville Romaine. In L. Ennabli (ed.), *Pour Sauver Carthage*. Tunis: UNESCO/INAA, pp.115–123.

Wickham, C. 1981. Early Medieval Italy. Central power and local society 400–1000. London: Macmillan.

And did those Feet in Ancient Time...
Feet and shoes as a material projection of the self

by Carol van Driel-Murray

Introduction

There is something uncanny about feet, footprints and shoes. Throughout prehistory, foot vessels, foot amulets and footprints engraved on rocks (Forrer 1942; Hald 1972:17–20) attest the symbolic power of the foot and shoe. The foot is a liminal extremity, on the cusp between us and the soil from which it was so long believed that we sprang; it is no coincidence that meta-morphosis begins with the feet, and it is in their feet that mermaids, centaurs, satyrs and the Devil himself are distinguished from humankind. Feet are on the frontier and it is around fron-tiers that rituals accumulate. This paper assesses the evidence for such rituals during the Roman period.

Much of the symbolism is seemingly literal and explicit, associated with the natural function of the foot and shoe – movement, hence travel and all journeys including that to the after-world, as well as trampling or crushing, hence the connotations of domination and violence. Addition-ally, for the shoe, come ideas of protection, something not to be underestimated in pre-penicillin days when wounds caused by stones, thorns, insect and snakebites could be fatal. Even on the simplest level implicit references abound.

Shoes for walking in

The sandals and footstools of Egyptian pharaohs were decorated with the figures of their bound and prone enemies (Forrer 1942:35, Taf. 2; Reeves 1990:155); thus, symbolically, the king daily trampled the foes of Egypt, no doubt a satisfying fiction, but one which embodies the concept of the just ruler subjugating the forces of cosmic chaos and establishing peace and prosperity for the land. By the Roman period, this message was no longer exclusive and depic-tions of bound captives on the feet of mummy cases are used in the sense of defeating those supernatural enemies who might hinder the path to the after-life (Simpson 1973).

The Egyptian evidence is explicit, but elsewhere we may also suspect that shoes in tombs carry the metaphor of the spiritual journey in addition to the simple and literal need to well-shod for a particularly difficult passage. Hobnails in Roman cremations and later, in burials, may have less to do with the clothing of the living than with the spiritual preparedness of the dead. This may well lie behind reported instances of adult shoes being provided in children's burials (Philpott 1991:172–3) [1].

Though usually only the presence of hobnails will be registered in cremation burials, the in-humations of the third and fourth centuries AD reveal considerable variation in the arrangement of shoes within the grave. Most commonly, the shoes were worn on the feet (e.g. Crummy 1983:51–3; Pirling 1997:grave 4349; Philpott 1991:168): here indeed, the body was dressed as for life, quite apart from any ritual significance attached to individual items of clothing. In other cases, a pair of shoes was neatly set out in readiness (Crummy 1983:fig. 56, no. G277; Pirling 1979:grave 2461). These bodies were presumably shrouded, and the symbolic nature of the footwear is more obvious. Very occasionally, the shoes are placed on either side of the body, usually with the toe pointing up towards the head (Laur-Belart 1952:Abb. 28). That the position of the footwear is not random is indicated by a coffined, prone burial at Kaiseraugst (Switzer-land) where the toe points *down* (Cat. Brugg 1997:23, Abb. 17). The ritual is structured, for body and gifts are all inverted. In this particular case, the care shown in burial and the provision

of shoes tell against a negative interpretation of the prone rite, and is rather a significant difference that needed to be marked in a special and consistent way. Structured minority rites such as
these are indicative of highly individual needs of expression, with fluid symbolism that can be
adapted by the participants to particular circumstances. Shoes are appropriate to widely differing situations and Laur-Belart (1952:99) records a touching recent superstition that focuses attention on the analytical depth required to elucidate individual rituals. In the region of Basle,
women who died in childbirth were buried with a pair of shoes specifically so that they could
return to care for the surviving baby. To recognise such a tradition in the archaeological record
would be difficult, but it reminds us that, in the case of Roman shod burials, we do not actually
know the *direction* the journey was intended to take – and we merely assume it was *to* the other
world because this accords with our modern perceptions.

The humble hobnail
    Thus in burials, attention needs to be paid to the position of the hobnails and, as will become
clear below, also to the patterns in which they lie. The proportions of burials with or without
hobnails is not so relevant, because many of the Roman shoe styles, particularly in the later period, were not nailed anyway and thus leave no trace, a fact not sufficiently appreciated by
Clark (1975) in his discussion of Winchester evidence (van Driel-Murray 1987), though recognised by Philpott (1991:171). Nevertheless, it is regrettable that so few cemetery reports (or any
others for that matter) treat hobnails with any respect, for these will, in the absence of organic
survivals, form the only evidence for the role of footwear in burial ritual and, if the pattern of
the nails can be distinguished, may even provide useful independent dating evidence.
    Outside burial contexts, hobnailed shoes are themselves carriers of additional messages in-
tended for the living [2]. The nailing patterns used on Roman shoes are remarkably consistent
over the entire Roman empire – not just in general terms, but in quite complex patterns, many of
which have only a short period of popularity (van Driel-Murray 1995; for decorative examples,
see Göpfrich 1986:Abb. 47–8). In this way, the nailing is a 'fashion accessory' in the same way
as the shoe itself and it is a highly visible one at that, for a person would have been instantly
identifiable by a track of distinctive footprints. The very fact that the patterns have such general
currency indicates that the iconography was widely understood, though what it was and why it
should be subject to such marked and rapid change requires further investigation. Swastikas,
circles and tridents may be general good luck symbols ('God-speed' Figure 1g, h), but it is difficult to discover significance in the lozenges of the late second century AD (Figure 1e), the S's
of the late second/early third, or the asymmetrical S of the period after *c.* AD 225 (Figure 1c, d).
With the appearance of arrangements of nails in groups of three in the late third and fourth
century (Figure 1f), it is clearly inadequate to dismiss these solely as 'decorative patterns'.
Something in the nature of protection is certainly indicated, and it is perhaps significant that this
need for protection was felt more strongly from the late second century onwards. Any piece of
personal material culture accumulates symbolic and emblematic meanings. If certain fibulae
functioned as badges or emblems, designs in some cases, such as swastikas, S's, lozenges, were
shared by the shoe nails. The exact meaning of symbols on footwear will remain elusive on account of the ambivalent nature of shoes: on the one hand positive (protective) on the other
negative (unclean, through the association with street dirt and oppressive). We can never know
what led to the individual choice, but can perhaps tend towards the positive and protective on
the basis of contextual evidence. A pair of sandals nailed with Neptune's trident was found
stowed away on a ship which sank with its full load of grain at Woerden (NL): the owner presumably hoped for better divine protection than they actually received (van Driel-Murray 1996,
fig. 11), but through his/her footprints, he/she would have been visibly under the protection of,
or committed to, the god as he/she walked the dusty streets.

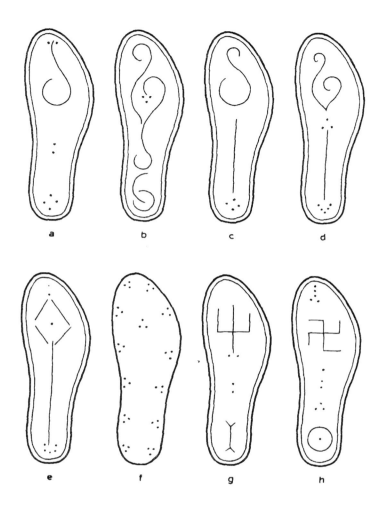

Figure 1 Diagram of third and fourth century AD nailing patterns from various sites. Not to scale.

Whatever their meaning, the belief that a person can be harmed by damaging their footprint, common throughout post-Medieval Europe, was not apparently shared by the Romans; indeed, they appear to have been proud to be identified as individuals by their footprints. In fact, the complex nailing could be regarded as a highly visible form of self-advertisement and the designs as widely recognised trade symbols. The function of the footprint as signature is implicit in the pottery lamps in the shape of a foot with the maker's name (frequently *Vitalis)*, picked out in retrograde by hobnails underneath (Fremersdorf 1926:46) or the *planta pedis* tile and samian stamps (Brunsting & Steures 1995:fig. 4). That hobnails did indeed carry legible messages is confirmed by the fulminations of Clement of Alexandria (*c.* AD 200), a misogynist moralist, who decried wicked women enticing young men to vice by the messages left by their hobnails in the sand (*Paedogogus* 11.11). If the nailing on a terracotta lamp in the Louvre is to be believed, these messages were of staggering simplicity and directness – 'Follow Me' in Greek (Heuzey 1877:94).

Cosmic forces?

For the Greeks and Romans contact with the soil was a source of strength, of inspiration for the barefooted priests of Dodona and, in certain rituals, feet were held to mediate between the individual and the earth. Students of foot symbolism wax lyrical about 'cosmic forces', and certain processions, like the Roman *nudipedalia* are claimed as evidence that barefoot contact with the soil was able to restore cosmic harmony in times of stress (Verhoeven 1957:55, 64–5, 83). Again, by extension of a natural function, the foot is seen to mediate between the individual, earth and heaven. I admit to being sceptical with regard to cosmological interpretations, but an accumulation of evidence drawn from my recent work with late Roman complexes of leatherwork compels my reconsideration.

Certain lightly impressed markings on sandal soles, predominantly third century AD types, occur too frequently and at too many different sites for them to be merely random doodles (Figure 2). Some of the markings are echoed in nailing patterns (e.g. the branch Figure 2e, arrows Figures 1d; 2h; and the 'squiggle', Figure 2j) and must, like them reflect shared perceptions. Moreover, certain signs, look suspiciously like the planetary symbols, Jupiter in particular (Figures 2a, 3; Gundel 1950:cols. 2034–5). Such specific signs shed a rather different light on the more common designs such as the dot-circle of both stamps and nail patterns (Figure 1h) and the cosmic significance of swastika, circle and S-patterns – all of which are common on footwear – is widely accepted, even if the reasons are not understood (Green 1986:45). Occasionally, astrological symbols of the heavens seem to be combined with the chthonic imagery of pits (Figure 2c, d?), branches (Figure 2e) and water (Figure 1g; 2b, g), perhaps signifying the intermediary role of the foot and shoe between heaven and earth. It must be stressed, however, that such symbols are relatively infrequent within the complexes concerned, although, with limited variations (e.g. Figure 2b, c, d, g), they do occur repeatedly.

The arrows of Figures 1d and 2h may signify Mercury and the design of Figure 2i may reflect the zodiac symbol of Pisces, the traditional protector of feet, but the absence of, perhaps more obvious, symbols such as Venus and Mars should introduce an element of caution. Nevertheless, such features are not accidental, nor simple decoration used in ignorance of meaning.

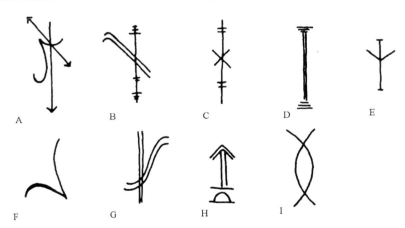

Figure 2 Selected designs impressed on third & fourth century soles. Not to scale. a. London, Aardenburg; b. London; c. Birdoswald (Mould 1997:fig 239, no. 16), Köln (Fremersdorf 1926:Abb.8), London (MacConnoran 1986:223, no. 8.23), Trier; d. Dalton Parlours (Mould 1990:fig. 143), Mainz (Göpfrich 1986:Abb. 39, no. 51); e. Dalton Parlours (Mould 1990:fig. 143), Vindolanda, Valkenburg; f. Köln (Fremersdorf 1926:Abb.8); g. Birdoswald (Mould 1997:fig 240, no. 19), Trier; h. Saalburg (Busch 1965:Taf 25 no. 393); i. Valkenburg, London, Mainz (Göpfrich 1986:Abb. 38, no. 34); j. Köln (Fremersdorf 1926:Abb. 8), Valkenburg.

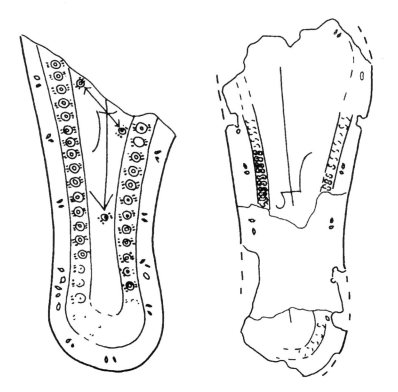

Figure 3 Slipper insoles from London (Dowgate) and Aardenburg (NL) with impressed and stamped designs (scale 1:2).

Shoes and sacrifice

Already in the late Neolithic, isolated shoes form part of the ritual complexes in and around the bogs of north-west Europe (van der Sanden 1990:224). They are usually found singly, but occasionally pairs are deposited and sometimes, more macabrely, the shoe is still on an amputated foot or leg (Marschalleck 1957:264–6). Clearly, there is no single explanation for deposits of this nature, but shoes evidently belong to a scale of offerings ranging from humans and weapons at one end, to foodstuffs and plaits of hair at the other (van der Sanden 1990:216–25). Unfortunately, shrinkage makes it impossible to size the shoes, so we cannot tell whether they belonged to men or women, though all do seem to be adult. To judge from the well-researched finds from Drenthe (NL) the practice of depositing shoes in bogs continued well into the middle ages (Groenman-van Waateringe 1970).

Shoes are deeply personal: they preserve the imprint of the soul, while footprints give clear, unequivocal proof of the actual presence of a living person – and thus function as a signature. In Roman Egypt pilgrims carved feet in the rock to register their presence and the prayers said on that spot for perpetuity (Wilson 1996: 113). Similarly, the footprints of gods or heroes were – and are – objects of intense devotion as evidence of divine presence. The gods can be traced on earth by their footprints, the only physical evidence for their passing. Dunbabin (1990) examines both aspects of this manifestation – the footprint as symbol of both god and supplicant – stressing that it is the context which imparts the meaning and showing how widespread this phenomenon is in the Mediterranean region. Representations of footprints seem to have been particularly significant in Egypt, and through the cult of Isis spread to the Western Empire

(Czysz 1995:280–1, Abb. 69), but the occurrence of footwear in ritual contexts such as springs (e.g. Coventina's Well, Allason Jones & Mckay 1985:37) or in wells associated with temples (e.g. Matagne-la-Petite, De Boe 1982: fig. 19 and, indeed the Cambridge shrine, cf. note 1) may be analogous records of presence and supplication.

In similar locations, coins and fibulae can be regarded as ex-voto offerings of thanks, within the standard ritual of the vow (Derks 1995) except that these, like animal sacrifice and altars, are gifts of intrinsic value, which is more than can be said of the average worn-out shoe. Yet the shoes are equally part of the ritual complex. The salient characteristics of footwear suggest that the deposition of shoes takes place at the beginning of a sequence of actions (*votum*), which is closed by the donation of the ex-voto (the *solutio*). As bearer of the individual's imprint, the shoe functions as a signature – a spiritual graffito, like the Egyptian pilgrim feet or the *planta pedis* tile stamps (Brunsting & Steures 1995:fig. 4). That shoes form a pair invites their use in contractual situations, primarily as a pledge of mutual obligations. The concept of signature, shoes and contract are neatly combined in a Samnite votive plaque from the temple at Pietrab-bondante where a vow is stated to be signed by both name and shoe prints (Poccetti 1979:42–3)[3]. Such pledges could have been deposited at any time during the life of a well and some of the rather exceptional shoes from the Saalburg (Busch 1965:nos. 220, 221) may be evidence of this practice.

From the Neolithic onwards, a preference for the left shoe can be discerned in shoes depos-ited in watery contexts [4]. This may represent no more than a statistically unsound group, but stands in sharp contrast to the foot models, lamps and votives which if not in pairs, are invaria-bly right. Here it would seem that the pair of shoes is being used in a contractual sense: one shoe (the left) being offered as a pledge to the deities while the other (the right) was retained by the supplicant. Symbolic of the contractual vow, the shoe becomes imbued with supernatural power and thereby becomes the earthly manifestation of divine protection. The promissory contract may concern an individual, and Forrer's (1942:219) record of a North German super-stition that as long as a child's first shoe was kept, the child would come to no harm, is an inter-esting example of the sort of guise in which footwear may be preserved above ground. More general protection for the homestead might also be requested and I would suggest that we should be looking for shoes (hobnails) under thresholds and in hearth constructions.

Foundation deposits and pars pro toto

These are the liminal locations within the house which require the protection offered by foundation deposits which may range from pits with now unidentifiable, presumably organic, contents (e.g. food, flowers, shoes), complete vessels (including food and drink), tools, weap-ons, animal and human sacrifices (Merrifield 1987:50–8). Once the meaning has been lost, the practice degenerates into superstition continued by force of habit, with the shoes a particularly tenacious element. Hearth and threshold are the favoured locations for the so-called 'concealed shoes' which turn up in surprisingly large numbers in more recent masonry structures (Merri-field 1987:129–34; Pitt 1998) and where the frequent association with chickens and cats – sometimes walled up alive – reinforces the connection with actual sacrifice.

In its symbolic role as signature, marker of actual physical presence and carrier of the im-print of the owner's personality, footwear readily assumes the guise of *pars pro toto*, function-ing as a substitute for that individual. Thus in certain contexts the shoe becomes a substitute or alternative for the human sacrifice which might, under different circumstances, have been of-fered there. In his discussion of recent 'concealed shoes', Merrifield (1987:134) with charac-teristic insight, already hinted at the possibility of interchangability as long ago as 1987 and patterns of depositions can be discerned in wells and shafts, which confirm the role of footwear in rituals of commencement and termination, situations in which human sacrifice is a prominent feature even in the Roman period.

Although the practice was condemned by Roman authorities some memory must have been retained, for the conclusion that human sacrifice re-emerges particularly strongly in Britain in the third and fourth centuries is inescapable. There are too many Romans tumbling down wells, too many strange and unnatural items amongst the contents of wells and pits for 'accident' to have any credible meaning (see most conveniently, Isserlin 1997; Merrifield 1987:40–8). Even some of the bog bodies belong to this period (e.g. Amcotts, dated by its shoes to the late third/fourth century AD (Turner & Rhodes 1992) and, given the choice in radiocarbon dates, possibly the Lindow man as well (Housley *et al.* 1995:4))[5]. Yet, whatever the contents in the way of children, horse skulls, dogs, owls, coins and complete vessels, most wells and pits are ultimately blocked with broken and incomplete material which we would still tend to regard as 'rubbish' (Clarke & Jones 1994) [6].

Until recently, I had always assumed that unlike the special contents, shoes in wells, pits and ditches were just part of the final fill of domestic refuse. However, since footwear can now be dated independently, it can be seen that the shoes themselves form part of the same ritual activity as the more obvious ritual items (van Driel-Murray 1987; 1995 and forthcoming). The intrinsic dates of the shoe, sole shape and nailing patterns reveal the various moments in time when shoes might serve a cultic purpose, quite separate from any refuse incorporated in the final fill. Votive or 'contract' shoes may be tossed in at any time to accompany a request or promise, but on the bottom of many wells lie shoes which can be dated rather earlier, to the period of construction, and which can be regarded as foundation offerings. Linking humans to the soil, shoes are particularly appropriate offerings to chthonic forces, especially in the case of commencement rituals for sources of water where a living sacrifice would be literally polluting.

A shoe sole was tucked at the back of the wooden construction of a well at Venray (Netherlands), while the fine (left!) child's sandal sole on the bottom of the well at Dalton Parlours can be dated to the mid/late third century AD, seventy to a hundred years before the well ceased to be used (Mould 1990:235, fig. 3) – it should also be noted that the shoe is unnailed and would have gone undetected in any other environment. What made these shoes special or appropriate to the supplicants is more difficult to assess: is it the nailing pattern which imparts a particular significance to the sole from Venray (pattern as Figure 1c), or are the shoes associated with particular individuals or events? These examples happened to be recognised and passed to competent finds specialists but there is clearly a need for greater awareness of the phenomenon during the excavation of wells, with proper recording of the location, depth and orientation of soles. Tantalising, but largely unrecorded, is the instance of structured deposition of numerous soles in the erroneously termed 'tannery' pit at Lullingstone villa (Meates 1979:107, Pl.22d); there must be many similar cases.

Conclusions

Shoes evidently form part of a ritual complex that, from the late Neolithic until at least the end of the Roman period, is associated with watery places as well as the foundations of buildings. Do all shoes therefore indicate 'ritual'? Of all items of dress, the most frequently discarded seems to be the shoe, as a glance at any modern beach or lay-by will make clear. It is hardly credible that some 3000 shoes from the disused ditches at Vindolanda, or the hundreds from the London quayside, were deposited with ritual intent. In the Roman period, shoes were rarely repaired and easily discarded, so the majority of shoes will indeed be refuse. On the other hand, shoes never look new or serviceable after 2000 years in the soil, so suspicions of ritual deposition are less easily aroused or substantiated, than would be the case with, for example metalwork. A complicating factor in the distinction between rubbish and ritual is that, as has been noted with more recent concealed shoes, *age* is of the essence. Something of the soul survives in the foot imprint and if the shoe is to function as a substitute, the imprint of the individual must be unambiguous. So almost *by definition* a shoe used ritually will be old and worn.

It will, therefore, be difficult to distinguish footwear used in a cultic sense from the mass of discarded refuse, except where reoccurring associations indicate regular patterning. The symbolism surrounding feet and shoes is present in latent form from prehistory, but seems to gather intensity in the later Roman period, with many layers of meaning being expressed in more or less public form via this medium. The repetition of symbols in both nailing patterns and the designs drawn on sandal soles point to deeper personal concerns than mere fashionable decoration, concerns which extended to the grave, where systematic variations in the placing of footwear reveal the metaphorical concepts behind what may seem to be simply corpses buried in their everyday clothing. The occurrence of footwear in sacrificial contexts – together with its inherent individuality – suggests shoes may serve both as a signature and a substitute. In bogs, wells or concealed behind chimney-breasts, shoes are a possible substitute for human sacrifice and thus allow the memory of the practice to be maintained during periods of political or religious unacceptability. And it is therefore perhaps, this ritual use of footwear that provides the link between Iron Age traditions of sacrifice and its apparent re-emergence in the later Roman period.

Instituut voor Pre- en Protohistorische Archelogie, University of Amsterdam

Endnotes

[1] I have not been able to confirm this independently, and the oft cited examples from the Cambridge shrine (*Current Archaeology* 1978 (61): 58–9) come from ritual shafts, not burials.

[2] Most of the examples of footwear are taken from my ongoing unpublished research on leather complexes from the Netherlands, the Museum of London collections and Vindolanda and no further references are given for such material.

[3] I am grateful to Rob Witcher for bringing this plaque to my notice.

[4] For example, Coventina's Well, three left, one right; Matagne-la-Petite all three soles left; nine of the twelve isolated bog finds in the Netherlands and Northern Germany.

[5] The almost desperate attempts to arrive at a pre-Roman date reveal how conceptually problematic human sacrifice is when dealing with the Roman period, even in 'hard' science.

[6] Characteristically, it is Merrifield (1987:44) who points out how frequently this material, often constructional debris, coincides with major alterations to structures and changes in function and/or ownership – thus again termination or commencement.

Bibliography

Allason-Jones, L. & B. Makay, 1985. *Coventina's Well: a shrine on Hadrian's Wall*. Oxford: Oxbow.

Boe, G. de, 1982. *Le sanctuaire Gallo-Romain dans la plaine de Bieure à Matagne-la-Petite*. Brussels: Archaeologia Belgica 251.

Brunsting, H. & D.C. Steures, 1995. De baksteenstempels van Romeins Nijmegen 1. *Oudheidkundige Mededelingen uit het Rijksmuseum van Oudheden te Leiden*, 75:85–117.

Busch, A.L. 1965. Die römerzeitlichen Schuh- und Lederfunde der Kastelle Saalburg, Zugmantel und Kleiner Feldberg. *Saalburg-Jahrbuch*, 22:158–210.

Cat. Brugg 1997. *Grenzen-Grenzenlos (100 Jahre Gesellschaft Pro Vindonissa/50 Jahre Kantonsarchäologie Aargau)*. Brugg: Aargauische Kantonsarchäologie.

Clarke, G.N. 1975. Popular movements and late Roman cemeteries. *World Archaeology*, 7:46–56.

Clarke, S. & R. Jones, 1994. The Newstead pits. In C. van Driel-Murray (ed.) *Military equipment in context (Journal of Roman Military Equipment Studies*, 5). Oxford: Oxbow, pp.109–124.

Crummy, N. 1983. *The Roman small finds from excavations in Colchester 1971–9*. Colchester: Colchester Archaeological Report 2.

Czysz, W. *et al.* 1995. *Die Römer in Bayern*. Stuttgart: Konrad Theiss Verlag.

Derks, T. 1995. The ritual of the vow in Gallo-Roman religion. In J. Metzler, M. Millett, N. Roymans & J. Slofstra (eds.) *Integration in the early Roman West*. Luxembourg: Musée National, pp.111– 127.

Driel-Murray, C. van, 1987. Roman footwear: a mirror of fashion and society. In D.E. Friendship-Taylor, J.M. Swann & S. Thomas (eds.) *Recent research in archaeological footwear.* Association of Archaeological Illustrators & Surveyors Technical Paper 8, pp.32–42.

Driel-Murray, C. van, 1995. Nailing Roman shoes. *Archaeological Leather Group Newsletter,* 1:6–7.

Driel-Murray, C. van, 1996. Die Schuhe aus Schiff I und ein lederner Schildüberzug. *Jahrbuch des Römische-Germanischen Zentralmuseums Mainz,* 43:493–498.

Driel-Murray, C. van, forthcoming. The leather trades in Roman Yorkshire. In J. Price & P. Wilson (eds.) *Crafts and industries in Roman Yorkshire.* Yorkshire Archaeological Society Monograph.

Dunbabin, K.M.D. 1990. *Ipsa deae vestigia...* Footprints divine and human on Graeco-Roman monuments. *Journal of Roman Archaeology,* 3:85–109.

Forrer, R. 1942. *Archäologisches zur Geschichte des Schuhes aller Zeiten.* Schönenwerd: Bally-Schuhmuseum.

Fremersdorf, F. 1926. Ein Fund römischer Ledersachen in Köln. *Germania,* 10:44–56.

Göpfrich, J. 1986. Römische Lederfunde aus Mainz. *Saalburg-Jahrbuch* 42:5–67.

Green, M. 1986. *The gods of the Celts.* Gloucester: Sutton.

Groenman-van Waateringe, W. 1970. Pre- en (proto)historisch schoeisel uit Drenthe. *Nieuwe Drentse Volksalmanak,* 88:241–262.

Gundel, W. 1950. Planeten. *Paulys Realencyclopädie der classischen Alertumswissenschaft* Stuttgart: Metzler, cols.2017–2185.

Hald, M. 1972. *Primitive shoes.* Copenhagen: National Museum of Denmark.

Heuzey, M.L. 1877. Une chaussure antique à inscription grecque. *Mémoires de la Sociéte National des Antiquaires de France.* 4ème série, 8:85–97.

Housley, R.A., Walker, A.J., Otlet, R.L. & R.E.M. Hedges 1995. Radiocarbon dating of the Lindow 3 bog body. In R.C. Turner & R.G. Scaife (eds.) *Bog bodies. New discoveries and new perspectives.* London: British Museum Press, pp.39–46.

Isserlin, R.M.J. 1997. Thinking the unthinkable: human sacrifice in Roman Britain. In K. Meadows, C. Lemke & J. Heron (eds.) *Proceedings of the sixth annual Theoretical Roman Archaeology Conference.* Oxford: Oxbow, p.91–100.

Laur-Belart, R. 1952. Kaiseraugst. *Jahrbuch Schweizerischen Gesellschaft für Urgeschichte,* 42:97–99.

MacConnoran, P. 1986. Footwear. In L. Millar, Schofield J. & Rhodes M. (eds.) *The Roman quay at St. Magnus House, London.* London: London & Middlesex Archaeological Society, Special Paper 8, pp.218–227.

Marschalleck, K.H. 1957. Zwei Opferfunde aus ostfriesischen Mooren. *Die Kunde* NF. 8:249–273.

Meates, G.W. 1979. *The Roman villa at Lullingstone, Kent.* Chichester: Kent Archaeological Society Monograph 1.

Merrifield, R. 1987 *The archaeology of ritual and magic.* London: Batsford.

Mould, Q. 1990. The leather objects. In S. Wrathmell & A. Nicholson (eds.) *Dalton Parlours. Iron Age settlement and Roman villa.* York: Yorkshire Archaeology 3, pp.231–235.

Mould, Q. 1997. Leather. In T. Wilmott (ed.) *Birdoswald: excavation of a Roman fort on Hadrian's Wall and its successor settlements, 1997.* London: English Heritage, pp.326–341.

Philpott, R. 1991. *Burial practices in Roman Britain. A survey of grave treatment and furnishing AD 43–410.* British Series 219. Oxford: BAR.

Pirling, R. 1979. *Das römisch-fränkische Gräberfeld von Krefeld-Gellep 1964–1965.* Germanische Denkmäler der Volkerwanderungszeit 10. Berlin: Mann.

Pirling, R. 1997. *Das römisch-fränkische Gräberfeld von Krefeld-Gellep 1975–1982.* Germanische Denkmäler der Volkerwanderungszeit 17. Stuttgart: Steiner Verlag.

Pitt, F. 1998. Builders, bakers and madhouses: some recent information from the Concealed Shoe Index. *Archaeological Leather Group Newsletter,* 7:3–6.

Poccetti, P. 1979. *Nuovi documenti italici: a complemento del Manuale di E. Vetter.* Pisa: Giardini.

Reeves, N. 1990. *The complete Tutankhamon.* New York: Thames & Hudson.

Sanden, W.A.B. van der (ed.) 1990. *Mens en Moeras: Veenlijken in Nederland van de Bronstijd tot en met de Romeinse Tijd.* Assen: Drents Museum.

Simpson, W.K. 1973. Ptolomaic-Roman Cartonnage footcases with prisoners bound and tied. *Zeitschrift für Ägyptische Sprache und Altertumskunde,* 100:50–54.

Turner, R.C. & M. Rhodes 1992. A bog body and its shoes from Amcotts, Lincolnshire. *Antiquaries Journal,* 72:76–90.

Verhoeven, C.W.M. 1957. *Symboliek van de Voet*. Assen: van Gorkum.

Wilson, P. 1996. Foot outlines and inscriptions. In P. Rose *Qasr Ibrim: the hinterland survey*. London: Egypt Exploration Society, pp.102–117.

Soranus and the Pompeii Speculum: the sociology of gynaecology and Roman perceptions of the female body

by Patricia Baker

Introduction

The speculum is a fascinating Roman surgical artefact because its precision design shows an acute awareness of the anatomy of the female body (Figure 1a). The priapiscus of the Roman specula is rounded, not pointed, so as not to rub or cut the cervix. Archigenes of Apamea, as recorded in Paul of Aegina (6.73), explains its use and states that before the instrument was placed in the vagina, the woman was measured to ensure the priapiscus was not too long, if it was, then compresses where placed on the labia to shorten the priapiscus thereby protecting the cervix from injury. The design of the instrument, and the proposed care taken in its use, is an indication that the female body was a respected concern in a medical context, suggesting the possibility that the Roman female was more highly regarded than often represented both in general works and in more detailed studies of Roman women, where the female is implicitly described as subordinate (e.g. Allason-Jones 1989). Here a focus on the philosophy and practice of Roman medicine will be employed to illustrate that these implicit assumptions are not always as unproblematic as often portrayed. The speculum only provides one indication of how Roman doctors perceived the body. To gain a more precise idea about the opinions held in medical thinking it is necessary to examine other aspects of Roman medicine such as medical literature, archaeological and epigraphic remains, and religion. The questions asked of these concern how the medical perspective influenced wider perceptions of the female body, and conversely how the popular understandings influenced the medical comprehension of the woman's body. It will be seen that the social constructs of the body for both men and woman are never clearly defined as there are many contradictions in the juxtaposition of the body and society (Turner 1996).

Anthropological studies of many different cultures – Native American Indians, South Pacific Islanders and African societies to name just a few – demonstrate that attitudes towards the natural functions of the female, such as menstruation, pregnancy and menopause, often reflect specific beliefs held towards females and influence the role and status which women hold in their societies (Moore 1988:16–7). This also applies to Greek and Roman women. Although this paper concentrates on the latter, the gynaecological literature of the Greeks must be considered for it creates a context, illustrating how medical ideas developed. Furthermore, the differences in medical texts dating from roughly the same periods are used to demonstrate the complexity of attitudes towards the female body in a single area of thought.

The Greek perception

Ideas are given about how the female body functioned in the medical texts of the *Hippocratic Corpus* (a collection of medical compositions from the late fifth century BC) and some of Aristotle's works. A lack of space prevents the detailed discussion this area deserves, but a few points will be drawn from this literature to show some of the ideas about the Greek female body and how these reflect general attitudes of the female's position in society. Generally, Greek women were identified with the *oikos* or home, while men were associated with the *polis* or city (Dean-Jones 1991:112), though there were exceptions, for example, Aspacia, the political confidant of Pericles. Yet for the majority of women in Greek society the structural dichotomy of her place in the private sphere against the public sphere of the male held many implications about the attitudes sustained towards the female role in society that were projected onto the medical conception of the Greek female body.

In some Greek medical philosophy the female body is assumed to have been something 'other' than that of the male body. It is stated by the author of the treatise *On Disease* in the *Hippocratic Corpus* that in specific cases a man differs from a woman in greater ease or difficulty when recovering from a disease (*Acut.* 1.22.6; 182, 22–184. 2L in Longrigg 1998:191). According to the author of *Airs, Waters and Places*, the contraction of disease is dependent upon environmental factors causing men and women's bodies to react differently (Hp. *Aër.* 3–4, 2 14, 21–22 9L in Longrigg 1998:191). Another instance of this distinction in the *Corpus* is quoted by the writer of *Diseases of Women*; if a woman was treated for the same disease with the same treatment as a man, the author considers the effects to have been potentially disastrous (Hp. *Mul.* 1.62,8 126, 14–19L in Longrigg 1998:192). This gendered differentiation of diseases is also found in mythological sources; according to Hesiod, when a plague was cast on a city: men died, but women became barren (*Op. Works and Days* 1.13). These earlier ideas may have carried over into later society and medical writings.

Childbirth reinforced the Greek woman's association with the home – one of her main duties was to bear children. Some descriptions of her anatomy describe her as a receptacle for holding children, for example, Aristotle's description of female body as a jar or pot to hold children (*GA.* 747a.4–23). The Hippocratic writer of the *Nature of Women* (3.7.314, 14–21L in Longrigg 1998:196) regarded the female body as a hollow tube that was connected by two orifices. In a discussion of the problem of the womb moving too close to the liver, the writer suggests attracting it back to its original place by pouring sweet smelling wines in the *os* or *uteri* while applying evil smelling ointments to the nostrils. This is supported by the author of *Diseases of Women*; here the fertility of a woman was tested by placing a clove of garlic in the womb – if the woman could taste the garlic in her mouth the following day she was able to conceive; if she could not, she was sterile (Hp. *Mul.* 3.214; 8.416, 3–5L in Longrigg 1998:197).

Menstruation is another female function that helped to define the separation of men and women in Greek society (Dean-Jones 1994:225). Menstrual blood was considered by some writers to determine the general health of the female, thereby enhancing her separation from men because men obviously cannot suffer from affects of menstruation. One differentiation in the cause of female illness was an excess of blood in the body due to amenorrhea. The Hippocratic writer of the *Diseases of Women* believed the blood would travel around the body making the woman ill; therefore, menstruation was a means of maintaining a healthy body and a catharsis for disease (*Mul* 1.1.8.12, 6–21L in Longrigg 1998:192). In spite of the conceptualized separation of men and women created by the ideas about the cause of disease, no health prevention appears to have existed to encourage men to avoid sexual contact during a woman's period. In fact, copulation was positively encouraged by some of the Hippocratic writers, and by Aristotle, because they believed menstruation was the best time for conception (Hp. *Mul.* 1.17 8.56.15–17; Hp. *Nat.Mul.* 8.7.324.5–7; Arist. *GA.* 727b.19–26). This implies that women were not ostracised or considered unclean during their cycle, such as amongst the Kaulong of New Britain who believe menstruating women must not touch anything that might come into male contact, because this will lend to the pollution of the male; in general, pollution spreads out from their bodies (Moore 1988:16–7). Similarly, south-eastern American Indian tribes sent women away from their villages during menstruation to stay in special dwellings so they could not pollute the area (Galloway 1998:199). Nothing so severe is suggested for Greek women. Perhaps her separation from the *polis* was symbolic of menstrual seclusion, just as some African cultures, in this case the Masakin Qisar of Sudan, do not physically separate themselves from women, in spite of their beliefs of menstrual taboos, but do so with painted symbols representing male virility (Hodder 1982:159).

Menstruation is only mentioned in medical texts and seems to have been excluded from general Greek literature. Dean-Jones (1994:226–32) suggests the reason for this is that menstruation was not experienced by men and, therefore, ignored in conversation. She alludes to Aristophanes, who poked fun at all natural bodily functions, including female genitalia, but not menstruation. Perhaps it is, as Dean-Jones claims, simply a matter in which men were unfamiliar. However, Aristophanes does refer to the female genitalia; and general male familiarity with the vagina during sexual intercourse would have made men aware of the menses. It is possible menstruation was not mentioned because it was merely not an agreeable topic of conversation. Pliny, writing five hundred years later, apologises for mentioning such terrible things when he discusses uses for menstrual blood (*HN.* 28.24.87). King (1995:142) argues that in the *Hippocratic Corpus* doctors who wrote about female conditions stated that what they knew came from conversations with women, implying that menstruation was not a taboo subject of conversation, at least in a medical context. Here we come to an impasse because we only have the surviving literary sources to study, and only medical texts state any attitude about menstruation. Yet, no explanatory myth for the origin of the menses exists. This may imply that one was not created because it was not experienced by men (Dean-Jones 1994:232–4), but this requires that we then ask why women did not invent one. Had menstruation been taboo, a myth most likely would have been told to warn men of its evils.

Menstruation clearly caused changes in a female's health; Aristotle (*Insom.* 459b–460a 23) was the first, that we are aware of, to remark on how it could alter things beyond the body. He claims that if a menstruating female looked into a mirror she would dim the reflective surface with a bloody cloud; the newer the mirror, the more difficult the stain was to remove. This alteration was caused by the blood vessels in the eyes being affected by menstruation. The eyes then moved the air that touched the mirror's surface and changed its quality. Since bronze reacts with the air, the surface becomes stained; the cleaner the surface, the deeper the stain will permeate. The transformation in the mirror, suggests that the changes in the female body were capable of affecting sense perceptions and in some respects has the ability to alter the quality of things around the body. It is plausible that this statement is a representation of the non-philosophical point of view in Greek society; however, without any mention in the extant literature one is forced to hypothesise about the statement's origin; it shows an intermingling of science and folk-lore that continues to appear in classical societies.

Medical philosophy changed during the Hellenistic era when Herophilus and Erasistratus began making anatomical studies through dissection and vivisection of human bodies. Herophilus stated men and women shared the same anatomy with one crucial difference, the male has his genitalia on the outside, while the female has hers on the inside of her body (von Staden 1989:165–9, 296–9; von Staden 1991:276). The 'magical' significance of menstruation is not mentioned in the anatomical studies, indicating that such popular beliefs were not accepted, or at least written about, by these scientific writers. The Hellenistic medical literature does not differentiate the males and females as much as some of the Hippocratic writers or Aristotelian philosophy; this appears to have influenced Roman medical thought.

The Roman female in medical literature
The construction of the female body in medicine, and its popular conception, may have served to inform one another. Roman women, especially during the imperial age, were not confined to the *domus* like their Greek counterparts. Their duties went beyond child-bearing – they were responsible for raising good Roman citizens by educating their children. To teach, the Roman female would need to have participated in some aspects of the male world to be educated herself. The duties of a Roman woman are only recorded for upper class females (Cantarella 1987:178); however, letters from soldiers, to their mothers suggest the latter knew how to read, indicating a degree of education in all classes of women. Soranus also requests that midwives, thought to be slaves or plebeians, be literate so they could stay abreast of the latest

medical theories (*Gyn.* 1,1,3; Jackson 1988:88). Roman women also gained freedoms that were denied their republican predecessors. She could seek a divorce, gain custody of her children if she could prove that the father was incapable of caring for them; there is also evidence that she could practise birth control and abortion, made apparent by Augustus, who was discouraged by the low numbers of upper-class children. He revised existing laws and created new ones on chastity and adultery, encouraged marriage between the various classes and is said to have given a lecture encouraging men of equestrian rank to procreate (Suet. *Aug.* 34). Roman women entered traditional male realms and pursued educational interests. Some learned to fight and hunt, others became gladiators and others doctors; the wife of the senator Licinius Buco was lawyer (Cantarella 1987:178). Literacy may also have been widespread, since there are records of many women holding jobs in areas that required reading, and not all of them were from the upper classes.

Celsus, a first century AD medical writer, used the male body as his model when he described medical treatment in his *de Medicina*, because the female body was something in need of separate discussion, her physiology and bodily functions were not shared by men (von Staden 1991:272). Celsus described the Roman female body in a similar manner to earlier Greek perceptions, seeing it as 'weaker [and] more liable and bloodier than the male body' (von Staden 1991:272; Celsus 7,29,1). Celsus, however, was apparently aware of the anatomical studies of Herophilus, who had discovered that the uterus was attached (*contra* Hippocratic writers, Hp. *Places in Man* 47, 6.344, 3–22L in Longrigg 1998:194–5; von Staden 1989:165–9, 296–9; 1991:274). The female body of Celsus, a combination of Hellenic and Hellenistic theories, was never as healthy as a man's. The female body was described as the *susceptible imbecilli* (weaker) rather than the *sani* or sound (Celsus 1.1–2; von Staden 1991:272–3).

This contradiction of attitude in the first century AD is also apparent beyond the medical texts. Menstrual blood is only mentioned once in Greek literature as having powers that extended beyond the body (Arist. above). However, more cases relating to its powers were mentioned in Roman literature. Columella, a second century BC agricultural writer, considers menstrual blood as having negative effects, stating his belief that if a menstruating woman walked near plants they died (*RR.* 10.357–63). In Pliny – who discusses conflicting points of views about the positive and negative factors of menstrual blood – there is a noticeable change in attitude from Columella about the menses and the female. Amongst his many stories of the mysterious and awful power of menstrual discharge, he claims whirlwinds and hail storms were supposedly driven away if exposed to menstrual blood (*HN.* 28.78.86). He also warns his readers about some negative aspects as well – he alerts men not to engage in sexual intercourse if a female is menstruating when the moon and sun are in eclipse because there will be irredeemable harm; thus indicating that it was not taboo to avoid intercourse during menstruation in general. Pliny also advises pregnant woman to avoid walking over or touching menstrual blood because a smear of blood could cause a miscarriage (*HN.* 28.73.82–84). Yet simultaneously, he also considered menstrual blood to be a life-force, believing it was collected by the semen, life beginning from the combination (Plin. *HN.* 7.15.66). He also claims curative power, for example, as a lineament for gout. Further, the touch of a menstruating woman could relieve parotid tumours, superficial abscesses, boils and eye fluxes; blood was also a cure for tertians and quartans if rubbed on the soles of the patients' feet – but the cure was more efficacious if it was the blood of the woman performing the treatment. Icatides, a doctor, said that quartans could be cured in men if they engaged in sexual intercourse with a woman on the first day of her cycle. Following this discussion, Pliny apologises – 'this is all the information it would be right for me to repeat most of which also needs an apology from me as the rest is detestable and unspeakable' (*HN.* 28.24.87). Clearly Pliny presents complex attitudes towards the beneficial and harmful qualities of menstruation, presumably reflecting those of Roman society as a whole.

Dean-Jones (1994:248, n.78) argues that menstruation only becomes an issue when the female began to challenge the role of male supremacy – it was a way of retaining male dominance. This statement can be contested on the basis of examples presented as illustrative of menstrual taboos. For example, Dean-Jones cites Tacitus (*Hist.* 5.6.5) who claims people who collected bitumen off a lake in Jerusalem could not cut it with a knife, but had to do so with a cloth soaked in menstrual blood. Further on, however, Tacitus says that the story was ridiculous and advises that the way to collect bitumen was to dry it in the sun; therefore demonstrating not everyone believed in the magical powers of menstrual blood.

Tacitus' rejection of the folklore about female blood provides a clue that in the late first century AD the menses was not always regarded as a magical device, but there would always have been an intermingling of tradition and science. Soranus of Ephesus wrote his gynaecological treatise about the same time as Tacitus and Soranus too, avoids discussing the magical beliefs about the female body, as he approaches the topic from a completely rational (here I mean non-magical) point of view. The only time magic is mentioned is when he discusses the practices of other cultures. His gynaecological treatise obviously discusses conditions which were specific to females, but his work was not intended as a means of enforcing particular sets of social values on the female's place in society, but merely to describe the physiological differences. Soranus, unlike the Hippocratics, understood that men and women could suffer the same disease with the same symptoms; however, in certain instances the females' expected role in society determined the embarrassment of her suffering. This is shown in Soranus' discussion of satyriasis. He states that both men and woman could suffer from it, but that the condition is more embarrassing for females because women are forced to scratch themselves in public, which must have been a social *faux pax*. Furthermore, satyriasis caused a desire for intercourse that a female should not be seen to want (Gourevitch 1995:162; *Gyn.* 3.25). Both bodies are the same medically, but there are social laws in Roman society that do not allow a female to be perfectly equal to a male and this is displayed in the way she is permitted to treat her body in public.

In some earlier medical texts menstruation has been explained as one of the factors separating Roman women from the male domain. Soranus, however, does not demonstrate this belief. To him menstruation was necessary if a woman wished to become pregnant; however, he did feel that menstruation was not always profitable for health as it causes headache, fever, chills and dimness of vision and he concludes it is not generally useful for maintaining a woman's health (*Gyn.* 1.6.27–9). He considered amenorrhea a physical demonstration that a woman is healthy because menstruation stops when a female is doing plenty of exercise (*Gyn.* 1.6.28). Yet if she wished to have children then it was suggested that she stop exercising, allowing her body to relax and regain her menstrual cycle. Soranus does not, therefore, appear to be interested in describing the differences in men and women as a means of judging who was superior or inferior.

Galen, who wrote in the late second century AD, does not perpetuate this approach. He considers women weaker because their bodies are colder than those of men, making women less motivated. This coolness is the result of the fact that the uterus is open during menstruation, allowing air to flow into her (*On the usefulness of parts of the body* 14.3–6; 5; Kühn 4.145–50). He also claims that temperature defines the side of a womb on which a child of a particular sex will develop. The female foetus developed on the left side of the uterus and the male on the right side (*On semen* 2.5,35–8). For Galen, the female was seen to exist within a separate realm.

From the Roman medical literature, it is obvious that contradictions in perceptions of the female body existed among the medical and non-medical writers alike, and that definitions are complex. The important point is that few actually describe such functions as wholly negative, (e.g. Columella), or those that do, emphasise positive aspects as well (e.g. Pliny).

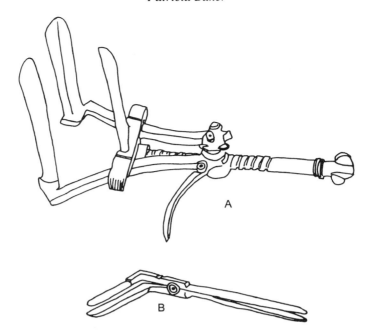

Figure 1. A) Vaginal Speculum. Based on Matthäus 1989 page 80 fig. 27b (actual size 23 cm).
B) Rectal Speculum. Based on Matthäus 1989 page 80 fig. 27a (actual size 15.5 cm)

Archaeological definitions

As illustrated above, medical writings reflect the perspective of individuals. Thus it is necessary to look beyond the literature for a fuller understanding of medical attitudes towards Roman women. Archaeologically, medical instruments demonstrate a developed understanding of female anatomy. The earliest known gynaecological instruments date to at least AD 79 – those found at Pompeii – showing that gynaecology was a developed field before Soranus wrote his treatise and presumably, long before the first century AD as well. The evidence of 'advanced' gynaecological care suggests that females were not always considered pollutants in the first century AD and the negative ideas mentioned by Pliny about menstruation cannot have been accepted by all. Nowhere is the evidence more indicative of a scientific understanding of female anatomy than in the vaginal speculum (Figure 1a). It comprises a projecting priapiscus composed of three prongs (in one case four) (Bliquez 1994:208). The prongs are prismatic on the inside and convex on the outside with a smooth surface and rounded tip. The lotus, at the opposite end of the priapiscus, is at a right angle and being operated by a worm screw situated at the back of the instrument (Muscio 2.34.94; Tert. *De anim.* 25.5 in Longfield-Jones 1986:83, n. 11). The instrument often has handles at the side (Muscio 2.34.94 in Longfield-Jones 1986:83 n 11). They were frequently forged of bronze, being easy to cast, strong, resistant to rust and also decorative (Hp. *De Medico* 2; Celsus 7.26.1; Oribas. 49.3. in Longfield-Jones 1986:84 n. 19); the worm screw was hand-made of brass.

The speculum is a rare find in the archaeological record, which is possibly surprising given the frequency with which it mentioned in medical texts (e.g. Muscio 2.33.91; Oribas *Syn.* 9.41; Gal. 19.110; Soranus *Gyn.* 2.40. in Longfield-Jones 1986:81, n.5). Only about seven are known, though they have been found around the Empire in Asia Minor, Varna, Madrid, Libya, and three from Pompeii, dating from the first to fourth centuries AD (Jackson 1988:94; Longfield-Jones 1986:81–2; Bliquez 1994:209; Künzl 1983:112). Jackson (1988:94) suggests that the rarity of the instrument may mean that it was only available to the wealthy. However, medical

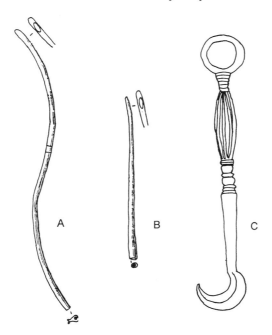

Figure 2. A) Male Catheter. Based on Milne 1907 Plate 45 fig. 1 (actual size 26.5 cm).
    B) Female Catheter. Based on Milne 1907 Plate 45 fig. 2 (actual size 20 cm)
    C) Decapitating Knife. Based on Milne 1907 Plate 50 fig. 2 (actual size 15.3 cm)

instruments have also been found at Roman fortifications, including a rectal speculum (Figure 1b) from the auxiliary fort at Vechten on the lower Rhine (Braadbart 1994:164). Rectal specula are normally used on both men and women and may have also been applied as vaginal specula for younger or smaller woman. Albucasis, who drew much of his medical information from Greek and Roman literature, mentioned the use of wooden or lacquered specula, which may also have been used by the Romans. These might have been more affordable and, therefore, widespread, but are less likely to have survived in the archaeological record than their metal counterparts (Spink & Lewis 1973:486, chapter 77).

The catheter is another instrument that demonstrates careful design for both male and female bodies (Gal. 14.787). The male instrument was longer and S-shaped (Figure 2a). The female catheter was shorter and straighter (Figure 2b) (Celsus 7.26–113; Milne 1907:144). Here it is important to note that female and male anatomy were clearly distinguished in terms of surgical implements; if not designs might not have differed.

For help in childbirth various instruments were developed specifically to keep the female alive in case of the threat of death to either the baby, mother or both. If a foetus died *in utero* during labour, the midwife or doctor was advised to use special traction hooks (steel hooks with bronze handles) that were to be inserted into an orifice of the foetus' body, generally the eyes or ears so that there would have been equal pull on both sides of the body (Sor. *Gyn.* 2.19; Celsus 7.29; Paul of Aegina 6.74). One of the more gruesome instruments to have been developed was the decapitating knife (Sor. *Gyn.* 4.19; Milne 1907:154). In case the traction hooks failed to work the decapitating knife was suggested. This curved knife with a long handle was used to separate the head of the infant from its body (Figure 2c). Two other instruments were also described in the literature being designed to crush the head of the foetus to make its removal from the uterus easier. The cranioclast was used to crush the skull, the fragments of bone being removed individually. The cephalotribe was used to again crush the skull, but without causing the bones to splinter. This was used especially in the removal of a child that was doubled on itself (Milne 1907:154–5). Forceps are thought to have been an Arab invention (Milne 1907:157). These instruments demonstrate the value placed on the life of the woman, even over that of a male child.

As artefacts were explicitly gendered they undoubtedly carried symbolic value that would have affected their use and deposition. In future, greater concern should be placed on the way that they might have been used in the negotiation of gender roles in society. There is always the possibility the Romans believed in female pollution – as mentioned, other cultures have segregated women physically or symbolically during menstruation. Modern western culture still hides the fact that women menstruate, by creating a menstrual etiquette that requires women to hide the fact of their periods, both in general, and in particular from men (Ginsburg 1996:365). Women are rarely seen to menstruate in western literature or films and when it is discussed it is usually under bizarre circumstances of young girls at menarche, such as in the *Exorcist,* where the onset of menstruation is clearly not treated as something normal (Galloway 1998:203). This western discrimination carries over into the archaeological record and menstruation and women's health are often disregarded or assumed to have been disregarded by the societies under study. In the literature it is clear that menstruation during the Roman era was not ignored and there is little in imperial literature that suggests it was considered polluting. Little is understood about how Roman women protected their clothing from blood stains, probably because we assume that things were hidden, so we do not look, as is also the case with the lack of 'menstrual huts' in the archaeological record. We are aware of their existence through historical sources, but such buildings have never been identified in the archaeological record as Galloway (1998:205) points out, because menstruation is hidden today it is expected to have been ignored in the past as well – this has implications for what is looked for in the archaeological record, including that of the Roman era. This is supported by the context in which the instruments were found. The specula from Pompeii and from Spain were found with sets of surgical instruments that consisted of scalpels, probes and other common instruments. This does not suggest that instruments concerned with female genitalia were considered polluting and kept separate from those used in the treatment of men (Bliquez 1995; Longfield-Jones 1986). Furthermore, the dual use of rectal specula emphasises the lack of concern for symbolic pollution. It is therefore, quite possible that the Romans did not hide menstruation as common today, especially since Pliny mentions the occurrence of drops of blood on the ground when he warns pregnant women not to come into contact with it.

Epigraphic and mythological evidence

Epigraphic evidence points to another aspect of attitudes towards women and medicine – their role as doctors. Women are mentioned as *medica* instead of *obstetrix* on fifteen known inscriptions from the first to third centuries AD, with one exception dating to *c.*350 BC. Five are from Asia Minor (Pleket 1969:10, 27–8, 32, 38–9). One was honoured with a statue by her city, Tlos in Lycia (Pleket 1969:27–8). Six inscriptions have been found at Rome (*CIL* 6, 6851, 8711, 8926, 9614, 9614 & 9616), one from Auximum in Italy (*CIL* 9, 5861) and three from other areas of the empire: Carthage (*CIL* 8, 24679) Lugdunum (*CIL* 13, 2019) and Belgica (*CIL* 13, 4334). The inscriptions show that women in all areas of the empire were permitted to learn the skills of a doctor rather than those of a midwife. Since females could become doctors it is implied that they could care for men – male doctors were allowed to help midwives in cases of difficult labour. In general, there is no evidence for the prohibition of women in medical practice.

Medically, there was an attitude that the female body in the Roman world was comparatively equal to that of the man, and this attitude was most apparently carried over into general society. This is perhaps seen in religious practices as well. In Greek religious sanctuaries, there do not seem to have been any prohibitions excluding woman from entering while they were menstruating; however giving birth was not permitted as the blood from childbirth was a pollutant. This has implications that there were differences in the attitudes about the two types of blood, though references are limited. However, some sanctuaries forbade women to enter at all times, a practice possibly deriving from Greek laws, though whether their original significance was fully understood in the Roman context is unclear (Parker 1983:20, B26–7).

Both Hecate and Diana may also be associated with the menstrual cycle. Diana was identified with the moon, itself associated with menstruation in many cultures. The moon was also associated with things that occur in the evening such as witch-craft and mysterious happenings. With these aspects, Diana is syncretic with Hecate, goddess of witch-craft, cross-roads and the underworld (Burkert 1985:171, 200). Once a month a sacrifice was made to Hecate that seems to suggest an association with the menstrual cycle. A food associated with her was the blood red mullet; could this also be a symbolic aspect menstrual blood? One might also ask whether these monthly sacrifices were simply to appease Hecate or a form of symbolic ritual purification. It is possible that there was an association with the menstrual cycle and religion. If so, these sacrifices are suggestive of purification. Whether this ritual was followed by all women is unclear – indeed, Pliny or perhaps Soranus might have commented on these practices if they had; nonetheless, there is the possibility that some women felt the need, or were required, to purify themselves.

Conclusions

In conclusion, Roman archaeology has rarely considered the conceptualisation of the body, despite the considerable potential for such work. From the literature, archaeology and religions of the Roman world, it seems that the functions of the female body were only occasionally considered harmful; they were also seen as life-giving. Unlike many societies, taboos of sexual pollution seem not to have been significant, and this has important implications for our understanding of the symbolism of gendered material culture and the organisation of domestic space. The intertwining of folklore, magical beliefs and scientific ideas make attitudes towards the Roman female body complex, but it is this richness and diversity of perspectives provided by the historical and archaeological evidence – as well as ethnographic parallels – which make this such a fruitful area of research.

Department of Classics, University of Newcastle upon Tyne

Acknowledgements

I am most grateful for the advice and numerous discussions about this paper and topic from Dr. J. Pollard and Professor Ph. J. van der Eijk. I am also grateful for comments from Dr. M. Gillings, R. Witcher and L. Allason-Jones. Needless to say, any mistakes are the author's own.

Bibliography

Allason-Jones, L. 1989. *Women in Roman Britain*. London: British Museum Press.

Aristotle *On dreams*. In J. Barnes 1984. (ed.) *The complete works of Aristotle*. Princeton: Princeton University Press.

Aristotle *On generation of animals*. (trans. A. C. Peck, 1943). Cambridge, USA & London: Harvard University Press & William Heinemann Press.

Bliquez, L. 1995. Gynecology in Pompeii. In Ph. J. van der Eijk, H.F.J. Horstmanshoff & P.H. Schrijvers (eds.) *Ancient medicine in its socio-cultural context*. Amsterdam and Atlanta: Rodopi, pp.209–224.

Braadbaart, S. 1994. Medical and cosmetic instruments in the collection of the 'Rijksmuseum van Oudheden' in Leiden, The Netherlands. *Oudheidkundige Mededelingen uit het Rijksmuseum van Oudheden te Leiden*, 74:163–175.

Burkert, W. 1985. *Greek religion*. (trans. J. Raffan). Cambridge, USA: Harvard University Press.

Cantarella, E. 1987. *Pandora's Daughters*. (trans M.B. Fant). Baltimore & London: Johns Hopkins University Press.

Celsus *De Medicina*. (trans W.G. Spencer, 1989). Cambridge, USA & London: Harvard University Press
    & William Heinemann Press.

Columella *De Re Rustica*. (trans. B. Ash, 1941–55). London: William Heinemann Press.

Corpus Inscriptionum Latinarum. Berlin: Berolini Apud W. de Gruyter et Socios.

Dean-Jones, L. 1991. The social construct of the female body in Classical Greek science. In S. Pomeroy
    (ed.) *Women's history and ancient history*. Chapel Hill & London: University of North Carolina Press,
    pp.111–137.

Dean-Jones, L. 1994. *Women's bodies in Classical Greek science*. Oxford: Clarendon Press.

Galen *Claudii Galeni Opera Omnia*. In C. G. Kühn (ed.) 1821–1823. *Comprehensive Greek-Latin edition
    of Galen's works*. Leipzig: Hildesheim.

Galen *De Simine*. (trans. P. De Lacy, 1992). Berlin: Akademie Verlag.

Galen *On usefulness of the parts of the body*. (trans. M. T. May, 1968). Ithaca: Cornell University Press.

Galloway, P. 1998. Where have all the menstrual huts gone? In K. Hays-Gilpin & D.S. Whitely (eds.)
    Reader in gender archaeology. London & New York: Routledge, pp.197–212.

Ginsburg, R. 1996. 'Don't tell dear'; the material culture of tampons and napkins. *Journal of Material
    Culture*, 1(3):365–375.

Gourevitch, D. 1995. Women who suffer from a man's disease: the example of Satyriasis and debate on
    affections specific to the sexes. In R. Hawley & B. Levick (eds.) *Women in antiquity: new assesments*.
    London & New York: Routledge, pp.149–164.

Hesiod *Theogony* and *Works and Days*. (trans. M.L. West, 1985). Oxford: Oxford University Press.

Hippocrates *Airs, waters, places*. (trans. J. Chadwick & W.N. Mann, 1978). Harmondsworth: Penguin.

Hodder, I. 1982. *Symbols in action: ethnoarchaeological studies of material culture*. Cambridge:
    Cambridge University Press.

Jackson, R. 1988. *Doctors and diseases in the Roman Empire*. Norman & London: University of
    Oklahoma Press.

King, H. 1995. Self-help and self-knowledge: in search of the patient in Hippocratic gynaecology. In R.
    Hawley & B. Levick (eds.) *Women in antiquity*. London: Routledge, pp.135–148.

Künzl, E. 1983. *Medizinische Instrumente aus Sepulkralfunden der römischen Kaiserzeit*. Cologne:
    Rhineland Verlag.

Longfield-Jones, G.M. 1986. A Graeco-Roman speculum in the Wellcome Museum. *Medical History*, 30:
    81–89.

Longrigg, J. 1998. *Greek medicine from the Heroic to the Hellenistic Age*. London: Duckworth Press.

Matthäus, H. 1989. *Der Arzt in Römische Zeit*. Stuttgart: Limes Museum Aalen.

Milne, J.S. 1907. *Surgical instruments in Greek and Roman times*. Oxford: Clarendon Press.

Moore, H.L. 1982. The interpretation of spatial patterning in settlement residues. In I. Hodder (ed.)
    Symbolic and structural archaeology. Cambridge: Cambridge University Press, pp.74–79.

Moore, H.L. 1988. *Feminism and anthropology*. Cambridge: Polity Press.

Oribas In Longfield-Jones 1986

Parker, R. 1983. *Miasma: pollution and purification in early Greek religion*. Oxford: Clarendon Press.

Paul of Aegina *Corpus Medicorum Graecorum*. (I.L. Heiberg, 1924). Berlin: B.G. Teubneri.

Pleket, H.W. 1969. Texts on the social history in the Greek world. *Epigraphica 2*. Leiden: E.J. Brill.

Pliny *Natural history*. (trans. W.H.S. Jones, 1956). Cambridge, USA & London: Harvard University Press
    & William Heinemann

Soranus *Gynecology*. (trans. Owsei Temkin, 1956). Baltimore & London: Johns Hopkins University Press.

Spink, M.S. & G.L. Lewis 1973. *Albucasis on surgery and instruments*. London: Wellcome Institute of
    the History of Medicine.

Suetonius *The Twelve Caesars*. (trans. J.C. Rolfe, 1989). Cambridge, USA & London: Harvard University
    Press.

Tacitus *Histories*. (trans. C.H. Moore, 1992). Cambridge, USA & London: Harvard University Press.

Turner, B.J. 1996. *The body and society*. Second edition. London: Sage.

von Staden, H. 1989. *Herophilus on the art of medicine in early Alexandria*. Cambridge: University Press.

von Staden, H. 1991. *Apud nos foediora verba*: Celsus' reluctant construction of the female body. *Centre
    Jean Palerne Le Latin Medical. La Constitution d'uns Language Scientifique*. Saint Etienne:
    Publications de l'Universite de Saint Etienne, pp.271–296.

The Dispersed Dead: preliminary observations on burial and settlement space in rural Roman Britain

by John Pearce

Introduction

Large scale excavation of Roman rural sites in Britain often reveals individual or small groups of burials dispersed across settlements, suggesting a recurring encounter of the living with the dead. The same is true of Roman Gaul (Ferdière 1993). Yet with occasional exceptions rural burials in Britain have remained relatively invisible in terms of the proportion of archaeological analysis devoted to them (Collis 1977; Esmonde-Cleary 1992; Philpott & Reece 1993). The subject is largely absent from general investigations of the Romano-British countryside (e.g. Hingley 1989; Millett 1990; Smith 1997) and in the rejuvenated study of rural Roman settlement space, burial and other depositional practice remain the poor relations of architecture, while students of mortuary practice are perhaps deterred by the small sample sizes and the frequent lack of large grave good assemblages to which detailed statistical analysis may be applied. The most explicit and influential model for the study of rural burial in Britain remains Collis' (1977) characterisation in terms of social status of the differences in burial type, furniture and location at Owslebury, Hampshire. In this scheme the individual or small groups of burials, not situated in a discrete cemetery area, and scattered across settlement sites, often within or close to other features, represent the lower echelons of the social hierarchy. It is the aim of this paper to re-evaluate this assumption that burial in such locations is an indicator of low social status within a Romano-British rural context.

The paper begins with a description of the sample area, Hampshire, and an assessment of the degree to which it is representative of other rural areas of Roman Britain. Rural sites are defined broadly as those at a lower level of the settlement hierarchy than 'local centres' or village sites (Hingley 1989), although in practice the Hampshire evidence is monopolised by a particular site type. The furnishing of these individual or small groups of burials is compared to those in urban cemeteries. The relationship of burial to its immediate archaeologically known environment is then examined in greater detail and recurring associations with particular settlement features proposed (to avoid repetition sites referred to more than once in the text are referenced in Appendix 1). The broader topographical context of burial (e.g. height, visibility, relation to slope), is not considered here although it will undoubtedly be a worthwhile area of future study (cf. Parker Pearson 1993). An alternative characterisation of the relationship of rural burials to settlement space is then offered.

The sample

Hampshire was chosen as a sample area not only to compare Owslebury to its regional context but also because the county possesses one of the largest sample of burials excavated in association with settlements from Roman Britain, although how small this sample is should be remembered. Approximately 150 burials are known from rural Hampshire, compared to over 1100 from Winchester (Kjølbye-Biddle 1992). Over 60 of the rural burials derive from one site, Owslebury. This low ratio of rural to urban burials characterises most other areas of southern England. The closest approximation to total recovery of burials from a rural site in the study area was achieved at Owslebury, but even there the expected burial population was not recovered from all periods of the site's use. The small size of other groups may sometimes be attributed to disturbance or small-scale excavation (e.g. Middle Wallop, Oakridge). However when conditions have been more propitious, large numbers of burials have not always been recovered (e.g. Burntwood Farm, Odiham, Snell's Corner), although there are occasional indications of larger rural cemeteries, for example at Itchen Abbas (Hampshire County Council 1992). Preferences in the location of burials around settlements will therefore be established as an aggregate derived from different sites, of which the quality and extent of excavation are highly diverse.

The evidence is largely derived from sites on the chalk downlands of northern and central Hampshire. For all periods recent archaeological activity, modern development and preservation environments have conspired to produce a bias in knowledge of the archaeological record of the county to this area (Cunliffe 1993). One particular site type also monopolises our knowledge of burial practice; large downland settlements, occupied, not necessarily continuously, from the early Iron Age into the Roman period, bounded at certain periods of their history by large enclosures ditches which make them highly archaeologically visible (Hughes 1994). Although knowledge of villa sites within the county is fairly extensive, save for infant burials and occasional post-Roman burials, the burial practice of their occupants remains largely unknown, even in the late Roman period when villa complexes are at their most extensive (Cunliffe 1993:255; Johnston 1978).

Although the best known Roman period burial groups from Hampshire, Owslebury and the various sites of the East Hampshire tradition (Millett 1987) are Late Pre-Roman Iron Age (LPRIA) and early Roman in date, the corpus of burial evidence is biased to the late Roman period by a ratio of over 2:1. This imbalance, which also characterises other counties (see below) is likely to be a complex product of mortuary ritual, taphonomy and recovery biases which requires further attention but cannot be considered in detail here. The dependency on grave goods for dating otherwise isolated rural burials is likely to exaggerate the proportion of burials furnished. The higher proportion of furnished burials at Owslebury is probably more typical. Given the known post-Roman practice of burial on Roman settlements (Esmonde Cleary 1989:185), Roman and post-Roman period burials are particularly difficult to distinguish.

The Hampshire sample is therefore the product of particular circumstances, but in some respects is currently representative of rural burial practice in counties from central southern England north to Lincolnshire and East Yorkshire. In these the available burial evidence is also biased to the late Roman period and derives substantially from non-villa settlements (Pearce in prep.). Initial examination also suggests that burials in other counties have been recovered in similar associations. In the description of burial location most attention is given to patterns which also characterise other counties, although particularities of the Hampshire sample will be signalled.

Principal trends in burial

For the majority of the Iron Age the visible burial practice in Hampshire comprised the deposition of fragments of bone, individual body parts, articulated limbs and whole corpses in a variety of depositional contexts around settlements (Wait 1985; Whimster 1981). The occasional deposition of individual body parts or skeletal fragments in non-grave deposits continued throughout the Roman period, for example adult skulls and skull fragments in late Roman settlement contexts at Owslebury, Cowdery's Down and Balksbury. In the late Iron Age the deposition of complete rather than part bodies formed an increasing part of the skeletal record and from the first century AD, the vast majority of archaeologically visible bodies were buried within separate graves (Wait 1985:116; Whimster 1981:191).

From the mid-first to early third centuries AD cremation was the dominant burial form and was superseded by extended inhumation in the late third or early fourth centuries. Early Roman burials were deposited most often in ceramic vessels and furnished with ceramics and more rarely other accessories. Most late Roman rural burials were deposited in wooden coffins, although more elaborate grave forms or containers have occasionally been recovered, for

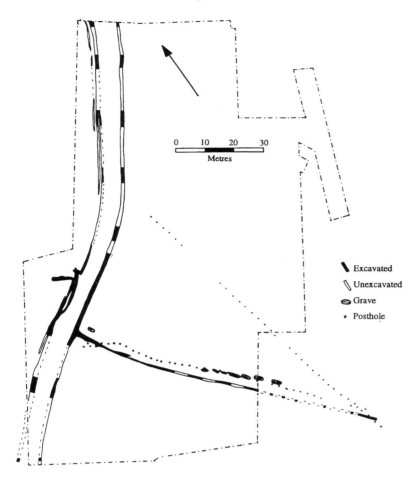

0   10   20   30

Metres

↘ Excavated

↖ Unexcavated

⬭ Grave

• Posthole

Figure 1. Burials and settlement features on Site P, Owslebury, Hampshire (after Collis 1968)

example the massive grave cuts with elaborate wooden coffins at Burntwood Farm and coffins of lead at Petersfield (Moray-Williams 1908) and stone at Binsted (Millett 1974). The commonest grave good categories of early and late Roman rural burials, respectively ceramics with the former and hobnails and ceramics with the latter, were the same as those of Winchester's cemeteries and throughout the proportion of furnished burials and the furnishing of the 'average' burial was equal to or higher than that from Winchester's cemeteries (Pearce in prep.), although the proportion of furnished burials in the rural sample is exaggerated by the dependency on grave goods for dating.

The spatial associations of rural burial

The concentration of LPRIA and early Roman cremation burials at Owslebury in a single enclosure is currently atypical of the Hampshire corpus. The majority of interments were recovered as single or small groups of burials in association with boundary features, usually the ditches and gullies which defined settlement and other enclosures, but also field boundaries and occasionally landscape features of greater antiquity. This association took several forms that are now illustrated.

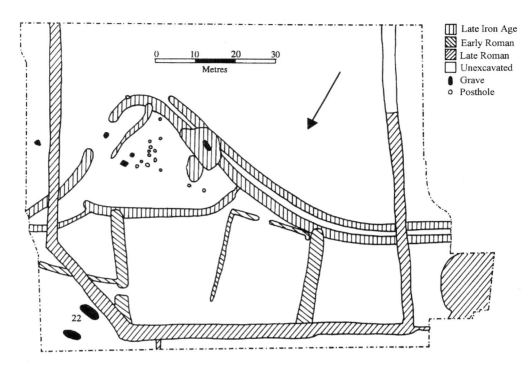

Figure 2. Burials and boundary features at Burntwood Farm, Itchen Valley, Hampshire (after Fasham 1980).

In some cases burials were located beyond the settlement boundary; the required distance seems to have varied from only a few metres at Ructstalls or Owslebury to 70m at Old Down Farm (Andover). The maintenance of distance is well illustrated on site P at Owslebury (Figure 1) where the northern corner of the large third century rectangular enclosure is cut off, seemingly to avoid disturbing burials 22 and 23 and in order that they remained outside the boundary feature. The unwillingness to excavate large areas outside enclosures is undoubtedly responsible for an under-representation of burials from this area. It is surely no accident that many such burials have been discovered beyond the limits of formal excavation (e.g. Cowdery's Down, Oakridge). The graves associated with the probable field boundary at Burntwood Farm represents the only occurrence within this sample of what is also likely to have been a frequent location for burial.

It is a commonplace that Roman burials at rural or small settlements were located within or close to enclosure ditches at the rear of settlements (Leech 1982; Philpott & Reece 1993; Smith 1987: 115–8). The front and rear of enclosures are not always easily established on these multi-period sites, but although some burials were placed to the rear of sites (e.g. Winnall Down), within the sample as a whole no preference for the latter was detected. In fact deposition in or close to entrances can be more commonly observed. On site P at Owslebury burial 24 was deposited at the entrance to a pre-Roman enclosure and burials 22 and 23 lay just beyond the entrance to the first century AD enclosure (Figure 1). During the brief salvage work at Old Down Farm (East Meon) single cremation burials were recovered from different entrances to the site. At Martin's Down a child burial was deposited at the enclosure entrance in the ditch terminal. Burials were also placed at internal entrances within settlements. A cremation in a mortared cist was deposited beneath the eastern doorway of the possible villa at Finkley, and the

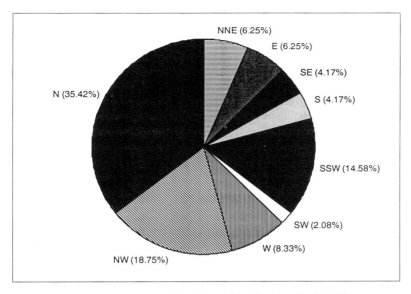

Figure 3.The Orientation of late Roman burials in Hampshire (head end); (N=48)

two cremation burials from Daneshill were located in the space between two enclosure ditches (3 & 4), possibly the entrance to a rear portion of the enclosure. A possibly analogous location for burial is at junctions of features, for example burial 54 at the junction of field boundary and trackway ditch at Burntwood Farm (Figure 2). The preferences for burial at points of access and in boundary features were united in the placing of burials in or alongside trackway and droveway ditches (Figure 2; Burntwood Farm). This is less well illustrated in Hampshire than elsewhere, for example Roden Downs (Berkshire) (Hood & Walton 1948) or Each End, Ash (Kent) (Bennett & Panton 1993).

The location of burials also appears to have been influenced by other features commonly occurring on settlement margins. Corn driers (the term is used here as shorthand for installations the function of which is most recently assessed by van der Veen (1989)) were sometimes associated not only with infant (Scott 1991) but also adult burials. Two adult inhumation burials were aligned on the north wall of the corn drier at Choseley Farm. Whether the burial was made while the corn drier was still in use is not possible to determine, but at Rockbourne the inhumation which cut the wall of the corn drier must have post-dated its use. A more spectacular example is the charred inhumation which had been placed head first in the flue of a drier at Welton Wold (East Yorkshire) (Wilson 1973: 282).

Infant burials comprise the most frequent exception to burial on settlement boundaries. From the late Iron Age to the late Roman period infants are more likely to have been buried in settlement interiors. However this interior/exterior distinction is by no means absolute, as others have noted (Struck 1993: 315). At Winnall Down and Cowdery's Down infant burials were located respectively beyond and within site enclosure ditches. Some examples of non-infant intrusion on site interiors have been noted above. The most spectacular is the deposition at Oakridge of a minimum of 24 adults and 3 children in several episodes in a well infill sequence from the late third to seventh centuries, although the nature and degree of contemporaneous occupation on the site is poorly understood. The excavator suggested that the human burials and many animal carcasses represented the hasty disposal of plague victims. However the bodies were deposited on several occasions and the skeletal sample did not represent a 'normal' population but, like other burial groups considered here, lacked infants, the age group most potentially susceptible to plague. The associations with complete pots and complete animals, sometimes in very large numbers, suggest that like the fill of other Roman period wells (Wait 1985) this deposit was carefully structured.

The spatial organisation of burial seems to be affected by gender as well as age. On all rural sites from Hampshire with four or more burials the sample is biased to either male or female burials (Table 1) although because of sample size the statistical significance of such patterns is not easily evaluated. No difference was noted in the relationship of burials of different gender to particular settlement features. Initial examination of other published rural samples from Britain has not so far found extensive parallels to this gender distinction.

The close relationship of burials to, and their alignment on, other features has implications for orientation. Figure 3 depicts the preferences for the end at which the head is placed in late Roman child and adult (but not infant) inhumations in Hampshire. The high degree of variability is best explained by the influence on orientation of features in the immediate locality of burials. Nevertheless general preferences can be identified for placing the head to the north or north-north-west end of the burial. This distinguishes this rural sample both from the preference for north and east of Iron Age crouched inhumations in the same region (Whimster 1981:12) and the predominant west-east orientation in Winchester's late Roman cemeteries (Clarke 1979: 131–2).

Site	Male burials	Female burials	Unknown
Burntwood Farm	2	5	1 (juvenile)
Balksbury	0	2	2 (juvenile)
Odiham	5	1	0
Owslebury (LPRIA & early Roman)	13	3	16
Owslebury (late Roman)	4	1	0
Snell's Corner	0	3	3 (adult)
Winnall	5	0	0

Table 1: Number of male and female burials at cemeteries in Hampshire with 4 or more graves.

It is important to note that burial represents one event in longer site and feature sequences. Burials could be integral to boundaries that were active in a very practical sense. The sequence at Burntwood Farm illustrates this well (Figure 2). The roadway and field boundaries, which divided up the landscape with little reference to their Iron Age predecessors, were probably in use throughout most of the Roman period. The fourth century graves were cut parallel to, and 3–5m to the north of, Feature 8, a ditched boundary. A late or sub-Roman period line of post-holes (Line 2) was later established later along the line of the graves rather than the earlier boundary. This line of postholes continued to respect the roadway to the west. Site P at Owslebury provides a further example of the influence of burial on settlement features (see above).

However burial was also commonly associated with 'deceased' features of differing degrees of antiquity. In some cases, for example at Welton Wold, such features had only recently gone out of use. At other times burials were placed alongside or within the fills of earlier Roman (e.g. Balksbury, Owslebury) or Iron Age enclosure ditches (Old Down Farm, (Andover)) although regrettably few reports record the stage during the formation of the fill at which the burials were placed. Phased site plans can obscure this relationship with the 'relict' landscape, as they omit older features that might influence the siting of burials, as for example at Balksbury. The dead were also interred on sites or parts of sites from which the main focus of activity had shifted away (e.g. Lain's Farm, Micheldever Wood), or occasionally placed within features of a much greater antiquity, for example in prehistoric barrows at South Wonston and in a Bronze Age boundary feature at Odiham, an association attested elsewhere in Britain (Williams 1998). The distinction between the choice of features one or two centuries old or one or two millennia should not perhaps be over-emphasised. The relative dating of different features in the palimpsest of surrounding landscapes must have become indistinct. The evidence assembled here suggests however that post-Roman burial on earlier settlements (e.g. Thruxton) continues a long-standing practice of placing the dead in close relation to 'antique' features.

Interpretation

Collis' characterisation of the differences in burial at Owsleybury in terms of social hierarchy is echoed in more recent explanatory models. Philpott & Reece (1993) have proposed a tenurial as well as social distinction on the basis of rural burial evidence in Britain. They argue that landowners maintained a formal burial space to legitimate their right to property, while tenants, slaves and workers had no formal cemetery on land to which they lacked a long-term attachment. The apparent minimal effort expended on burial by using existing features has prompted an interpretation of individuals buried at such locations as outcasts:

> the substantial group of burials in disused features such as ditches, corn-drying ovens, pottery kilns or wells may be the result of indifference or laziness on the part of the grave-diggers, violent or illicit death, or disapprobation on the part of the family or community.

(Philpott 1991:232).

It is tempting to link this model to social change extrapolated from the study of settlement space. The Hampshire burials might be argued to be those of the variously characterised subordinate groups, slaves, workers, or 'degraded kin', which emerged in an increasingly hierarchical rural Romano-British society (Hingley 1989:155).

However while it is possible to identify a hierarchy of burial practice based on numbers of grave goods and / or burial containers in the early and late Roman period within this rural sample, the majority of burials on settlement margins were as often contained or coffined and provided with grave goods as contemporary burials in urban cemeteries. The repeated favouring of certain locations for burial and the regularities in orientation, influenced but not determined by the relationship to local features, have been outlined above. To explain these burials as the product of indifference does not take sufficient account of these characteristics.

An alternative analysis of these burials is suggested by recent approaches to settlement space. Of these the basic principle is that the organisation of space is not the static product of social relationships, but is also an active medium through which experience and social relationships are created and re-negotiated (Parker Pearson & Richards 1994a). Students of Iron Age settlement have used both evidence of architecture and depositional practice to identify principles behind the structure of settlement space (Hill 1995; Fitzpatrick 1997). Similar studies in a Romano-British rural context have been based on the analysis of villa art and architecture to a much greater extent than depositional practice (Hingley 1990; Rippengal 1993; Scott 1990; Scott 1994). Here the organisation of settlement space of non-villa sites, in particular the structure of settlement space through time, is explored through burial as a component of depositional practice.

When beginning this study it was assumed that the distribution of burial favoured the rear of settlement sites (see above), but in this sample a more satisfactory characterisation of the relationship of burial to settlement space is as a 'concentric' ordering (cf. Hingley 1990:143; Parker Pearson & Richards 1994b). Innermost were infant burials, closer to the interior of settlement space and within structures. Adult and older child burials on the settlement boundaries and at more distant locations were the outer rings of this concentric arrangement. On these outer rings a possible difference in male and female burial locations was identified, but further samples must be examined to establish this differentiation with greater confidence.

The locations identified provide a classic illustration of liminality (van Gennep 1960). The ambiguous object, the corpse or cremated bone, was distanced from the living by its deposition in locations on the limits of the domestic sphere, boundaries, entrances, and trackways. The location of burial on abandoned or prehistoric sites distanced the dead in time as well as space.

Burial sometimes appears to be the final act in a sequence of deposits like other 'rites of termination' identified by Merrifield (1987). However graves and by implication the dead also impinged on the experience of a settlement. Their influence on the siting of other features around them implies that graves were marked and visible for some time after burial. Their impact was also realised through the obviousness of the larger features like boundary ditches with which burials were associated. Rural burial in the Roman world has been associated with the marking of property boundaries (e.g. Miles 1985: 40), but more complex relationships between burial, personal and group identity and landscape can be proposed.

The ceremony of burial and the grave can be argued to have integrated the lifecycle of bodies and persons within a variety of temporal rhythms (cf. Bloch & Parry 1982). Burial close to corn driers, or in field boundaries could have been linked to the promotion or control of fertility and to cycles of social and agricultural reproduction. The placing of burials on parts of the site, either recently disused, or related to a more distant past, connected the dead to long-term or ancestral occupation. Some burial groups of this period whether or not aligned along ditches or other features, possess a head to toe linear layout (e.g. Burntwood Farm, Odiham and Snell's Corner). These physical arrangements were powerful metaphors for lineages that allowed the living to define their own genealogical position. To those inhabiting the settlement, graves demarcated an area with which a particular group were affiliated from spaces of a different quality. The memory of a ceremony or physical marker of an interment could also have conditioned the experience of the 'outsider' arriving or passing through by alerting them that the space they were entering or traversing was differentiated from that whence they had come.

This intimate connection of burial to settlement was not a timeless constant, but within the Hampshire sample and other parts of southern and central England, may have characterised the late Roman period to a greater degree than the earlier. Given the complexity of factors that may make later Roman burial more visible and the need for further research to establish this trend more securely, potential avenues of approach are simply indicated here. The late Roman period in Britain was characterised by changes in exchange relationships and by agricultural innovation within an increasingly dis-embedded economy (Scott 1990; Millett 1990). The functions of urban public spaces were also increasingly usurped by villas (Scott 1994). These processes have been argued to be reflected in the increased architectural and artistic elaboration of villa space in the fourth century, through which the encounters of inhabitants and strangers were structured. The greater frequency of visible burial, emphasising settlement boundaries, in the fourth century may be one component of an analogous elaboration of the space of non-villa sites. In other contexts similar changes at a macro-level have been argued to have transformed gender roles within the organisation of household production (Hasdorf 1991). The gender distinction noted in the Hampshire burials may therefore relate to broader changes in engendered space on settlement sites which reflected such transformations, although attempts (e.g. Hingley 1989:43–5) to identify gender-based activity patterning in Romano-British rural space are not convincing. The Owslebury data also suggests that spatial divisions in burial based on gender did not characterise the late Roman period alone.

Conclusions

Recurring locations have been identified in the placing of burials on rural settlement sites in Hampshire. The importance of site boundaries for the location of burial has been confirmed and a number of further preferences proposed, both for the rear of, and the entrances to, settlements and fields, close to 'corn driers', by or in the ditches of roads and trackways, and in abandoned and prehistoric sites. Within the small number of sites it is difficult to evaluate the strength of different associations. It is suggested here that the significance of the rear of settlement enclosures have been hitherto exaggerated. Burials outside the settlement area are likely to be under-represented in the currently available sample, as such areas are rarely privileged in excavation, especially under rescue conditions. That burial in these various locations signified lower status within the hierarchy of rural burial has been challenged. An alternative characterisation has been offered which places burial within the evolving structure of settlement space and suggests its influence on contemporary perceptions of the landscape. This characterisation provides a further challenge to the hypothesis that formal bounded cemetery areas alone connect groups to resources and property (cf. Morris 1991).

The provisional nature of conclusions must however be emphasised. Publication of large-scale recent excavations (e.g. Frocester Court, Stanwick, Stansted) will undoubtedly enhance our understanding of rural Roman burial practice and will hopefully prompt the future collection of larger and better samples. With such information regional and chronological differences which are suggested by currently available information will be more satisfactorily characterised; in Cambridgeshire for example individual burials associated with field boundaries or entrances seem to be more typical than in Hampshire (J. Taylor pers. comm.) whilst excavations in Somerset and the Thames Valley have revealed late Roman cemeteries with several tens or hundreds of burials which possibly acted as the communal cemetery for a number of settlements (Philpott & Reece 1993). Regular scientific dating of small groups of burials without grave goods should facilitate the distinction between late and post-Roman burials. In this analysis burial has also been isolated from the broader context of deposition. Hill (1995) has demonstrated the value for the interpretation of Iron Age settlement space of the comparison of the deposition of human remains with other types of deposit. Although unlike the Iron Age the Roman period is largely characterised by the discrete deposition of whole bodies, a change which Hill has set within a broader context of the increasing separation of ritual from settlement space, the study of burial within the context of general depositional practice remains an area of unexploited value. Nevertheless, while there is much potential for further work, this paper has shown that burial on settlement boundaries, a commonplace of Romano-British archaeology, can sustain re-investigation and suggests a further dimension to a different rather than over-familiar Roman Britain.

Department of Archaeology, University of Durham

Acknowledgements

I would like to thank John Collis for information on Owslebury in advance of publication, and Rosemary Braithwaite for help in assembling relevant references from the Hampshire County Council SMR. Thanks are also extended to Martin Millett for commenting on draft work for a doctoral thesis from which this paper is taken, and to the audience of this paper in a research seminar in Durham, to delegates at TRAC and to the anonymous referee for their observations. Responsibility for the contents remains my own.

Appendix 1

Site	Reference	Site	Reference
Alton	Millett 1986	Old Down Farm, Andover	Davies 1981
Balksbury	Wainwright & Davies 1995	Old Down, East Meon	Whinney & Walker 1980
Burntwood Farm	Fasham 1980	Owslebury	Collis 1968, 1970, 1977
Choseley Farm	Morris 1986	Rockbourne	Sumner 1914
Cowdery's Down	Millett & James 1983	Ructstalls Hill	Oliver & Applin 1979
Finkley	Stevens 1872	Snell's Corner	Knocker 1956
Lain's Farm	Bellamy 1992	South Wonston	Whinney 1987
Micheldever Wood	Fasham 1987	Thruxton	Colt Hoare 1829
Middle Wallop	Piggott 1949	Winnall	Collis 1978
Oakridge	Oliver 1992	Winnall Down	Fasham 1985
Odiham	Jenkins 1990		

Bibliography
PHFCAS: Proceedings of the Hampshire Field Club and Archaeological Society

Bellamy, P. 1992. An investigation of the prehistoric landscape along the route of the A303 road improvement between Andover, Hampshire and Amesbury, Wiltshire 1984–1987. *PHFCAS*, 47:5–82.

Bennett, P. & Panton, F. 1993. Interim report on work carried out in 1993 by the Canterbury Archaeological Trust. *Archaeologia Cantiana*, 112:355–403.

Bloch, M. and Parry, J. (eds.) 1982. *Death and the regeneration of life*. Cambridge: University Press.

Clarke, G. 1979. *Pre-Roman and Roman Winchester, part 2: the Roman cemetery at Lankhills*. Oxford: Oxford University Press.

Collis, J. 1968. Excavations at Owslebury, Hants: an interim report. *Antiquaries Journal*, 48:18–31.

Collis, J. 1970. Excavations at Owslebury, Hants: second interim report. *Antiquaries Journal*, 50:246–61.

Collis, J. 1977. Owslebury and the problems of burials on rural settlements. In R. Reece (ed.) *Burial in the Roman world*. London: Council for British Archaeology Research Report 22, pp. 39–52.

Collis, J. 1978. *Winchester excavations, 1949–1960, II. Excavations in the suburbs and the western parts of the town*. Winchester: Winchester City Museums.

Colt Hoare, R. 1829. Observations upon four mosaic pavements in the county of Hampshire. *Archaeologia*, 22:49–54.

Cunliffe, B. 1993. *Wessex to AD 1000*. London: Longman.

Davies, S.M. 1981. Excavations at Old Down Farm, Andover, 2. Prehistoric and Roman. *PHFCAS*, 37:81–163.

Esmonde Cleary, S. 1989. *The ending of Roman Britain*. London: Batsford

Esmonde Cleary, S. 1992. Town and country. In S. Bassett (ed.) *Death in towns: urban responses to the living and the dead, 100–1600*. Leicester: Leicester University Press, pp.28–42.

Fasham, P.J. 1980. Excavations on Bridget's and Burntwood Farms, Itchen Valley Parish, Hampshire, 1974. MARC 3 Sites R5 and R6. *PHFCAS*, 36:37–86.

Fasham, P.J. 1985. *The prehistoric settlement at Winnall Down, Winchester: excavations of MARC 3 site R17 in 1976 and 1977*. Hampshire Field Club and Archaeological Society Monograph 2, Southampton: Hampshire Field Club.

Fasham, P.J. 1987. *A 'Banjo' enclosure in Micheldever Wood, Hampshire (MARC 3 site R27)*. Hampshire Field Club and Archaeological Society Monograph 5, Southampton: Hampshire Field Club.

Ferdière, A. ed. 1993. *Monde des morts, monde des vivants en Gaule rurale*. Tours: Université de Tours.

Fitzpatrick, A. 1997. Everyday life in the Iron Age. In A. Gwilt and C. Haselgrove (eds.) *Reconstructing Iron Age societies*. Oxford: Oxbow, pp. 73–86.

Gennep, A. van 1960. *The rites of passage*. London: Routledge & Kegan Paul.

Hampshire County Council 1992. *Archaeology annual report for 1991*. Winchester: Hampshire County Council.

Hasdorf, C. 1991. Gender, space and food in prehistory. In J. Gero and M. Conkey (eds.) *Engendering archaeology: women and prehistory*. Oxford: Blackwell, pp.132–63.

Hill, J.D. 1995. *Ritual and rubbish in the Iron Age of Wessex. A study in the formation of a specific archaeological record*. Oxford: BAR (Tempus Reparatum) British Series 242.

Hingley, R. 1989. *Rural settlement in Roman Britain*. London: Seaby.

Hingley, R. 1990. Public and private space: domestic organisation and gender relations among Iron Age and Romano-British households. In R. Samson (ed.) *The social archaeology of houses*. Edinburgh: Edinburgh University Press, pp. 125–149.

Hood, S. and Walton, H. 1948. A Romano-British cremating place and burial ground on Roden Downs, Compton, Berkshire. *Transactions of the Newbury and District Field Club*, 9:1–62.

Hughes, M.F. 1994. The impact of development on the Iron Age in Hampshire. In A.P. Fitzpatrick and E. Morris (eds.) *The Iron Age in Wessex: recent work*. Salisbury: Trust for Wessex Archaeology, pp.33–35.

Jenkins, A.V.C. 1990. An archaeological investigation of a cropmark at Odiham, Hampshire. *PHFCAS*, 46:5–16.

Johnston, D.E. 1978. Villas of Hampshire and the Isle of Wight. In M. Todd (ed.) *Studies in the Romano-British Villa*. Leicester: Leicester University Press, pp. 71–92.

Knocker, G.M. 1956. Early burials and an Anglo-Saxon cemetery at Snell's Corner near Horndean, Hampshire. *PHFCAS*, 19.2:117–170.

Kjølbye-Biddle, B. 1992. Dispersal or concentration: the disposal of the Winchester dead over 2000 years. In S. Bassett (ed.) *Death in towns: urban responses to the living and the dead, 100–1600.* Leicester: Leicester University Press, pp. 210–48.

Leech, R. 1982. *Excavations at Catsgore, 1970–73: a Romano-British village.* Bristol: Western Archaeological Trust.

Merrifield, R. 1987. *The archaeology of ritual and magic.* London: Batsford.

Miles, D. 1985. *Archaeology at Barton Court Farm, Abingdon, Oxfordshire.* Council for British Archaeology Research Reports 50, London: Council for British Archaeology.

Millett, M. 1974. A Romano-British burial from Binsted, Hampshire. *PHFCAS,* 30:39–40.

Millett, M. 1986. An early cemetery at Alton, Hampshire. *PHFCAS,* 42:43–87.

Millett, M. 1987. An early Roman burial tradition in Central Southern England. *Oxford Journal of Archaeology,* 6:63–68.

Millett, M. 1990. *The Romanization of Britain.* Cambridge: Cambridge University Press.

Millett, M. and James, S. 1983. Excavations at Cowdery's Down. *Archaeological Journal,* 140:151–279.

Moray Williams, A. 1908. The Stroud Roman villa, Petersfield, Hampshire, 1907. *Archaeological Journal,* 65:57–60.

Morris, M. 1986. An Iron Age and Romano-British site at Choseley Farm, Odiham. The excavations of Dorothy Liddell 1937. *PHFCAS,* 42:89–108.

Morris, I. 1991. The archaeology of ancestors: the Saxe-Goldstein hypothesis revisited. *Cambridge Archaeological Journal,* 1(2):147–169.

Oliver, M. 1992. The Iron Age and Romano-British settlement at Oakridge. *PHFCAS,* 48:55–94.

Oliver, M. & Applin, B. 1979. Excavations of an Iron Age and Romano-British settlement at Ructstalls Hill, Basingstoke, Hampshire. *PHFCAS,* 35:41–92.

Parker Pearson, M. 1993. The powerful dead: archaeological relationships between the living and the dead. *Cambridge Archaeological Journal,* 3(2):203–229.

Parker Pearson, M. & Richards, C. (eds.) 1994a. *Architecture and order: approaches to social space.* London: Routledge.

Parker Pearson, M. & Richards, C. 1994b. Ordering the world: perceptions of architecture, space and time. In M. Parker Pearson & C. Richards (eds.) *Architecture and order: approaches to social space.* London: Routledge, pp.1–37.

Pearce, J. (in prep.) *Case studies in a contextual archaeology of burial practice in Roman Britain.* Ph.D. thesis, Durham University.

Philpott, R. 1991. *Burial practices in Roman Britain. A survey of grave treatment and furnishing AD 43–410.* Oxford: BAR British Series 219.

Philpott, R. & Reece, R. 1993. Sépultures rurales en Bretagne romaine. In A. Ferdière (ed.) *Monde des morts, monde des vivants en Gaule rurale.* Tours: FERACF, pp.417–423.

Piggott, S. 1949. Roman burials at Middle Wallop, Hampshire. *PHFCAS,* 17:60–3.

Rippengal, R. 1993. 'Villas as a key to social structure'? Some comments on recent approaches to the Romano-British villa and some suggestions towards an alternative. In E. Scott (ed.) *Theoretical Roman archaeology: first conference proceedings.* Aldershot: Avebury, pp.79–101.

Scott, E. 1990. Romano-British villas and the social construction of space. In R. Samson (ed.) *The social archaeology of houses.* Edinburgh: Edinburgh University Press, pp.149–173.

Scott, E. 1991. Animal(s) and infant burials in Romano-British villas: a revitalization movement. In P. Garwood *et al.* (eds.) *Sacred and profane.* Oxford: Oxford University Committee for Archaeology, pp.115–122.

Scott, S. 1994. Patterns of movement: architectural design and visual planning in the Romano-British villa. In M. Locock (ed.) 1994. *Meaningful architecture: social interpretations of buildings.* Aldershot: Avebury, pp.86–98.

Smith, J.T. 1997. *Roman villas: a study in social structure.* London: Routledge.

Smith, R.F. 1987. *Roadside settlements in lowland Roman Britain.* Oxford: BAR British Series 157.

Stevens, J. 1872. On newly discovered Roman and Saxon remains at Finkley near Andover. *Journal of the British Archaeological Association,* 28:327–36.

Struck, M. 1993. Kinderbestattungen in romano-britischen Siedlungen–der Archäologische Befund. In M. Struck (ed.) *Römerzeitliche Gräber als Quellen zur Religion, Bevölkerungsstruktur und Sozialgeschichte.* Mainz: Johannes Gutenberg Institut für Vor- und Frühgeschichte, pp.313–319.

Sumner, H. 1914. *Excavations at Rockbourne Down, Hampshire.* London: Chiswick Press.

van der Veen, M. 1989. Charred grain assemblages from Roman period corn driers in Britain. *Archaeological Journal*, 146: 302–19

Wainwright, G.J. & Davies, S.M. 1995. *Balksbury Camp, Hampshire: excavations 1973 and 1981*. London: English Heritage.

Wait, G. A. 1985. *Ritual and religion in Iron Age Britain*. Oxford: BAR British Series 149.

Whimster, R. 1981. *Burial practice in Iron Age Britain*. Oxford: BAR British Series 90.

Whinney, R. 1987. Rescue excavations on Bronze Age sites in the South Wonston area. *PHFCAS*, 43:5–14.

Whinney, R. & Walker, G. 1980. Salvage excavations at Old Down Farm, East Meon. *PHFCAS*, 36:153–60.

Williams, H. 1998. The ancient monument in Romano-British ritual practices. In C. Forcey, J. Hawthorne & R. Witcher (eds.) *TRAC97. Proceedings of the seventh annual Theoretical Roman Archaeology Conference*. Oxford: Oxbow, pp. 71–86.

Wilson, D.R. 1973. Roman Britain in 1972. Sites explored. *Britannia*, 4: 270–323.

Ideological Biases in the Urban Archaeology of Rome: a quantitative approach

by Giovanni Ricci & Nicola Terrenato

Introduction

This paper intends to take stock of the situation of urban archaeology in Rome. It is based on a comparatively detailed review (enabled by a new systematisation of the evidence through the means of a Geographical Information System (GIS)) of all the stratigraphic excavations carried out in the city in the last century or so, within the perimeter of the Aurelian walls. The data collection includes quantitative parameters such as the volume of excavated deposits, the number of contexts and the periods represented. This work allows us to assess reliably for the first time the situation after two of decades of intensive work in the city. Recent strategies and tendencies can now be understood in the light provided by a retrospective review of the origins and development of urban archaeology in Rome. What is clearly emerging is the existence of strong theoretical standpoints that characterise various periods and 'schools'; standpoints which, as usual in Italian classical archaeology, are very seldom made explicit. These hidden agendas have strongly influenced the planning and conduct of excavations, and ideological biases in favour of certain periods, type of remains, and even taboos, will become apparent.

The evolution of urban archaeology in Rome, which obviously represents a central theme for Roman archaeology, has not yet been studied in detail, especially within English-speaking scholarship. Yet the case of Rome holds great potential, both in substantive terms and as one of the most complex examples of the questions posed by the study of Roman urbanism. To begin illustrating this case-study, archaeological fieldwork conducted in the city over the last century must be synthesized. As a tool to facilitate the processing of such a massive amount of data, a rough typology of excavations has been defined. These four types will be described below, deriving from a comprehensive review of methods and strategies in the urban archaeology of Rome (Table 1). The same types will also be used for the graphs presented in this paper.

Excavations have been conducted in Rome ever since the Renaissance, and they have had a particular intensity and scale in the last century or so. During the first decade of this century some effort was devoted, mainly by Rodolfo Lanciani, to retracing the main phases of earlier field work in the city (Lanciani 1989). Since then, however, no further historiographical attempt has been made to analyse the developments of this century, so that, paradoxically, less is known about what was happening in the 1930s than in the 1600s. Further, when compared with other large urban centres, the situation in Rome appears to be rather peculiar, without doubt leaving much room for improvement. The present paper will attempt to take some initial steps towards filling in this gap in the literature, beginning with a brief retrospective review of the main events and trends in the urban archaeology of Rome over the last hundred years. This is connected with the recent collection of a database of the main excavations carried out in this period, the new *Forma Urbis Romae*. This high-sounding name (derived from that of a map of ancient Rome published by Lanciani in 1901) will designate a new and massive GIS archive for the archaeology of Rome, which has been promoted by the Comune di Roma [1]. Building on this new information a series of quantitative assessments has been derived, and some of the most relevant will be presented here, as an interim report on ongoing work.

A retrospective review

Before examining the actual body of data collected, it is worthwhile to review briefly the development of urban archaeology in Rome; a good starting point is provided by the introduction of large scale excavation and the massive intensification of archaeological work brought about by the incorporation, in 1870, of the Eternal City into the recently created Kingdom of Italy. Papal archaeology had been mainly concerned with just a few of the most striking monuments (such as the Colosseum or the Arch of Titus). Much attention was also paid, for obvious reasons, to early Christian archaeology – catacombs, churches and early cult places (Barbanera 1998:7–9). The new capital became the seat of both King and government, and as a result underwent enormous expansion. This led to the reurbanization of large areas of the ancient city, which had been unoccupied since the late Roman period. Not surprisingly, a vast quantity of new archaeological remains was brought to light in the process, mainly through rescue work. In addition, large scale excavations were undertaken in some central areas of the ancient city, such as in the Roman Forum and on the Palatine Hill, with the aim of unearthing the glory of the ancient city (Barbanera 1998:82–92). The general attitude, throughout this period, was indeed that of emphasising the imperial Roman past in contrast with the Christian and Medieval periods. Churches such as Saint Hadrian were entirely demolished to reveal the underlying Roman monuments (in this case, the *Curia Senatus*, Tortorici 1993).

At the turn of the century, the Positivist trend briefly exerted some influence over the archaeology of Rome. As a consequence, the excavation procedures, which had beforehand been purely directed at bringing to light as much Roman masonry as possible, became rather more systematic, and began to include some recording of the stratigraphy encountered (Manacorda 1982: 89–90). In some cases, such as at the Comitium or at the Forum, deep soundings into the republican and archaic levels were carried out below the imperial horizon (Ammerman 1990, 1996); the latter had been, as a matter of fact, the final objective of the digging in almost every case. Detailed written documentation (and even photographs) of each layer, together with stratigraphic sections, illustrate the impact of these new methods on this work, representing the earliest example of what is defined here as a type C excavation (see Table 1). Their author, the Venetian architect Giacomo Boni, is rightfully considered the father of Italian archaeological stratigraphy (he even wrote a short methodological essay on the subject, Boni 1901).

Type	Period	Description
A1	1980–present	large-scale sites with up to date Barker/Harris methodology
A2	1975–present	small-scale modern sites with a stratigraphic approach
B	1950–1975	rescue excavations and other mid-century Soprintendenza digs
C	1900–1960	early stratigraphic excavations

Table 1. Typology of urban excavations adopted for the quantitative assessments.

With the advent of Fascism in the 20s and 30s, the nationalist stance of the late nineteenth century found new strength and influenced archaeological agendas to an unparalleled extent. The imperial past was now an essential ideological ingredient in the propaganda of the regime. Through massive destruction of entire quarters of the medieval and Renaissance centre, space was made for new grandiose Fascist architecture (Manacorda & Tamassia 1985; Quatermaine 1995). Roman monuments were often incorporated in new projects, as in the case of the decontextualised Ara Pacis and Mausoleum of Augustus complex, where Mussolini himself had planned apparently to be buried. In this context, archaeology reverted to recording nothing but Roman imperial monuments. For instance, both medieval and late Roman structures were mercilessly destroyed without trace. Even the imperial topography was distorted to serve the vision of the architects of the regime. The Via dell'Impero, flanked by Trajan's column and statues of the emperors, was cut across the Imperial Fora and through the hill of the Velia, forever confusing the original morphology (Terrenato 1992).

After the Second World War, even if the imperialist overtones were abandoned, the quality of the few excavations carried out by the Italian *Soprintendenza* did not improve significantly. It was mainly through foreign practitioners working in Rome that new approaches were introduced to the field. Again, the best stratigraphical investigation seemed to concentrate on the earlier periods: the Swede Einar Gjerstad and the American Frank Brown directed crucial excavations on archaic Rome in the Forum and at the Regia during the 50s and 60s (Brown 1974–75; Gjerstad 1953–73). Although still small in area, these sites were the first in the city to be excavated with modern methods. Contemporary Italian excavations adopted only in part these new techniques, more so in the case of the exploration of archaic deposits, such as that of Sant'Omobono (Pisani Sartorio 1989). At most other sites, which constitute our type B, only rudimentary stratigraphic information was recorded.

The appointment of Adriano La Regina as Superintendent in the early 80s, led to radical changes to the practice of archaeology in Rome: several massive large scale excavations were opened in the centre of the city, in which the Barker/Harris methods were largely employed. These include the Crypta Balbi (directed by D. Manacorda since 1981), the Northern Slope of the Palatine (A. Carandini, since 1985), the Meta Sudans (C. Panella, since 1986), those at Piazza Celimontana (C. Pavolini, since 1984), at Via della Consolazione (G. Maetzke, since 1980) and at the Temple of Magna Mater (P. Pensabene, since 1977). Sites of this type, which we call A1, witnessed the participation of university staff, students and the slow emergence of a group of professional urban diggers (Terrenato 1998:180). Besides these sites, the tradition of small scale excavations has continued, mostly for rescue purposes, and represents our type A2 (see Table 1). This new phase of activity, which has declined somewhat over the last five years, can only be compared in terms of size and effort to two earlier periods: that at the beginning of the century and the Fascist one.

The data collection

The current collection of data on the urban archaeology of Rome is concerned with the range of work reviewed above. Some attention has been paid to the implementation of elementary quantitative assessments for a better understanding of the development of this fieldwork. A database of sites has been gathered, containing records for all the excavations within the Aurelian walls whose published reports include some stratigraphic information. To these, all the unpublished data that was reasonably accessible was added, producing a total of 87 sites. For each of these the following information was collected: a) the dates of activity, b) the surface-area investigated, c) the number of stratigraphic contexts for which records were accessible, d) the number of those published, e) the main chronological horizons exposed, f) their levels, g) the relevant bibliographic and archival references. It can be reckoned that this represents only a sample of the total number of excavations in Rome. An unknown number of rescue sites, investigated by the *Soprintendenza*, and of which little or no stratigraphic records exist or are accessible must be acknowledged; but while their number may be fairly high, their contribution to the present analysis, even if they could be included, would not be particularly significant. Their potential for a reconstruction of urban history is in fact severely limited by their small size, the quality of the records and the difficulty of piecing together composite plans. This problem, by the way, may be rectified in the future by the planned creation of a general GIS archive [1].

Referring to Figure 1, the first interesting trend concerns the spatial distribution of sites within the Aurelian walls. Rescue sites (open circles) are the only ones to be spread almost uniformly across the city, while the large-scale sites (diamonds) are strongly concentrated in the Roman Forum and Palatine areas. This bias in favour of the monumental centre of the city is also brought out when the data are broken down by region. Figure 2 shows the totals of excavated sites for each of the wards in to which Augustus subdivided the city. The central regions, even if they are smaller, contain by far the majority of sites, while the south-western part of the city is still virtually untouched. When the investigated surface-areas of excavations are taken into consideration (Figure 3), some regions appear to contain particularly large sites; the Palatine, for instance, has an average of almost a thousand square metres per excavation; the average figure is only around half this.

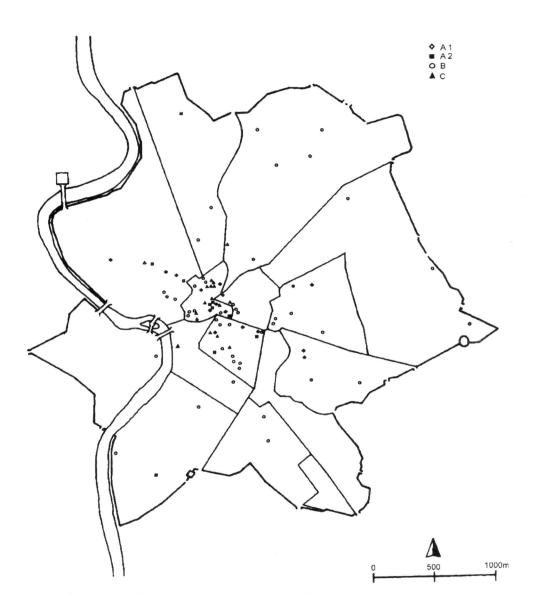

◇ A 1
■ A 2
○ B
▲ C

Figure 1 Map of Rome within the Aurelian Walls (thick line), showing the fourteen Augustan regions (thin lines) and the location of the urban excavations discussed in the paper. The symbols correspond to the types of site identified (see Table 1).

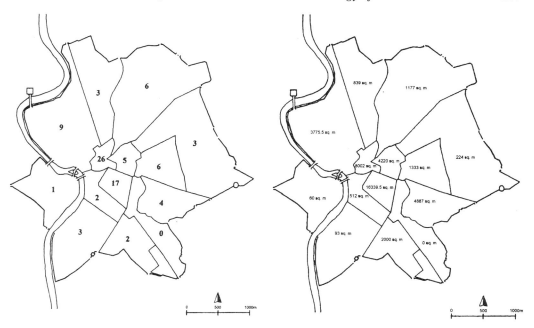

Figure 2 Map of Rome showing the number of sites for each of the Augustan regions.

Figure 3 Map of Rome showing the surface-area investigated for each of the Augustan regions

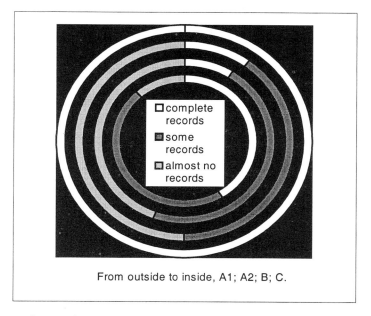

From outside to inside, A1; A2; B; C.

Figure 4 Histogram showing the proportion of well-documented sites for each of the excavation types in Table 1.

There are also marked differences, concerning the quality of the excavation records; as indicated above, the sites have been divided into four types (see Table 1). Figure 4 shows a breakdown of sites for each type on the basis of the existing information. For type A1, all the contexts have complete, accessible records. For type A2, however, only around half of the sites have context records, but only one is completely accessible. For the remaining half, some records have been collected, but they are no longer existent or accessible. Similar proportions exist for type B, while for type C the proportion is significantly closer to type A1. When we look at the number of contexts documented for each of the four types (Figure 5), it is clear that the vast majority of them have been identified at the large-scale A1 sites. Also of significance is that the sites of type C, even if they are chronologically the oldest, have a higher average of known contexts per site than many later small-scale excavations of type A2. In conclusion, these numbers strongly suggest that the best quality in the recording and dissemination of stratigraphic data was obtained during the positivist movement at the beginning of the century and, after that, only since the 1980s. The intervening decades witnessed instead an entirely unsatisfactory level of stratigraphic analysis.

Finally, useful observations can be made when the chronological horizons reached by the excavations are taken into consideration. We have defined a horizon as being reached when a sizeable stretch of its surface had been exposed, dated stratigraphically to a given century and documented with levels. Figure 6 shows the number of instances in which this has happened for the bedrock and for the centuries from the eighth BC through to the seventh AD. It is immediately obvious that most of our information concerns the period between the first century BC and the second AD. This can be easily explained when the ideological biases against the preceding and following phases are recalled. The later Republic and early Empire were considered the golden age of Rome and nothing else was considered worth exposing and preserving. Late Roman and Medieval remains were dug away without record, as disturbing material correlates of a period of decadence that was best forgotten. Even the third and fourth centuries AD were apparently perceived as already demonstrating the decline of the great city. Pre-first century BC horizons, on the other hand, were simply not reached, because the exploration of a site was deemed finished when the imperial floor-levels were brought to light. It must be kept in mind that taking the investigation further would have involved the destruction of the cherished imperial remains. While it was perfectly acceptable to destroy whole medieval towers (sometimes even with the use of dynamite), it was sacrilege to remove a few imperial stone floor slabs to reach the earlier sequences beneath them.

When the same graph is considered in terms of type of excavation, the results are even more striking. This chronological bias characterises not only types A2 and B, as may be expected, but notably type A1 as well, that is, those results which are supposed to derive from the most methodologically advanced excavations. It is fair to say that, in proportion, there seems to be a slight trend towards correcting this bias, but there is still a long way to go before the imbalance is completely redressed. It must be said that when A1 sites are located in areas already excavated in the last century, the post-imperial levels have often been irretrievably lost. It is significant that rescue sites (B) have produced more evidence for these periods, as they are often opened in previously unexcavated areas. As far as the archaic phases are concerned, it must be noted that the high water-table prevailing in Rome since the modern channelling of the Tiber often makes the early horizons much harder to reach (Ammerman 1990:n. 64). In this respect, however, it is still striking that the majority of information comes from type C, showing clearly the serious attempts made at the beginning of the century to throw light on the origins of Rome.

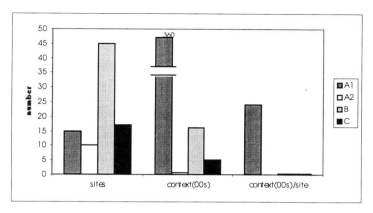

Figure 5 Histogram showing the number of sites (left), the aggregate number of well-documented contexts (in hundreds, centre), the average of well-documented contexts (in hundreds) per site (right) for each of the excavation types in Table 1.

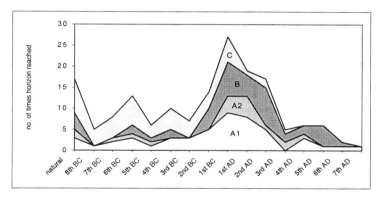

Figure 6 Histogram showing the number of times a horizon dating to each century was reached and documented for each of the excavation types in Table 1.

Conclusions

This new review of the situation makes it possible to draw some conclusions about the state of the art as far as urban archaeology in Rome is concerned. There appears to be a tension between the influence of the traditional approaches and the new methodological developments stimulated by wider debates on the issue. Old-fashioned preconceptions have been mentioned in the previous discussion: heavy biases have affected the collection of data for most of the century; they have favoured the central part of the city, where most of the public architecture is concentrated, and the periods in which these monuments were built – the early Empire. These biases are also evident in the taboo placed on the destruction of masonry of a certain type and date and in the unevenness of the stratigraphical recording. Most of the urban archaeology carried out in Rome has been guided by agendas explicitly or implicitly based on these preconceptions. Against this set of beliefs, which have been successfully challenged in the past only by scholars like Boni, a structured reaction has been developing ever since the 1980s. Theorists working within a Marxist framework, such as Daniele Manacorda and Andrea Carandini have advocated the introduction of standard stratigraphic procedures for all phases, open area excavations and exhaustive study of all finds (Carandini 1981; Manacorda 1983). This new approach has met with heavy criticism and resistance, and has only partially succeeded in bringing about a moderate amount of change (Terrenato 1998). As the diagrams suggest, even the most up-to-date projects (A1) are still influenced by old biases and preconceptions, to an extent that is sometimes even greater than the brave new projects of the beginning of the century. The deeply rooted idealist and nationalist framework, in which the heyday of Rome is assigned priority over all the other periods, is still hampering the renovation of urban archaeology in Rome.

When this picture is compared with what is happening elsewhere, the peculiarity, and in this perspective the shortcomings, of the situation in Rome become evident. There are nowadays many approaches that are ordinarily applied in many European contexts, but are still virtually non-existent in Italy. It is enough to mention a few aspects that are completely lacking in the study of Rome: the definition of clear and pragmatic research agendas at a city level, which has been recently advocated by Martin Carver (1990); the connected issue of the urban deposit model, which has been guiding urban excavation in many British and French cases (Carver 1987); the computerisation of stratigraphic data, which is a standard procedure at MOLAS and many other urban units; the systematic collection and processing of environmental samples, which is now standard almost everywhere, from Exeter (Maltby 1979) to Saint Petersburg; advanced conservation and analysis of artefacts of the kind that has been carried out in Genoa and elsewhere (Mannoni & Giannichedda 1996); adequate logistic and accounting techniques to efficiently operate archaeological excavations, as exemplified by the case of Milan (Caporusso 1991); creative ways of presenting the remains, integrating them within new architectural layouts, as has been done brilliantly in Paris (at the Cour Carrée of the Louvre). The list could go on and on with many other minor points. What seems to be radically missing, is a central structure that can ensure a steady accumulation of information, experience and procedures; from the high level of research questions and updated databases, down to the creation of reference collections, skilled expertise and administrative tools; in other words, there is not enough permanent build-up of local knowledge (in the sense of Geertz 1983).

This tirade may sound a bit out of tune to British ears at a time when theorists like Martin Carver (1993:100) are predicting 'that urban archaeologists will be forced to abandon their large municipal units and work in small partnerships'. While flexibility and research-oriented structures certainly present major advantages, it must be kept in mind that in Britain they can build on the firm basis of a generation or more of systematic centralised action. In Rome, on the other hand, no sustained attempt has ever been made to integrate strategies, methods, archives and presentation to the public. Even when large-scale project have been undertaken, they have largely relied on *ad hoc* solutions and ephemeral co-operations. Rather than venturing into deregulation right now, Rome first needs, for the next few years at least, a focused attempt to develop a modern urban archaeology. One in which the distortions introduced by biases and taboos of the nationalist past are finally corrected, and updated methods consistently adopted; one in which a solid body of experience and knowledge of the entire material past of the city is organised in an integrated and accessible way; one in which the rich heritage of the city is finally allowed to express its full potential as an object for innovative research, as a component of social memory, and as a productive and renewable resource.

Coop. ASTRA, Pisa (GR)
University of North Carolina at Chapel Hill (NT)

Acknowledgements

Our acknowledgements go to the technical committee of the *Forma Urbis Romae*, composed of Giovanni Azzena, Paolo Carafa, Luca D'Elia, Antonio Mucci, Carlo Pavolini, Susanna Le Pera, and to the other members of the screening team, Stefano Ferri, Anna Misiani, Domenico Palombi, Manuela Tascio, Pierluigi Tucci. Anna Gallone contributed to the research on which this paper is based. Martin Millett kindly commented on a draft of the text.

Endnote

[1] The present reflexive work has been spurred on by the active involvement of the authors in the project, still in its preliminary phase, and directed by Eugenio La Rocca, Adriano La Regina, Andrea Carandini and Paolo Sommella. It aims at collecting all the information relevant to the ancient topography of the city, from structures and finds to inscriptions and literary and iconographic sources. The stratigraphic information has been reviewed as part of the preliminary work in order to obtain an estimate of the resources needed to store it within the archive. Similar work has been carried out for the other types of data, and the results are now contained in an unpublished internal document entitled 'La nuova *Forma Urbis Romae*'. The actual work will take into account the guidelines contained in it.

Bibliography

Ammerman, A. J. 1990. On the origins of the Forum Romanum. *American Journal of Archaeology*, 94:627–645.

Ammerman, A. J. 1996. The Comitium in Rome from the beginning. *American Journal of Archaeology*, 100:121–136.

Barbanera, M. 1998. *L'archeologia degli Italiani*. Roma: Editori Riuniti.

Boni, G. 1901. Il metodo negli scavi archeologici. *Nuova Antologia* 16.

Brown, F. 1974–75, La protostoria della Regia. *Rendiconti della Pontificia Accademia di Archeologia* 47:15–36.

Caporusso D. 1991. (ed.) *Scavi MM3. Ricerche di archeologia urbana a Milano durante la costruzione della linea 3 della Metropolitana 1982–1990*. (5 volumes). Milano: ET.

Carandini, A. 1981, *Storie dalla Terra*. Bari: De Donato

Carver, M. O. H. 1987. *Underneath English towns*. London: Fitzhouse Books.

Carver, M. O. H. 1990. Digging for data: archaeological approaches to data definition, acquisition and analysis. In R. Francovich & D. Manacorda (eds.) *Lo scavo. Dalla diagnosi all'edizione*, Firenze: Insegna del Giglio, pp. 45–120.

Carver, M. O. H. 1993. *Arguments in stone*. Oxford: Oxbow.

Geertz, C. 1983. *Local knowledge*. New York: Basic Books.

Gjerstad, E. 1953–73. *Early Rome*. (6 volumes). Lund: Acta Instituti Romani Regni Sueciae.

Lanciani R. 1989. [1903] *Storia degli scavi di Roma*. (6 volumes). Roma: Quasar.

Maltby M. 1979. *The animal bones from Exeter*. Sheffield: University of Sheffield.

Manacorda, D. 1982. Cento anni di ricerche archeologiche italiane: il dibattito sul metodo, *Quaderni di Storia*, 6:85–119.

Manacorda, D. 1983. Introduzione. In E. C. Harris *Principi di stratigrafia archeologica*, Roma: Nuova Italia Scientifica, pp. 9–36.

Manacorda, D. & Tamassia R. 1985. *Il piccone del regime*. Roma: Laterza.

Mannoni T. & Giannichedda E., 1996. *Archeologia della produzione*. Torino: Einaudi.

Pisani Sartorio, G. 1989. *Il viver quotidiano in Roma arcaica*. Roma: Procom.

Quatermaine, L. 1995. 'Slouching towards Rome': Mussolini's imperial vision. In T. J. Cornell & K. Lomas (eds.) *Urban society in Roman Italy*. London: UCL Press, pp.203–216.

Terrenato, N. 1992. Velia and Carinae: some observations on an area of archaic Rome. In E. Herring, R. Whitehouse & J. Wilkins (eds.) *New developments in Italian archaeology. Papers of the fourth conference of Italian archaeology* 4. London: Accordia, pp.31–47.

Terrenato, N. 1998. Fra tradizione e *trend*. Gli ultimi venti anni (1975–1995). In M. Barbanera *L'archeologia degli Italiani*. Roma: Editori Riuniti, pp.175–192.

Tortorici, E. 1993. Curia Iulia. In E. Steinby *Lexicon Topographicum Urbis Romae* 1, Roma: Quasar, pp.332–335.